W9-BCK-837

COMPOUND INTEREST TABLES

A handy pocket guide for investment analysis.

Michael Sherman, Ph.D.

C O N T E M P O R A R Y
BOOKS, INC.
CHICAGO

Published by Contemporary Books, Inc.
180 North Michigan Avenue, Chicago, Illinois 60601
Manufactured in the United States of America
International Standard Book Number: 0-8092-5704-1

This edition published by arrangement with Delphi Information
    Sciences Corporation

Contributions

Edited by Suzanne Gardner – California State University
at Northridge

Cover design by Lyn Mayer - Design Consultant

Computer Analyst - David R. Warren
Delphi Information Sciences Corporation

Content organization - Thomas D. Kinsey
Marketing and Computer Consultant

About the Author

Michael Sherman, Ph.D.

EXPERIENCE: 15 years Computer Research, Theoretical and Applied Mathematics

SPECIALIST IN: Financial Mathematics

Real Estate Finance

SPECIFIC PROJECTS INCLUDE:

- Consultant to Major California Financial Institutions

- Consulting Mathematician to:
  - Federal Reserve Board
  - Federal Trade Commission
  - California Department of Real Estate
  - California Department of Corporations
  - Courts of the State of California
  - Federal Deposit Insurance Corp.
  - Federal Home Loan Bank
  - Legal Aid Society

- Author and Holder of 12 copyrights on Real Estate Publications

- Author of 6 papers published in:
  - Real Estate Review
  - Real Estate Syndication Digest
  - California Real Estate Magazine

- Speaker & Lecturer to:
  - Property Improvement Lenders' Council
  - California Independent Finance Association

EDUCATION: PhD Case Institute of Technology
MS Stanford University
BS New York University

Introduction

The purpose of this book is to show how time affects the value of invested money. Our tables and explanations are appropriate for people in business, finance, real estate, or in any aspect of investment analysis. This handy pocket guide is also useful to students in the investment field. No advanced mathematical skills are required to understand these tables. You need only the ability to read and follow directions.

Since people in diverse professions and financial positions are often intimidated by successive columns of fractional numbers, our tables offer a simple approach. We present the following six different effects of time on money. Then for clarity and for easy use, we have placed each of the different effects of time on money, into sections.

Section 6. Partial Payment to Amortize $1.00, page 106.

Each respective section explains the use of each concept and includes practical questions. Also, each section is separated into four compounding periods: monthly, quarterly, semi-annual, and annual. In each period, the interest is either compounded or calculated according to the duration of the period.

The above categories include the use of $1.00 as the simplest monetary factor for calculation of value. However, if your investment is greater than $1.00, simply multiply the table factor given, by the dollar amount invested.

Your first and most important job in correctly using these tables, will be to select the appropriate section for analysis o´ your investment. This should be an easy task after careful reading of the summaries within each classification.

Section 1. Future Value of $1.00:

This represents the growth of $1.00 including interest over a designated period of time. In this section it is important to understand that the date of your original $1.00 investment constitutes the beginning of the investment period. The factors presented in this section are based on the fact that no additional investments may be made, and that the future growth of this fund depends upon the interest paid. These factors are based on the assumption that no funds will be withdrawn at any point, for the duration of the investment.

In this section, the following four (4) periods are presented in detail: monthly, quarterly, semiannual, and annual.

Monthly:

The factors presented on pages 9 through 14 will indicate the value of a $1.00 investment at the end of each stated monthly interval. That is, the original $1.00 plus the interest earned for each monthly period. The interest is compounding each month. This is interest earned on interest.

Example A

If you invest $1250.00 on a certain date, what will be the value of that investment in 20 years? We assume an earned annual interest of 8%, and a monthly compounding.

Turn to page 10 and locate the 8.0% column. Proceed down that column until you locate the point where the 20 year row intersects the 8.0%

interest column The number is 4.926803 for each $1.00 invested. So, to determine your answer, multiply 4.926803 by $1250. The correct answer is $6,158.50. That is, the value of that $1250 investment is $6,158.50 in 20 years.

Note: If your investment period is less than 2 years, we have provided all the $1.00 amounts for each monthly period. Over 2 years, only the annual figures are provided.

Quarterly:

The factors presented on pages 15 through 17, will indicate the value of a $1.00 investment at the end of each stated quarterly interval. That is, the original $1.00 plus the interest earned for each quarterly period. The interest is compounding each quarter. This is interest earned on interest.

Example B

You deposit $500.00 in the credit union every quarter. What is the value of that account at the end of 2 years or eight quarters? Assume an interest rate of 7.0% and quarterly compounding.

Turn to page 15 and locate the 7.0% column. Proceed down that column until you locate the point where the 8 quarters row intersects the 7% interest column. The number is 1.148882 for each $1.00 invested. So, to determine your answer, multiply 1.148882 by $500.00. The correct answer is $574.44. That is, the value of that $500.00 account is $574.44 in 2 years (or eight quarters).

Note: For investments of 5 years and more, only the annual amounts are shown.

Semiannual:

The factors on pages 18 tnrough 19 cover semiannual compounding (or the interest being compounded every 6 months). They are used the same way as the monthly or quarterly tables.

Annual:

The factors on pages 20 through 25 cover annual compounding (or the interest being compounded every year. They are used the same way as the monthly, quarterly, and semiannual tables.

In case you want to know how it is done, here's the formula . . .

$$S = (1+i)^n$$
S = The future value of $1.00
i = interest rate per period
n = number of compounding periods

	5.0%	6.0%	7.0%	7.5%	
	ANNUAL RATE	ANNUAL RATE	ANNUAL RATE	ANNUAL RATE	
MOS					MOS
1	1.004 167	1.005 000	1.005 833	1.006 250	1
2	1.008 351	1.010 025	1.011 701	1.012 539	2
3	1.012 552	1.015 075	1.017 602	1.018 867	3
4	1.016 771	1.020 151	1.023 538	1.025 235	4
5	1.021 008	1.025 251	1.029 509	1.031 643	5
6	1.025 262	1.030 378	1.035 514	1.038 091	6
7	1.029 534	1.035 529	1.041 555	1.044 579	.
8	1.033 824	1.040 707	1.047 631	1.051 108	8
9	1.038 131	1.045 911	1.053 742	1.057 677	9
10	1.042 457	1.051 140	1.059 889	1.064 287	10
11	1.046 800	1.056 396	1.066 071	1.070 939	11
12	1.051 162	1.061 678	1.072 290	1.077 633	12
13	1.055 542	1.066 986	1.078 545	1.084 368	13
14	1.059 940	1.072 321	1.084 837	1.091 145	14
15	1.064 356	1.077 683	1.091 165	1.097 965	15
16	1.068 791	1.083 071	1.097 530	1.104 827	16
17	1.073 244	1.088 487	1.103 932	1.111 732	17
18	1.077 716	1.093 929	1.110 372	1.118 681	18
19	1.082 207	1.099 399	1.116 849	1.125 672	19
20	1.086 716	1.104 896	1.123 364	1.132 708	20
21	1.091 244	1.110 420	1.129 917	1.139 787	21
22	1.095 791	1.115 972	1.136 508	1.146 911	22
23	1.100 357	1.121 552	1.143 138	1.154 079	23
YRS					
2	1.104 941	1.127 160	1.149 806	1.161 292	24
3	1.161 472	1.196 681	1.232 926	1.251 446	36
4	1.220 895	1.270 489	1.322 054	1.348 599	48
5	1.283 359	1.348 850	1.417 625	1.453 294	60
6	1.349 018	1.432 044	1.520 106	1.566 117	72
7	1.418 036	1.520 370	1.629 994	1.687 699	84
8	1.490 585	1.614 143	1.747 826	1.818 720	96
9	1.566 847	1.713 699	1.874 177	1.959 912	108
10	1.647 009	1.819 397	2.009 661	2.112 065	120
11	1.731 274	1.931 613	2.154 940	2.276 030	132
12	1.819 849	2.050 751	2.310 721	2.452 724	144
13	1.912 956	2.177 237	2.477 763	2.643 135	156
14	2.010 826	2.311 524	2.656 881	2.848 329	168
15	2.113 704	2.454 094	2.848 947	3.069 452	180
16	2.221 845	2.605 457	3.054 897	3.307 741	192
17	2.335 519	2.766 156	3.275 736	3.564 530	204
18	2.455 008	2.936 766	3.512 539	3.841 254	216
19	2.580 611	3.117 899	3.766 461	4.139 460	228
20	2.712 640	3.310 204	4.038 739	4.460 817	240
21	2.851 424	3.514 371	4.330 700	4.807 122	252
22	2.997 308	3.731 129	4.643 766	5.180 311	264
23	3.150 656	3.961 257	4.979 464	5.582 472	276
24	3.311 850	4.205 579	5.339 430	6.015 854	288
25	3.481 290	4.464 970	5.725 418	6.482 880	300
26	3.659 400	4.740 359	6.139 309	6.986 163	312
27	3.846 622	5.032 734	6.583 120	7.528 517	324
28	4.043 422	5.343 142	7.059 015	8.112 976	338
29	4.250 291	5.672 696	7.569 311	8.742 807	348
30	4.467 744	6.022 575	8.116 497	9.421 534	360

SECTION 1

	8.0% ANNUAL RATE	8.5% ANNUAL RATE	9.0% ANNUAL RATE	9.5% ANNUAL RATE	
MOS					MOS
1	1.006 667	1.007 083	1.007 500	1.007 917	1
2	1.013 378	1.014 217	1.015 056	1.015 896	2
3	1.020 134	1.021 401	1.022 669	1.023 939	3
4	1.026 935	1.028 636	1.030 339	1.032 045	4
5	1.033 781	1.035 922	1.038 067	1.040 215	5
6	1.040 673	1.043 260	1.045 852	1.048 450	6
7	1.047 610	1.050 650	1.053 696	1.056 750	7
8	1.054 595	1.058 092	1.061 599	1.065 116	8
9	1.061 625	1.065 586	1.069 561	1.073 548	9
10	1.068 703	1.073 134	1.077 583	1.082 047	10
11	1.075 827	1.080 736	1.085 664	1.090 614	11
12	1.083 000	1.088 391	1.093 807	1.099 248	12
13	1.090 220	1.096 100	1.102 010	1.107 950	13
14	1.097 488	1.103 864	1.110 276	1.116 721	14
15	1.104 804	1.111 683	1.118 603	1.125 562	15
16	1.112 170	1.119 558	1.126 992	1.134 473	16
17	1.119 584	1.127 488	1.135 445	1.143 454	17
18	1.127 048	1.135 474	1.143 960	1.152 506	18
19	1.134 562	1.143 517	1.152 540	1.161 630	19
20	1.142 125	1.151 617	1.161 184	1.170 826	20
21	1.149 740	1.159 775	1.169 893	1.180 096	21
22	1.157 404	1.167 990	1.178 667	1.189 438	22
23	1.165 120	1.176 263	1.187 507	1.198 854	23
YRS					
2	1.172 888	1.184 595	1.196 414	1.208 345	24
3	1.270 237	1.289 302	1.308 645	1.328 271	36
4	1.375 666	1.403 265	1.431 405	1.460 098	48
5	1.489 846	1.527 301	1.565 681	1.605 009	60
6	1.613 502	1.662 300	1.712 553	1.764 303	72
7	1.747 422	1.809 232	1.873 202	1.939 406	84
8	1.892 457	1.969 152	2.048 921	2.131 887	96
9	2.049 530	2.143 207	2.241 124	2.343 472	108
10	2.219 640	2.332 647	2.451 357	2.576 055	120
11	2.403 869	2.538 832	2.681 311	2.831 723	132
12	2.603 389	2.763 242	2.932 837	3.112 764	144
13	2.819 469	3.007 487	3.207 957	3.421 699	156
14	3.053 484	3.273 321	3.508 886	3.761 294	168
15	3.306 921	3.562 653	3.838 043	4.134 593	180
16	3.581 394	3.877 559	4.198 078	4.544 942	192
17	3.878 648	4.220 300	4.591 887	4.996 016	204
18	4.200 574	4.593 337	5.022 638	5.491 859	216
19	4.549 220	4.999 346	5.493 796	6.036 912	228
20	4.926 803	5.441 243	6.009 152	6.636 061	240
21	5.335 725	5.922 199	6.572 851	7.294 674	252
22	5.778 588	6.445 667	7.189 430	8.018 653	264
23	6.258 207	7.015 406	7.863 848	8.814 485	276
24	6.777 636	7.635 504	8.601 532	9.689 302	288
25	7.340 176	8.310 413	9.408 415	10.650 941	300
26	7.949 407	9.044 978	10.290 989	11.708 022	312
27	8.609 204	9.844 472	11.256 354	12.870 014	324
28	9.323 763	10.714 634	12.312 278	14.147 332	336
29	10.097 631	11.661 710	13.467 255	15.551 421	348
30	10.935 730	12.692 499	14.730 576	17.094 862	360

	10.0% ANNUAL RATE	10.5% ANNUAL RATE	11.0% ANNUAL RATE	11.5% ANNUAL RATE	
MOS					MOS
1	1.008 333	1.008 750	1.009 167	1.009 583	1
2	1.016 736	1.017 577	1.018 417	1.019 259	2
3	1.025 209	1.026 480	1.027 753	1.029 026	3
4	1.033 752	1.035 462	1.037 174	1.038 888	4
5	1.042 367	1.044 522	1.046 681	1.048 844	5
6	1.051 053	1.053 662	1.056 276	1.058 895	6
7	1.059 812	1.062 881	1.065 958	1.069 043	7
8	1.068 644	1.072 182	1.075 730	1.079 288	8
9	1.077 549	1.081 563	1.085 591	1.089 631	9
10	1.086 529	1.091 027	1.095 542	1.100 074	10
11	1.095 583	1.100 573	1.105 584	1.110 616	11
12	1.104 713	1.110 203	1.115 719	1.121 259	12
13	1.113 919	1.119 918	1.125 946	1.132 005	13
14	1.123 202	1.129 717	1.136 267	1.142 853	14
15	1.132 562	1.139 602	1.146 683	1.153 805	15
16	1.142 000	1.149 574	1.157 194	1.164 863	16
17	1.151 516	1.159 632	1.167 802	1.176 026	17
18	1.161 112	1.169 779	1.178 507	1.187 296	18
19	1.170 788	1.180 015	1.189 310	1.198 675	19
20	1.180 545	1.190 340	1.200 212	1.210 162	20
21	1.190 383	1.200 755	1.211 214	1.221 759	21
22	1.200 303	1.211 262	1.222 317	1.233 468	22
23	1.210 305	1.221 860	1.233 521	1.245 288	23
YRS					
2	1.220 391	1.232 552	1.244 829	1.257 222	24
3	1.348 182	1.368 383	1.388 879	1.409 672	36
4	1.489 354	1.519 184	1.549 598	1.580 608	48
5	1.645 309	1.686 603	1.728 916	1.772 272	60
6	1.817 594	1.872 472	1.928 984	1.987 176	72
7	2.007 920	2.078 825	2.152 204	2.228 140	84
8	2.218 176	2.307 919	2.401 254	2.498 323	96
9	2.450 448	2.562 260	2.679 124	2.801 268	108
10	2.707 041	2.844 630	2.989 150	3.140 948	120
11	2.990 504	3.158 118	3.335 051	3.521 817	132
12	3.303 649	3.506 153	3.720 979	3.948 870	144
13	3.649 584	3.892 543	4.151 566	4.427 707	156
14	4.031 743	4.321 515	4.631 980	4.964 608	168
15	4.453 920	4.797 761	5.167 988	5.566 613	180
16	4.920 303	5.326 491	5.766 021	6.241 617	192
17	5.435 523	5.913 488	6.433 259	6.998 471	204
18	6.004 693	6.565 175	7.177 708	7.847 101	216
19	6.633 463	7.288 680	8.008 304	8.798 635	228
20	7.328 074	8.091 918	8.935 015	9.865 552	240
21	8.095 419	8.983 675	9.968 965	11.061 842	252
22	8.943 115	9.973 707	11.122 562	12.403 194	264
23	9.879 576	11.072 844	12.409 652	13.907 196	276
24	10.914 097	12.293 109	13.845 682	15.593 574	288
25	12.056 945	13.647 852	15.447 889	17.484 440	300
26	13.319 465	15.151 893	17.235 500	19.604 591	312
27	14.714 187	16.821 684	19.229 972	21.981 831	324
28	16.254 954	18.675 491	21.455 242	24.647 333	336
29	17.957 060	20.733 595	23.938 018	27.636 052	348
30	19.837 399	23.018 509	26.708 098	30.987 181	360

11

MOS	12.0% ANNUAL RATE	12.5% ANNUAL RATE	13.0% ANNUAL RATE	13.5% ANNUAL RATE	MOS
1	1.010 000	1.010 417	1.010 833	1.011 250	1
2	1.020 100	1.020 942	1.021 784	1.022 627	2
3	1.030 301	1.031 577	1.032 853	1.034 131	3
4	1.040 604	1.042 322	1.044 043	1.045 765	4
5	1.051 010	1.053 180	1.055 353	1.057 530	5
6	1.061 520	1.064 150	1.066 786	1.069 427	6
7	1.072 135	1.075 235	1.078 343	1.081 458	7
8	1.082 857	1.086 436	1.090 025	1.093 625	8
9	1.093 685	1.097 753	1.101 834	1.105 928	9
10	1.104 622	1.109 188	1.113 770	1.118 370	10
11	1.115 668	1.120 742	1.125 836	1.130 951	11
12	1.126 825	1.132 416	1.138 032	1 143 674	12
13	1.138 093	1.144 212	1.150 361	1.156 541	13
14	1.149 474	1.156 131	1.162 823	1.169 552	14
15	1.160 969	1.168 174	1.175 421	1.182 709	15
16	1.172 579	1.180 342	1.188 154	1.196 015	16
17	1.184 304	1.192 638	1.201 026	1.209 470	17
18	1.196 147	1.205 061	1.214 037	1.223 077	18
19	1.208 109	1.217 614	1.227 189	1.236 836	19
20	1.220 190	1.230 297	1.240 484	1.250 751	20
21	1.232 392	1.243 113	1.253 922	1.264 821	21
22	1.244 716	1.256 062	1.267 507	1.279 051	22
23	1.257 163	1.269 146	1.281 238	1.293 440	23

YRS					
2	1.269 735	1.282 366	1.295 118	1.307 991	24
3	1.430 769	1.452 172	1.473 886	1.495 916	36
4	1.612 226	1.644 463	1.677 330	1.710 841	48
5	1.816 697	1.862 216	1.908 857	1.956 645	60
6	2.047 099	2.108 803	2.172 341	2.237 765	72
7	2.306 723	2.388 043	2.472 194	2.559 275	84
8	2.599 273	2.704 258	2.813 437	2.926 977	96
9	2.928 926	3.062 345	3.201 783	3.347 509	108
10	3.300 387	3.467 849	3.643 733	3.828 460	120
11	3.718 959	3.927 048	4.146 687	4.378 512	132
12	4.190 616	4.447 052	4.719 064	5.007 593	144
13	4.722 091	5.035 913	5.370 448	5.727 056	156
14	5.320 970	5.702 748	6.111 745	6.549 887	168
15	5.995 802	6.457 884	6.955 364	7.490 939	180
16	6.756 220	7.313 011	7.915 430	8.567 195	192
17	7.613 078	8.281 371	9.008 017	9.798 082	204
18	8.578 606	9.377 958	10.251 416	11.205 816	216
19	9.666 588	10.619 750	11.666 444	12.815 805	228
20	10.892 554	12.025 975	13.276 792	14.657 109	240
21	12.274 002	13.618 407	15.109 421	16.762 961	252
22	13.830 653	15.421 703	17.195 012	19.171 370	264
23	15.584 726	17.463 783	19.568 482	21.925 805	276
24	17.561 259	19.776 269	22.269 568	25.075 983	288
25	19.788 466	22.394 964	25.343 491	28.678 761	300
26	22.298 139	25.360 417	28.841 716	32.799 166	312
27	25.126 101	28.718 543	32.822 810	37.511 568	324
28	28.312 720	32.521 339	37.353 424	42.901 021	336
29	31.903 481	36.827 686	42.509 410	49.064 802	348
30	35.949 641	41.704 262	48.377 089	56.114 160	360

	14.0%	14.5%	15.0%	16.0%	
	ANNUAL RATE	ANNUAL RATE	ANNUAL RATE	ANNUAL RATE	
MOS					MOS
1	1.011 667	1.012 083	1.012 500	1.013 333	1
2	1.023 469	1.024 313	1.025 156	1.026 844	2
3	1.035 410	1.036 690	1.037 971	1.040 536	3
4	1.047 490	1.049 216	1.050 945	1.054 410	4
5	1.059 710	1.061 894	1.064 082	1.068 468	5
6	1.072 074	1.074 726	1.077 383	1.082 715	6
7	1.084 581	1.087 712	1.090 850	1.097 151	7
8	1.097 235	1.100 855	1.104 486	1.111 779	8
9	1.110 036	1.114 157	1.118 292	1.126 603	9
10	1.122 986	1.127 620	1.132 271	1.141 625	10
11	1.136 088	1.141 245	1.146 424	1.156 846	11
12	1.149 342	1.155 035	1.160 755	1.172 271	12
13	1.162 751	1.168 992	1.175 264	1.187 901	13
14	1.176 316	1.183 117	1.189 955	1.203 740	14
15	1.190 040	1.197 413	1.204 829	1.219 790	15
16	1.203 924	1.211 882	1.219 890	1.236 053	16
17	1.217 970	1.226 526	1.235 138	1.252 534	17
18	1.232 179	1.241 346	1.250 577	1.269 235	18
19	1.246 555	1.256 346	1.266 210	1.286 158	19
20	1.261 098	1.271 527	1.282 037	1.303 307	20
21	1.275 811	1.286 891	1.298 063	1.320 684	21
22	1.290 695	1.302 441	1.314 288	1.338 293	22
23	1.305 753	1.318 179	1.330 717	1.356 137	23
YRS					
2	1.320 987	1.334 107	1.347 351	1.374 219	24
3	1.518 266	1.540 940	1.563 944	1.610 957	36
4	1.745 007	1.779 841	1.815 355	1.888 477	48
5	2.005 610	2.055 779	2.107 181	2.213 807	60
6	2.305 132	2.374 497	2.445 920	2.595 181	72
7	2.649 385	2.742 628	2.839 113	3.042 255	84
8	3.045 049	3.167 833	3.295 513	3.566 347	96
9	3.499 803	3.658 959	3.825 282	4.180 724	108
10	4.022 471	4.226 227	4.440 213	4.900 941	120
11	4.623 195	4.881 441	5.153 998	5.745 230	132
12	5.313 632	5.638 237	5.982 526	6.734 965	144
13	6.107 180	6.512 363	6.944 244	7.895 203	156
14	7.019 239	7.522 010	8.060 563	9.255 316	168
15	8.067 507	8.688 187	9.356 334	10.849 737	180
16	9.272 324	10.035 163	10.860 408	12.718 830	192
17	10.657 072	11.590 968	12.606 267	14.909 912	204
18	12.248 621	13.387 978	14.632 781	17.478 455	216
19	14.077 855	15.463 588	16.985 067	20.489 482	228
20	16.180 270	17.860 991	19.715 494	24.019 222	240
21	18.596 664	20.630 076	22.884 848	28.157 032	252
22	21.373 928	23.828 467	26.563 691	33.007 667	264
23	24.565 954	27.522 721	30.833 924	38.693 924	276
24	28.234 683	31.789 716	35.790 617	45.359 757	288
25	32.451 308	36.718 246	41.544 120	53.173 919	300
26	37.297 652	42.410 872	48.222 525	62.334 232	312
27	42.867 759	48.986 057	55.974 514	73.072 600	324
28	49.269 718	56.580 627	64.972 670	85.660 875	336
29	56.627 757	65.352 625	75.417 320	100.417 742	348
30	65.084 661	75.484 592	87.540 995	117.716 787	360

MOS	17.0% ANNUAL RATE	18.0% ANNUAL RATE	19.0% ANNUAL RATE	20.0% ANNUAL RATE	MOS
1	1.014 167	1.015 000	1.015 833	1.016 667	1
2	1.028 534	1.030 225	1.031 917	1.033 611	2
3	1.043 105	1.045 678	1.048 256	1.050 838	3
4	1.057 882	1.061 364	1.064 853	1.068 352	4
5	1.072 869	1.077 284	1.081 714	1.086 158	5
3	1.088 068	1.093 443	1.098 841	1.104 260	6
7	1.103 482	1.109 845	1.116 239	1.122 665	7
8	1.119 115	1.126 493	1.133 913	1.141 376	8
9	1.134 969	1.143 390	1.151 866	1.160 399	9
10	1.151 048	1.160 541	1.170 104	1.179 739	10
11	1.167 354	1.177 949	1.188 631	1.199 401	11
12	1.183 892	1.195 618	1.207 451	1.219 391	12
13	1.200 664	1.213 552	1.226 569	1.239 714	13
14	1.217 673	1.231 756	1.245 990	1.260 376	14
15	1.234 923	1.250 232	1.265 718	1.281 382	15
16	1.252 418	1.268 986	1.285 758	1.302 739	16
17	1.270 161	1.288 020	1.306 116	1.324 451	17
18	1.288 155	1.307 341	1.326 796	1.346 525	18
19	1.306 403	1.326 951	1.347 804	1.368 967	19
20	1.324 911	1.346 855	1.369 144	1.391 784	20
21	1.343 680	1.367 058	1.390 822	1.414 980	21
22	1.362 716	1.387 564	1.412 844	1.438 563	22
23	1.382 021	1.408 377	1.435 214	1.462 539	23

YRS					
2	1.401 600	1.429 503	1.457 938	1.486 915	24
3	1.659 342	1.709 140	1.760 389	1.813 130	36
4	1.964 482	2.043 478	2.125 583	2.210 915	48
5	2.325 733	2.443 220	2.566 537	2.695 970	60
6	2.753 417	2.921 158	3.098 968	3.287 442	72
7	3.259 747	3.492 590	3.741 852	4.008 677	84
8	3.859 188	4.175 804	4.518 103	4.888 145	96
9	4.568 860	4.992 667	5.455 388	5.960 561	108
10	5.409 036	5.969 323	6.587 114	7.268 255	120
11	6.403 713	7.137 031	7.953 617	8.862 845	132
12	7.581 303	8.533 164	9.603 603	10.807 275	144
13	8.975 441	10.202 406	11.595 879	13.178 294	156
14	10.625 951	12.198 182	14.001 456	16.069 495	168
15	12.579 975	14.584 368	16.906 072	19.594 998	180
16	14.893 329	17.437 335	20.413 254	23.893 966	192
17	17.632 089	20.848 395	24.648 004	29.136 090	204
18	20.874 484	24.926 719	29.761 257	35.528 288	216
19	24.713 129	29.802 839	35.935 259	43.322 878	228
20	29.257 669	35.632 816	43.390 065	52.827 531	240
21	34.637 912	42.603 242	52.391 377	64.417 420	252
22	41.007 538	50.937 210	63.260 020	78.550 028	264
23	48.548 485	60.901 454	76.383 375	95.783 203	276
24	57.476 150	72.814 885	92.229 182	116.797 184	288
25	68.045 538	87.058 800	111.362 218	142.421 445	300
26	80.558 550	104.089 083	134.464 421	173.667 440	312
27	95.372 601	124.450 799	162.359 199	211.768 529	324
28	112.910 833	148.795 637	196.040 777	258.228 656	336
29	133.674 202	177.902 767	236.709 632	314.881 721	348
30	158.255 782	212.703 781	285.815 282	383.963 963	360

	5.0%	6.0%	7.0%	8.0%	
	ANNUAL RATE	ANNUAL RATE	ANNUAL RATE	ANNUAL RATE	
QTRS					QTRS
1	1.012 500	1.015 000	1.017 500	1.020 000	1
2	1.025 156	1.030 225	1.035 306	1.040 400	2
3	1.037 971	1.045 678	1.053 424	1.061 208	3
4	1.050 945	1.061 364	1.071 859	1.082 432	4
5	1.064 082	1.077 284	1.090 617	1.104 081	5
6	1.077 383	1.093 443	1.109 702	1.126 162	6
7	1.090 850	1.109 845	1.129 122	1.148 686	7
8	1.104 486	1.126 493	1.148 882	1.171 659	8
9	1.118 292	1.143 390	1.168 987	1.195 093	9
10	1.132 271	1.160 541	1.189 444	1.218 994	10
11	1.146 424	1.177 949	1.210 260	1.243 374	11
12	1.160 755	1.195 618	1.231 439	1.268 242	12
13	1.175 264	1.213 552	1.252 990	1.293 607	13
14	1.189 955	1.231 756	1.274 917	1.319 479	14
15	1.204 829	1.250 232	1.297 228	1.345 868	15
16	1.219 890	1.268 986	1.319 929	1.372 786	16
17	1.235 138	1.288 020	1.343 028	1.400 241	17
18	1.250 577	1.307 341	1.366 531	1.428 246	18
19	1.266 210	1.326 951	1.390 445	1.456 811	19
YRS					
5	1.282 037	1.346 855	1.414 778	1.485 947	20
6	1.347 351	1.429 503	1.516 443	1.608 437	24
7	1.415 992	1.517 222	1.625 413	1.741 024	28
8	1.488 131	1.610 324	1.742 213	1.884 541	32
9	1.563 944	1.709 140	1.867 407	2.039 887	36
10	1.643 619	1.814 018	2.001 597	2.208 040	40
11	1.727 354	1.925 333	2.145 430	2.390 053	44
12	1.815 355	2.043 478	2.299 599	2.587 070	48
13	1.907 839	2.168 873	2.464 846	2.800 328	52
14	2.005 034	2.301 963	2.641 967	3.031 165	56
15	2.107 181	2.443 220	2.831 816	3.281 031	60
16	2.214 532	2.593 144	3.035 308	3.551 493	64
17	2.327 353	2.752 269	3.253 422	3.844 251	68
18	2.445 920	2.921 158	3.487 210	4.161 140	72
19	2.570 529	3.100 411	3.737 797	4.504 152	76
20	2.701 485	3.290 663	4.006 392	4.875 439	80
21	2.839 113	3.492 590	4.294 287	5.277 332	84
22	2.983 753	3.706 907	4.602 871	5.712 354	88
23	3.135 761	3.934 376	4.933 629	6.183 236	92
24	3.295 513	4.175 804	5.288 154	6.692 933	96
25	3.463 404	4.432 046	5.668 156	7.244 646	100
26	3.639 849	4.704 012	6.075 464	7.841 838	104
27	3.825 282	4.992 667	6.512 041	8.488 258	108
28	4.020 162	5.299 034	6.979 990	9.187 963	112
29	4.224 971	5.624 202	7.481 565	9.945 347	116
30	4.440 213	5.969 323	8.019 183	10.765 163	120

	9.0%	10.0%	11.0%	12.0%	
	ANNUAL RATE	ANNUAL RATE	ANNUAL RATE	ANNUAL RATE	
QTRS					QTRS
1	1.022 500	1.025 000	1.027 500	1 030 000	1
2	1.045 506	1.050 625	1.055 756	1.060 900	2
3	1.069 030	1.076 891	1.084 790	1.092 727	3
4	1.093 083	1.103 813	1.114 621	1.125 509	4
5	1.117 678	1.131 408	. 145 273	1.159 274	5
6	1.142 825	1.159 693	1.176 768	1.194 052	6
7	1.168 539	1.188 686	1.209 129	1.229 874	7
8	1.194 831	1.218 403	1.242 381	1.266 770	8
9	1.221 715	1.248 863	1.276 546	.304 773	9
10	1.249 203	1.280 085	1.311 651	1.343 916	10
11	1.277 311	1.312 087	1.347 721	1.384 234	11
12	1.306 050	1.344 889	1.384 784	1.425 761	12
13	1.335 436	1.378 511	1.422 865	1.468 534	13
14	1.365 483	1.412 974	1.461 994	1.512 590	14
15	1.396 207	1.448 298	1.502 199	1.557 967	15
16	1.427 621	1.484 506	1.543 509	1.604 706	16
17	1.459 743	1.521 618	1.585 956	1.652 848	17
18	1.492 587	1.559 659	1.629 570	1.702 433	18
19	1.526 170	1.598 650	1.674 383	1.753 506	19
YRS					
5	1.560 509	1.638 616	1.720 428	1.806 111	20
6	1.705 767	1.808 726	1.917 626	2.032 794	24
7	1.864 545	1.996 495	2.137 427	2.287 928	28
8	2.038 103	2.203 757	2.382 421	2.575 083	32
9	2.227 816	2.432 535	2.655 498	2.898 278	36
10	2.435 189	2.685 064	2.959 874	3.262 038	40
11	2.661 864	2.963 808	3.299 138	3.671 452	44
12	2.909 640	3.271 490	3.677 290	4.132 252	48
13	3.180 479	3.611 112	4.098 785	4.650 886	52
14	3.476 528	3.985 992	4.568 593	5.234 613	56
15	3.800 135	4.399 790	5.092 251	5.891 603	60
16	4.153 864	4.856 545	5.675 932	6.631 051	64
17	4.540 519	5.360 717	6.326 514	7.463 307	68
18	4.963 166	5.917 228	7.051 667	8.400 017	72
19	5.425 154	6.531 513	7.859 938	9.454 293	76
20	5.930 145	7.209 568	8.760 854	10.640 891	80
21	6.482 143	7.958 014	9.765 034	11.976 416	84
22	7.085 522	8.784 158	10.884 315	13.479 562	88
23	7.745 066	9.696 067	12.131 889	15.171 366	92
24	8.466 003	10.702 644	13.522 461	17.075 506	96
25	9.254 046	11.813 716	15.072 422	19.218 632	100
26	10.115 444	13.040 132	16.800 042	21.630 740	104
27	11.057 023	14.393 866	18.725 684	24.345 588	108
28	12.086 247	15.888 135	20.872 046	27.401 174	112
29	13.211 275	17.537 528	23.264 426	30.840 262	116
30	14.441 024	19.358 150	25.931 024	34.710 987	120

16

QTRS	13.0% ANNUAL RATE	14.0% ANNUAL RATE	15.0% ANNUAL RATE	16.0% ANNUAL RATE	QTRS
1	1.032 500	1.035 000	1.037 500	1.040 000	1
2	1.066 056	1.071 225	1.076 406	1.081 600	2
3	1.100 703	1.108 718	1.116 771	1.124 864	3
4	1.136 476	1.147 523	1.158 650	1.169 859	4
5	1.173 411	1.187 686	1.202 100	1.216 653	5
6	1.211 547	1.229 255	1.247 179	1.265 319	6
7	1.250 923	1.272 279	1.293 948	1.315 932	7
8	1.291 578	1.316 809	1.342 471	1.368 569	8
9	1.333 554	1.362 897	1.392 813	1.423 312	9
10	1.376 894	1.410 599	1.445 044	1.480 244	10
11	1.421 643	1.459 970	1.499 233	1.539 454	11
12	1.467 847	1.511 069	1.555 454	1.601 032	12
13	1.515 552	1.563 956	1.613 784	1.665 074	13
14	1.564 807	1.618 695	1.674 301	1.731 676	14
15	1.615 663	1.675 349	1.737 087	1.800 944	15
16	1.668 173	1.733 986	1.802 265	1.872 981	16
17	1.722 388	1.794 676	1.869 811	1.947 900	17
18	1.778 366	1.857 489	1.939 929	2.025 817	18
19	1.836 163	1.922 501	2.012 677	2.106 849	19

YRS					
5	1.895 838	1.989 789	2.088 152	2.191 123	20
6	2.154 574	2.283 328	2.419 438	2.563 304	24
7	2.448 622	2.620 172	2.803 283	2.998 703	28
8	2.782 800	3.006 708	3.248 025	3.508 059	32
9	3.162 585	3.450 266	3.763 326	4.103 933	36
10	3.594 201	3.959 260	4.360 379	4.801 021	40
11	4.084 723	4.543 342	5.052 155	5.616 515	44
12	4.642 190	5.213 589	5.853 681	6.570 528	48
13	5.275 737	5.982 713	6.782 370	7.686 589	52
14	5.995 748	6.865 301	7.858 396	8.992 222	56
15	6.814 023	7.878 091	9.105 134	10.519 627	60
16	7.743 974	9.040 291	10.549 667	12.306 476	64
17	8.800 840	10.373 941	12.223 376	14.396 836	68
18	10.001 942	11.904 336	14.162 620	16.842 262	72
19	11.366 967	13.660 500	16.409 525	19.703 065	76
20	12.918 284	15.675 738	19.012 903	23.049 799	80
21	14.681 319	17.988 269	22.029 308	26.965 005	84
22	16.684 965	20.641 953	25.524 267	31.545 242	88
23	18.962 061	23.687 116	29.573 702	36.903 471	92
24	21.549 926	27.181 510	34.265 582	43.171 841	96
25	24.490 973	31.191 408	39.701 831	50.504 948	100
26	27.833 401	35.792 858	46.000 543	59.083 646	104
27	31.631 990	41.073 128	53.298 548	69.119 509	108
28	35.948 995	47.132 359	61.754 385	80.860 049	112
29	40.855 168	54.085 466	71.551 744	94.594 821	116
30	46.430 915	62.064 316	82.903 458	110.662 561	120

	5.0%	6.0%	7.0%	8.0%	
	ANNUAL RATE	ANNUAL RATE	ANNUAL RATE	ANNUAL RATE	
HALF YRS					HALF YRS
1	1.025 000	1.030 000	1.035 000	1.040 000	1
2	1.050 625	1.060 900	1.071 225	1.081 600	2
3	1.076 891	1.092 727	1.108 718	1.124 864	3
4	1.103 813	1.125 509	1.147 523	1.169 859	4
5	1.131 408	1.159 274	1.187 686	1.216 653	5
6	1.159 693	1.194 052	1.229 255	1.265 319	6
7	1.188 686	1.229 874	1.272 279	1.315 932	7
8	1.218 403	1.266 770	1.316 809	1.368 569	8
9	1.248 863	1.304 773	1.362 897	1.423 312	9
10	1.280 085	1.343 916	1.410 599	1.480 244	10
11	1.312 087	1.384 234	1.459 970	1.539 454	11
12	1.344 889	1.425 761	1.511 069	1.601 032	12
13	1.378 511	1.468 534	1.563 956	1.665 074	13
14	1.412 974	1.512 590	1.618 695	1.731 676	14
15	1.448 298	1.557 967	1.675 349	1.800 944	15
16	1.484 506	1.604 706	1.733 986	1.872 981	16
17	1.521 618	1.652 848	1.794 676	1.947 900	17
18	1.559 659	1.702 433	1.857 489	2.025 817	18
19	1.598 650	1.753 506	1.922 501	2.106 849	19
20	1.638 616	1.806 111	1.989 789	2.191 123	20
21	1.679 582	1.860 295	2.059 431	2.278 768	21
22	1.721 571	1.916 103	2.131 512	2.369 919	22
23	1.764 611	1.973 587	2.206 114	2.464 716	23
24	1.808 726	2.032 794	2.283 328	2.563 304	24
25	1.853 944	2.093 778	2.363 245	2.665 836	25
26	1.900 293	2.156 591	2.445 959	2.772 470	26
27	1.947 800	2.221 289	2.531 567	2.883 369	27
28	1.996 495	2.287 928	2.620 172	2.998 703	28
29	2.046 407	2.356 566	2.711 878	3.118 651	29
YRS					
15	2.097 568	2.427 262	2.806 794	3.243 398	30
16	2.203 757	2.575 083	3.006 708	3.508 059	32
17	2.315 322	2.731 905	3.220 860	3.794 316	34
18	2.432 535	2.898 278	3.450 266	4.103 933	36
19	2.555 682	3.074 783	3.696 011	4.438 813	38
20	2.685 064	3.262 038	3.959 260	4.801 021	40
21	2.820 995	3.460 696	4.241 258	5.192 784	42
22	2.963 808	3.671 452	4.543 342	5.616 515	44
23	3.113 851	3.895 044	4.866 941	6.074 823	46
24	3.271 490	4.132 252	5.213 589	6.570 528	48
25	3.437 109	4.383 906	5.584 927	7.106 683	50
26	3.611 112	4.650 886	5.982 713	7.686 589	52
27	3.793 925	4.934 125	6.408 832	8.313 814	54
28	3.985 992	5.234 613	6.865 301	8.992 222	56
29	4.187 783	5.553 401	7.354 282	9.725 987	58
30	4.399 790	5.891 603	7.878 091	10.519 627	60

HALF YRS	9.0% ANNUAL RATE	10.0% ANNUAL RATE	11.0% ANNUAL RATE	12.0% ANNUAL RATE	HALF YRS
1	1.045 000	1.050 000	1.055 000	1.060 000	1
2	1.092 025	1.102 500	1.113 025	1.123 600	2
3	1.141 166	1.157 625	1.174 241	1.191 016	3
4	1.192 519	1.215 506	1.238 825	1.262 477	4
5	1.246 182	1.276 282	1.306 960	1.338 226	5
6	1.302 260	1.340 096	1.378 843	1.418 519	6
7	1.360 862	1.407 100	1.454 679	1.503 630	7
8	1.422 101	1.477 455	1.534 687	1.593 848	8
9	1.486 095	1.551 328	1.619 094	1.689 479	9
10	1.552 969	1.628 895	1.708 144	1.790 848	10
11	1.622 853	1.710 339	1.802 092	1.898 299	11
12	1.695 881	1.795 856	1.901 207	2.012 196	12
13	1.772 196	1.885 649	2.005 774	2.132 928	13
14	1.851 945	1.979 932	2.116 091	2.260 904	14
15	1.935 282	2.078 928	2.232 476	2.396 558	15
16	2.022 370	2.182 875	2.355 263	2.540 352	16
17	2.113 377	2.292 018	2.484 802	2.692 773	17
18	2.208 479	2.406 619	2.621 466	2.854 339	18
19	2.307 860	2.526 950	2.765 647	3.025 600	19
20	2.411 714	2.653 298	2.917 757	3.207 135	20
21	2.520 241	2.785 963	3.078 234	3.399 564	21
22	2.633 652	2.925 261	3.247 537	3.603 537	22
23	2.752 166	3.071 524	3.426 152	3.819 750	23
24	2.876 014	3.225 100	3.614 590	4.048 935	24
25	3.005 434	3.386 355	3.813 392	4.291 871	25
26	3.140 679	3.555 673	4.023 129	4.549 383	26
27	3.282 010	3.733 456	4.244 401	4.822 346	27
28	3.429 700	3.920 129	4.477 843	5.111 687	28
29	3.584 036	4.116 136	4.724 124	5.418 388	29
YRS					
15	3.745 318	4.321 942	4.983 951	5.743 491	30
16	4.089 981	4.764 941	5.547 262	6.453 387	32
17	4.466 362	5.253 348	6.174 242	7.251 025	34
18	4.877 378	5.791 816	6.872 085	8.147 252	36
19	5.326 219	6.385 477	7.648 803	9.154 252	38
20	5.816 365	7.039 989	8.513 309	10.285 718	40
21	6.351 615	7.761 588	9.475 525	11.557 033	42
22	6.936 123	8.557 150	10.546 497	12.985 482	44
23	7.574 420	9.434 258	11.738 515	14.590 487	46
24	8.271 456	10.401 270	13.065 260	16.393 872	48
25	9.032 636	11.467 400	14.541 961	18.420 154	50
26	9.863 865	12.642 808	16.185 566	20.696 885	52
27	10.771 587	13.938 696	18.014 940	23.255 020	54
28	11.762 842	15.367 412	20.051 079	26.129 341	56
29	12.845 318	16.942 572	22.317 352	29.358 927	58
30	14.027 408	18.679 186	24.839 770	32.987 691	60

SECTION 1

YRS	5.0% ANNUAL RATE	6.0% ANNUAL RATE	7.0% ANNUAL RATE	7.5% ANNUAL RATE	YRS
1	1.050 000	1.060 000	1.070 000	1.075 000	1
2	1.102 500	1.123 600	1.144 900	1.155 625	2
3	1.157 625	1.191 016	1.225 043	1.242 297	3
4	1.215 506	1.262 477	1.310 796	1.335 469	4
5	1.276 282	1.338 226	1.402 552	1.435 629	5
6	1.340 096	1.418 519	1.500 730	1.543 302	6
7	1.407 100	1.503 630	1.605 781	1.659 049	7
8	1.477 455	1.593 848	1.718 186	1.783 478	8
9	1.551 328	1.689 479	1.838 459	1.917 239	9
10	1.628 895	1.790 848	1.967 151	2.061 032	10
11	1.710 339	1.898 299	2.104 852	2.215 609	11
12	1.795 856	2.012 196	2.252 192	2.381 780	12
13	1.885 649	2.132 928	2.409 845	2.560 413	13
14	1.979 932	2.260 904	2.578 534	2.752 444	14
15	2.078 928	2.396 558	2.759 032	2.958 877	15
16	2.182 875	2.540 352	2.952 164	3.180 793	16
17	2.292 018	2.692 773	3.158 815	3.419 353	17
18	2.406 619	2.854 339	3.379 932	3.675 804	18
19	2.526 950	3.025 600	3.616 528	3.951 489	19
20	2.653 298	3.207 135	3.869 684	4.247 851	20
21	2.785 963	3.399 564	4.140 562	4.566 440	21
22	2.925 261	3.603 537	4.430 402	4.908 923	22
23	3.071 524	3.819 750	4.740 530	5.277 092	23
24	3.225 100	4.048 935	5.072 367	5.672 874	24
25	3.386 355	4.291 871	5.427 433	6.098 340	25
26	3.555 673	4.549 383	5.807 353	6.555 715	26
27	3.733 456	4.822 346	6.213 868	7.047 394	27
28	3.920 129	5.111 687	6.648 838	7.575 948	28
29	4.116 136	5.418 388	7.114 257	8.144 144	29
30	4.321 942	5.743 491	7.612 255	8.754 955	30
31	4.538 039	6.088 101	8.145 113	9.411 577	31
32	4.764 941	6.453 387	8.715 271	10.117 445	32
33	5.003 189	6.840 590	9.325 340	10.876 253	33
34	5.253 348	7.251 025	9.978 114	11.691 972	34
35	5.516 015	7.686 087	10.676 581	12.568 870	35
36	5.791 816	8.147 252	11.423 942	13.511 536	36
37	6.081 407	8.636 087	12.223 618	14.524 901	37
38	6.385 477	9.154 252	13.079 271	15.614 268	38
39	6.704 751	9.703 507	13.994 820	16.785 339	39
40	7.039 989	10.285 718	14.974 458	18.044 239	40
41	7.391 988	10.902 861	16.022 670	19.397 557	41
42	7.761 588	11.557 033	17.144 257	20.852 374	42
43	8.149 667	12.250 455	18.344 355	22.416 302	43
44	8.557 150	12.985 482	19.628 460	24.097 524	44
45	8.985 008	13.764 611	21.002 452	25.904 839	45
46	9.434 258	14.590 487	22.472 623	27.847 702	46
47	9.905 971	15.465 917	24.045 707	29.936 279	47
48	10.401 270	16.393 872	25.728 907	32.181 500	48
49	10.921 333	17.377 504	27.529 930	34.595 113	49
50	11.467 400	18.420 154	29.457 025	37.189 746	50

YRS	8.0% ANNUAL RATE	8.5% ANNUAL RATE	9.0% ANNUAL RATE	9.5% ANNUAL RATE	YRS
1	1.080 000	1.085 000	1.090 000	1.095 000	1
2	1.166 400	1.177 225	1.188 100	1.199 025	2
3	1.259 712	1.277 289	1.295 029	1.312 932	3
4	1.360 489	1.385 859	1.411 582	1.437 661	4
5	1.469 328	1.503 657	1.538 624	1.574 239	5
6	1.586 874	1.631 468	1.677 100	1.723 791	6
7	1.713 824	1.770 142	1.828 039	1.887 552	7
8	1.850 930	1.920 604	1.992 563	2.066 869	8
9	1.999 005	2.083 856	2.171 893	2.263 222	9
10	2.158 925	2.260 983	2.367 364	2.478 228	10
11	2.331 639	2.453 167	2.580 426	2.713 659	11
12	2.518 170	2.661 686	2.812 665	2.971 457	12
13	2.719 624	2.887 930	3.065 805	3.253 745	13
14	2.937 194	3.133 404	3.341 727	3.562 851	14
15	3.172 169	3.399 743	3.642 482	3.901 322	15
16	3.425 943	3.688 721	3.970 306	4.271 948	16
17	3.700 018	4.002 262	4.327 633	4.677 783	17
18	3.996 019	4.342 455	4.717 120	5.122 172	18
19	4.315 701	4.711 563	5.141 661	5.608 778	19
20	4.660 957	5.112 046	5.604 411	6.141 612	20
21	5.033 834	5.546 570	6.108 808	6.725 065	21
22	5.436 540	6.018 028	6.658 600	7.363 946	22
23	5.871 464	6.529 561	7.257 874	8.063 521	23
24	6.341 181	7.084 574	7.911 083	8.829 556	24
25	6.848 475	7.686 762	8.623 081	9.668 364	25
26	7.396 353	8.340 137	9.399 158	10.586 858	26
27	7.988 061	9.049 049	10.245 082	11.592 610	27
28	8.627 106	9.818 218	11.167 140	12.693 908	28
29	9.317 275	10.652 766	12.172 182	13.899 829	29
30	10.062 657	11.558 252	13.267 678	15.220 313	30
31	10.867 669	12.540 703	14.461 770	16.666 242	31
32	11.737 083	13.606 663	15.763 329	18.249 535	32
33	12.676 050	14.763 229	17.182 028	19.983 241	33
34	13.690 134	16.018 104	18.728 411	21.881 649	34
35	14.785 344	17.379 642	20.413 968	23.960 406	35
36	15.968 172	18.856 912	22.251 225	26.236 644	36
37	17.245 626	20.459 750	24.253 835	28.729 126	37
38	18.625 276	22.198 828	26.436 680	31.458 393	38
39	20.115 298	24.085 729	28.815 982	34.446 940	39
40	21.724 521	26.133 016	31.409 420	37.719 399	40
41	23.462 483	28.354 322	34.236 268	41.302 742	41
42	25.339 482	30.764 439	37.317 532	45.226 503	42
43	27.366 640	33.379 417	40.676 110	49.523 020	43
44	29.555 972	36.216 667	44.336 960	54.227 707	44
45	31.920 449	39.295 084	48.327 286	59.379 340	45
46	34.474 085	42.635 166	52.676 742	65.020 377	46
47	37.232 012	46.259 155	57.417 649	71.197 313	47
48	40.210 573	50.191 183	62.585 237	77.961 057	48
49	43.427 419	54.457 434	68.217 908	85.367 358	49
50	46.901 613	59.086 316	74.357 520	93.477 257	50

YRS	10.0% ANNUAL RATE	10.5% ANNUAL RATE	11.0% ANNUAL RATE	11.5% ANNUAL RATE	YRS
1	1.100 000	1.105 000	1.110 000	1.115 000	1
2	1.210 000	1.221 025	1.232 100	1.243 225	2
3	1.331 000	1.349 233	1.367 631	1.386 196	3
4	1.464 100	1.490 902	1.518 070	1.545 608	4
5	1.610 510	1.647 447	1.685 058	1.723 353	5
6	1.771 561	1.820 429	1.870 415	1.921 539	6
7	1.948 717	2.011 574	2.076 160	2.142 516	7
8	2.143 589	2.222 789	2.304 538	2.388 905	8
9	2.357 948	2.456 182	2.558 037	2.663 629	9
10	2.593 742	2.714 081	2.839 421	2.969 947	10
11	2.853 117	2.999 059	3.151 757	3.311 491	11
12	3.138 428	3.313 961	3.498 451	3.692 312	12
13	3.452 271	3.661 926	3.883 280	4.116 928	13
14	3.797 498	4.046 429	4.310 441	4.590 375	14
15	4.177 248	4.471 304	4.784 589	5.118 268	15
16	4.594 973	4.940 791	5.310 894	5.706 869	16
17	5.054 470	5.459 574	5.895 093	6.363 159	17
18	5.559 917	6.032 829	6.543 553	7.094 922	18
19	6.115 909	6.666 276	7.263 344	7.910 838	19
20	6.727 500	7.366 235	8.062 312	8.820 584	20
21	7.400 250	8.139 690	8.949 166	9.834 951	21
22	8.140 275	8.994 357	9.933 574	10.965 971	22
23	8.954 302	9.938 764	11.026 267	12.227 057	23
24	9.849 733	10.982 335	12.239 157	13.633 169	24
25	10.834 706	12.135 480	13.585 464	15.200 983	25
26	11.918 177	13.409 705	15.079 865	16.949 096	26
27	13.109 994	14.817 724	16.738 650	18.898 243	27
28	14.420 994	16.373 585	18.579 901	21.071 540	28
29	15.863 093	18.092 812	20.623 691	23.494 768	29
30	17.449 402	19.992 557	22.892 297	26.196 666	30
31	19.194 342	22.091 775	25.410 449	29.209 282	31
32	21.113 777	24.411 412	28.205 599	32.568 350	32
33	23.225 154	26.974 610	31.308 214	36.313 710	33
34	25.547 670	29.806 944	34.752 118	40.489 787	34
35	28.102 437	32.936 673	38.574 851	45.146 112	35
36	30.912 681	36.395 024	42.818 085	50.337 915	36
37	34.003 949	40.216 501	47.528 074	56.126 776	37
38	37.404 343	44.439 234	52.756 162	62.581 355	38
39	41.144 778	49.105 354	58.559 340	69.778 211	39
40	45.259 256	54.261 416	65.000 867	77.802 705	40
41	49.785 181	59.958 864	72.150 963	86.750 016	41
42	54.763 699	66.254 545	80.087 569	96.726 268	42
43	60.240 069	73.211 272	88.897 201	107.849 788	43
44	66.264 076	80.898 456	98.675 893	120.252 514	44
45	72.890 484	89.392 794	109.530 242	134.081 553	45
46	80.179 532	98.779 037	121.578 568	149.500 932	46
47	88.197 485	109.150 836	134.952 211	166.693 539	47
48	97.017 234	120.611 674	149.796 954	185.863 296	48
49	106.718 957	133.275 900	166.274 619	207.237 575	49
50	117.390 853	147.269 869	184.564 827	231.069 896	50

YRS	12.0% ANNUAL RATE	12.5% ANNUAL RATE	13.0% ANNUAL RATE	13.5% ANNUAL RATE	YRS
1	1.120 000	1.125 000	1.130 000	1.135 000	1
2	1.254 400	1.265 625	1.276 900	1.288 225	2
3	1.404 928	1.423 828	1.442 897	1.462 135	3
4	1.573 519	1.601 807	1.630 474	1.659 524	4
5	1.762 342	1.802 032	1.842 435	1.883 559	5
6	1.973 823	2.027 287	2.081 952	2.137 840	6
7	2.210 681	2.280 697	2.352 605	2.426 448	7
8	2.475 963	2.565 785	2.658 444	2.754 019	8
9	2.773 079	2.886 508	3.004 042	3.125 811	9
10	3.105 848	3.247 321	3.394 567	3.547 796	10
11	3.478 550	3.653 236	3.835 861	4.026 748	11
12	3.895 976	4.109 891	4.334 523	4.570 359	12
13	4.363 493	4.623 627	4.898 011	5.187 358	13
14	4.887 112	5.201 580	5.534 753	5.887 651	14
15	5.473 566	5.851 778	6.254 270	6.682 484	15
16	6.130 394	6.583 250	7.067 326	7.584 619	16
17	6.866 041	7.406 156	7.986 078	8.608 543	17
18	7.689 966	8.331 926	9.024 268	9.770 696	18
19	8.612 762	9.373 417	10.197 423	11.089 740	19
20	9.646 293	10.545 094	11.523 088	12.586 855	20
21	10.803 848	11.863 231	13.021 089	14.286 080	21
22	12.100 310	13.346 134	14.713 831	16.214 701	22
23	13.552 347	15.014 401	16.626 629	18.403 686	23
24	15.178 629	16.891 201	18.788 091	20.888 184	24
25	17.000 064	19.002 602	21.230 542	23.708 088	25
26	19.040 072	21.377 927	23.990 513	26.908 680	26
27	21.324 881	24.050 168	27.109 279	30.541 352	27
28	23.883 866	27.056 438	30.633 486	34.664 435	28
29	26.749 930	30.438 493	34.615 839	39.344 133	29
30	29.959 922	34.243 305	39.115 898	44.655 591	30
31	33.555 113	38.523 718	44.200 965	50.684 096	31
32	37.581 726	43.339 183	49.947 090	57.526 449	32
33	42.091 533	48.756 581	56.440 212	65.292 520	33
34	47.142 517	54.851 153	63.777 439	74.107 010	34
35	52.799 620	61.707 547	72.068 506	84.111 457	35
36	59.135 574	69.420 991	81.437 412	95.466 503	36
37	66.231 843	78.098 615	92.024 276	108.354 481	37
38	74.179 664	87.860 942	103.987 432	122.982 336	38
39	83.081 224	98.843 559	117.505 798	139.584 951	39
40	93.050 970	111.199 004	132.781 552	158.428 920	40
41	104.217 087	125.098 880	150.043 153	179.816 824	41
42	116.723 137	140.736 240	169.548 763	204.092 095	42
43	130.729 914	158.328 270	191.590 103	231.644 528	43
44	146.417 503	178.119 303	216.496 816	262.916 539	44
45	163.987 604	200.384 216	244.641 402	298.410 272	45
46	183.666 116	225.432 243	276.444 784	338.695 659	46
47	205.706 050	253.611 274	312.382 606	384.419 573	47
48	230.390 776	285.312 683	352.992 345	436.316 215	48
49	258.037 669	320.976 768	398.881 350	495.218 904	49
50	289.002 190	361.098 864	450.735 925	562.073 456	50

YRS	14.0% ANNUAL RATE	14.5% ANNUAL RATE	15.0% ANNUAL RATE	16.0% ANNUAL RATE	YRS
1	1.140 000	1.145 000	1.150 000	1.160 000	1
2	1.299 600	1.311 025	1.322 500	1.345 600	2
3	1.481 544	1.501 124	1.520 875	1.560 896	3
4	1.688 960	1.718 787	1.749 006	1.810 639	4
5	1.925 415	1.968 011	2.011 357	2.100 342	5
6	2.194 973	2.253 372	2.313 061	2.436 396	6
7	2.502 269	2.580 111	2.660 020	2.826 220	7
8	2.852 586	2.954 227	3.059 023	3.278 415	8
9	3.251 949	3.382 590	3.517 876	3.802 961	9
10	3.707 221	3.873 066	4.045 558	4.411 435	10
11	4.226 232	4.434 660	4.652 391	5.117 265	11
12	4.817 905	5.077 686	5.350 250	5.936 027	12
13	5.492 411	5.813 950	6.152 788	6.885 791	13
14	6.261 349	6.656 973	7.075 706	7.987 518	14
15	7.137 938	7.622 234	8.137 062	9.265 521	15
16	8.137 249	8.727 458	9.357 621	10.748 004	16
17	9.276 464	9.992 940	10.761 264	12.467 685	17
18	10.575 169	11.441 916	12.375 454	14.462 514	18
19	12.055 693	13.100 994	14.231 772	16.776 517	19
20	13.743 490	15.000 638	16.366 537	19.460 759	20
21	15.667 578	17.175 731	18.821 518	22.574 481	21
22	17.861 039	19.666 212	21.644 746	26.186 398	22
23	20.361 585	22.517 812	24.891 458	30.376 222	23
24	23.212 207	25.782 895	28.625 176	35.236 417	24
25	26.461 916	29.521 415	32.918 953	40.874 244	25
26	30.166 584	33.802 020	37.856 796	47.414 123	26
27	34.389 906	38.703 313	43.535 315	55.000 382	27
28	39.204 493	44.315 293	50.065 612	63.800 444	28
29	44.693 122	50.741 011	57.575 454	74.008 515	29
30	50.950 159	58.098 457	66.211 772	85.849 877	30
31	58.083 181	66.522 734	76.143 538	99.585 857	31
32	66.214 826	76.168 530	87.565 068	115.519 594	32
33	75.484 902	87.212 967	100.699 829	134.002 729	33
34	86.052 788	99.858 847	115.804 803	155.443 166	34
35	98.100 178	114.338 380	133.175 523	180.314 073	35
36	111.834 203	130.917 445	153.151 852	209.164 324	36
37	127.490 992	149.900 474	176.124 630	242.630 616	37
38	145.339 731	171.636 043	202.543 324	281.451 515	38
39	165.687 293	196.523 269	232.924 823	326.483 757	39
40	188.883 514	225.019 143	267.863 546	378.721 158	40
41	215.327 206	257.646 919	308.043 078	439.316 544	41
42	245.473 015	295.005 722	354.249 540	509.607 191	42
43	279.839 237	337.781 552	407.386 971	591.144 341	43
44	319.016 730	386.759 877	468.495 017	685.727 436	44
45	363.679 072	442.840 059	538.769 269	795.443 826	45
46	414.594 142	507.051 868	619.584 659	922.714 838	46
47	472.637 322	580.574 389	712.522 358	1070.349 212	47
48	538.806 547	664.757 675	819.400 712	1241.605 086	48
49	614.239 464	761.147 538	942.310 819	1440.261 900	49
50	700.232 988	871.513 931	1083.657 442	1670.703 804	50

	17.0%	18.0%	19.0%	20.0%	
	ANNUAL RATE	ANNUAL RATE	ANNUAL RATE	ANNUAL RATE	
YRS					YRS
1	1.170 000	1.180 000	1.190 000	1.200 000	1
2	1.368 900	1.392 400	1.416 100	1.440 000	2
3	1.601 613	1.643 032	1.685 159	1.728 000	3
4	1.873 887	1.938 778	2.005 339	2.073 600	4
5	2.192 448	2.287 758	2.386 354	2.488 320	5
6	2.565 164	2.699 554	2.839 761	2.985 984	6
7	3.001 242	3.185 474	3.379 315	3.583 181	7
8	3.511 453	3.758 859	4.021 385	4.299 817	8
9	4.108 400	4.435 454	4.785 449	5.159 780	9
10	4.806 828	5.233 836	5.694 684	6.191 736	10
11	5.623 989	6.175 926	6.776 674	7.430 084	11
12	6.580 067	7.287 593	8.064 242	8.916 100	12
13	7.698 679	8.599 359	9.596 448	10.699 321	13
14	9.007 454	10.147 244	11.419 773	12.839 185	14
15	10.538 721	11.973 748	13.589 530	15.407 022	15
16	12.330 304	14.129 023	16.171 540	18.488 426	16
17	14.426 456	16.672 247	19.244 133	22.186 111	17
18	16.878 953	19.673 251	22.900 518	26.623 333	18
19	19.748 375	23.214 436	27.251 616	31.948 000	19
20	23.105 599	27.393 035	32.429 423	38.337 600	20
21	27.033 551	32.323 781	38.591 014	46.005 120	21
22	31.629 255	38.142 061	45.923 307	55.206 144	22
23	37.006 228	45.007 632	54.648 735	66.247 373	23
24	43.297 287	53.109 006	65.031 994	79.496 847	24
25	50.657 826	62.668 627	77.388 073	95.396 217	25
26	59.269 656	73.948 980	92.091 807	114.475 460	26
27	69.345 497	87.259 797	109.589 251	137.370 552	27
28	81.134 232	102.966 560	130.411 208	164.844 662	28
29	94.927 051	121.500 541	155.189 338	197.813 595	29
30	111.064 650	143.370 638	184.675 312	237.376 314	30
31	129.945 641	169.177 353	219.763 621	284.851 577	31
32	152.036 399	199.629 277	261.518 710	341.821 892	32
33	177.882 587	235.562 547	311.207 264	410.186 270	33
34	208.122 627	277.963 805	370.336 645	492.223 524	34
35	243.503 474	327.997 290	440.700 607	590.668 229	35
36	284.899 064	387.036 802	524.433 722	708.801 875	36
37	333.331 905	456.703 427	624.076 130	850.562 250	37
38	389.998 329	538.910 044	742.650 594	1020.674 700	38
39	456.298 045	635.913 852	883.754 207	1224.809 640	39
40	533.868 713	750.378 345	1051.667 507	1469.771 568	40
41	624.626 394	885.446 447	1251.484 333	1763.725 882	41
42	730.812 881	1044.826 807	1489.266 356	2116.471 058	42
43	855.051 071	1232.895 633	1772.226 964	2539.765 269	43
44	1000.409 753	1454.816 847	2108.950 087	3047.718 323	44
45	1170.479 411	1716.683 879	2509.650 603	3657.261 988	45
46	1369.460 910	2025.686 977	2986.484 218	4388.714 386	46
47	1602.269 265	2390.310 633	3553.916 219	5266.457 263	47
48	1874.655 040	2820.566 547	4229.160 301	6319.748 715	48
49	2193.346 397	3328.268 525	5032.700 758	7583.698 458	49
50	2566.215 284	3927.356 860	5988.913 902	9100.438 150	50

Section 2. The Future Value of $1.00 per period:

These factors represent the growth of the investment of $1.00 per period. It is important to understand that each investment is made at the end of each period. Convention dictates this technique.

That is, if we begin an investment period at a particular time, then the first $1.00 investment is made at the end of the first period. An example: If the investment intervals are to be monthly, and the beginning period is January 1, then the first regular investment of $1.00 will be made at the end of January. All investments are made in equal amounts ($1) and at the exact same intervals (monthly, quarterly, annual, and semiannual).

These factors are based on the assumption that no funds will be withdrawn at any point during the investment.

In this section the following four (4) periods are presented in detail: monthly, quarterly, semiannual, and annual.

Monthly:

The factors presented on pages 29 through 34 indicate the value of a $1 investment made at the end of each stated monthly interval. That is, the regular monthly investment, plus interest earned on the interest and on the investment.

Example C

If you invest $150 at the end of each month, what will be the value of your investment in 10 years? Assume an annual interest rate of 12.0% and monthly compounding of interest.

Turn to page 32 and locate the 12% column. Proceed down that column until you locate the point where the 10 year row intersects the 12.0% interest column. The number is 230.038689 for ech $1 invested. So, to determine your answer, multiply 230.038689 by $150. The correct answer is $34,505.80. That is, the value of that monthly investment of $150 is $34,505.80 in 10 years.

Note: if your investment period is less than two (2) years, we have provided all the monthly payment amounts for each monthly period; over two (2) years only the annual figures are provided.

Quarterly:

The factors presented on pages 35 through 37 indicate the value of a $1 investment, made at the end of each stated quarterly interval. That is, the regular quarterly interval, plus interest earned on the interest and on the investment.

Example D

If you deposit $500 in a savings account at the end of every quarter, what is the value of that account at the end of 30 years? Assume an interest rate of 5.0% and quarterly compounding.

Turn to page 35 and locate the 5.0% column. Proceed down that column until you locate the point where the 30 years row intersects the 5.0% interest column. The number is 275.217058 for each $1 invested. So, to determine your answer, multiply 275.217058 by $500. The correct answer is $137,608.53. That is, the value of that $500 per quarter investment is $137,608.53 in 30 years.

Note: For investments of 5 years and more, only the annual amounts are shown.

Semiannual:

The factors on pages 38 through 39 cover semiannual compounding, or the interest being compounded every 6 months. They are used the same way as the monthly or quarterly tables.

Annual:

The factors on pages 40 through 45 cover annual compounding (or the interest being compounded every year). They are used the same way as the monthly, quarterly, and semiannual tables.

For you formula buffs . . .

$$S_{\overline{n}|} = \frac{(1 + i)^n - 1}{i}$$

$S_{\overline{n}|}$ = The future value of \$1.00 per period
i = Interest rate per period
n = number of compounding periods

FUTURE VALUE OF
$1 PER PERIOD
MONTHLY COMPOUNDING

MOS	5.0% ANNUAL RATE	6.0% ANNUAL RATE	7.0% ANNUAL RATE	7.5% ANNUAL RATE	MOS
1	1.000 000	1.000 000	1.000 000	1.000 000	1
2	2.004 167	2.005 000	2.005 833	2.006 250	2
3	3.012 517	3.015 025	3.017 534	3.018 789	3
4	4.025 070	4.030 100	4.035 136	4.037 656	4
5	5.041 841	5.050 251	5.058 675	5.062 892	5
6	6.062 848	6.075 502	6.088 184	6.094 535	6
7	7.088 110	7.105 879	7.123 698	7.132 626	7
8	8.117 644	8.141 409	8.165 253	8.177 205	8
9	9.151 467	9.182 116	9.212 883	9.228 312	9
10	10.189 599	10.228 026	10.266 625	10.285 989	10
11	11.232 055	11.279 167	11.326 514	11.350 277	11
12	12.278 855	12.335 562	12.392 585	12.421 216	12
13	13.330 017	13.397 240	13.464 875	13.498 848	13
14	14.385 559	14.464 226	14.543 420	14.583 216	14
15	15.445 499	15.536 548	15.628 257	15.674 361	15
16	16.509 855	16.614 230	16.719 422	16.772 326	16
17	17.578 646	17.697 301	17.816 952	17.877 153	17
18	18.651 891	18.785 788	18.920 884	18.988 885	18
19	19.729 607	19.879 717	20.031 256	20.107 566	19
20	20.811 814	20.979 115	21.148 105	21.233 238	20
21	21.898 529	22.084 011	22.271 469	22.365 946	21
22	22.989 773	23.194 431	23.401 386	23.505 733	22
23	24.085 564	24.310 403	24.537 894	24.652 644	23

YRS

YRS	5.0%	6.0%	7.0%	7.5%	MOS
2	25.185 921	25.431 955	25.681 032	25.806 723	24
3	38.753 336	39.336 105	39.930 101	40.231 382	36
4	53.014 885	54.097 832	55.209 236	55.775 864	48
5	68.006 083	69.770 031	71.592 902	72.527 105	60
6	83.764 259	86.408 856	89.160 944	90.578 789	72
7	100.328 653	104.073 927	107.998 981	110.031 871	84
8	117.740 512	122.828 542	128.198 821	130.995 147	96
9	136.043 196	142.739 900	149.858 909	153.585 857	108
10	155.282 279	163.879 347	173.084 807	177.930 342	120
11	175.505 671	186.322 629	197.989 707	204.164 753	132
12	196.763 730	210.150 163	224.694 985	232.435 809	144
13	219.109 391	235.447 328	253.330 789	262.901 620	156
14	242.598 299	262.304 766	284.036 677	295.732 572	168
15	267.288 944	290.818 712	316.962 297	331.112 276	180
16	293.242 809	321.091 337	352.268 112	369.238 599	192
17	320.524 523	353.231 110	390.126 188	410.324 767	204
18	349.202 021	387.353 194	430.721 027	454.600 560	216
19	379.346 715	423.579 854	474.250 470	502.313 599	228
20	411.033 669	462.040 895	520.926 660	553.730 725	240
21	444.341 787	502.874 129	570.977 075	609.139 496	252
22	479.354 011	546.225 867	624.645 640	668.849 794	264
23	516.157 528	592.251 446	682.193 909	733.195 558	276
24	554.843 982	641.115 782	743.902 347	802.536 650	288
25	595.509 708	692.993 962	810.071 693	877.260 872	300
26	638.255 971	748.071 876	881.024 427	957.786 129	312
27	683.189 213	806.546 875	957.106 339	1044.562 771	324
28	730.421 325	868.628 484	1038.688 219	1138.076 109	336
29	780.069 922	934.539 150	1126.167 659	1238.849 131	348
30	832.258 635	1004.515 042	1219.970 996	1347.445 425	360

FUTURE VALUE OF
$1 PER PERIOD
MONTHLY
COMPOUNDING

	8.0%	8.5%	9.0%	9.5%	
	ANNUAL RATE	ANNUAL RATE	ANNUAL RATE	ANNUAL RATE	
MOS					MOS
1	1.000 000	1.000 000	1.000 000	1.000 000	1
2	2.006 667	2.007 083	2.007 500	2.007 917	2
3	3.020 044	3.021 300	3.022 556	3.023 813	3
4	4.040 178	4.042 701	4.045 225	4.047 751	4
5	5.067 113	5.071 337	5.075 565	5.079 796	5
6	6.100 893	6.107 259	6.113 631	6.120 011	6
7	7.141 566	7.150 519	7.159 484	7.168 461	7
8	8.189 176	8.201 168	8.213 180	8.225 211	8
9	9.243 771	9.259 260	9.274 779	9.290 328	9
10	10.305 396	10.324 846	10.344 339	10.363 876	10
11	11.374 099	11.397 980	11.421 922	11.445 923	11
12	12.449 926	12.478 716	12.507 586	12.536 537	12
13	13.532 926	13.567 107	13.601 393	13.635 785	13
14	14.623 145	14.663 207	14.703 404	14.743 734	14
15	15.720 633	15.767 072	15.813 679	15.860 456	15
16	16.825 437	16.878 755	16.932 282	16.986 018	16
17	17.937 606	17.998 313	18.059 274	18.120 490	17
18	19.057 191	19.125 801	19.194 718	19.263 944	18
19	20.184 238	20.261 276	20.338 679	20.416 450	19
20	21.318 800	21.404 793	21.491 219	21.578 081	20
21	22.460 925	22.556 410	22.652 403	22.748 907	21
22	23.610 665	23.716 185	23.822 296	23.929 003	22
23	24.768 069	24.884 174	25.000 963	25.118 441	23
YRS					
2	25.933 190	26.060 437	26.188 471	26.317 295	24
3	40.535 558	40.842 659	41.152 716	41.465 760	36
4	56.349 915	56.931 495	57.520 711	58.117 673	48
5	73.476 856	74.442 437	75.424 137	76.422 249	60
6	92.025 325	93.501 188	95.007 028	96.543 509	72
7	112.113 308	114.244 559	116.426 928	118.661 756	84
8	133.868 583	136.821 455	139.856 164	142.975 186	96
9	157.429 535	161.393 943	165.483 223	169.701 665	108
10	182.946 035	188.138 416	193.514 277	199.080 682	120
11	210.580 392	217.246 858	224.174 837	231.375 495	132
12	240.508 387	248.928 220	257.711 570	266.875 491	144
13	272.920 390	283.409 927	294.394 279	305.898 776	156
14	308.022 574	320.939 504	334.518 079	348.795 027	168
15	346.038 222	361.786 353	378.405 769	395.948 628	180
16	387.209 149	406.243 693	426.410 427	447.782 110	192
17	431.797 244	454.630 657	478.918 252	504.759 939	204
18	480.086 128	507.294 589	536.351 674	567.392 681	216
19	532.382 966	564.613 533	599.172 747	636.241 570	228
20	589.020 416	626.998 951	667.886 870	711.923 546	240
21	650.358 746	694.898 672	743.046 852	795.116 775	252
22	716.788 127	768.800 112	825.257 358	886.566 731	264
23	788.731 114	849.233 766	915.179 777	987.092 874	276
24	866.645 333	936.777 024	1013.537 539	1097.595 994	288
25	951.026 395	1032.058 310	1121.121 937	1219.066 282	300
26	1042.411 042	1135.761 595	1238.798 495	1352.592 202	312
27	1141.380 571	1248.631 307	1367.513 924	1499.370 247	324
28	1248.564 521	1371.477 676	1508.303 750	1660.715 659	336
29	1364.644 687	1505.182 546	1662.300 631	1838.074 212	348
30	1490.359 449	1650.705 711	1830.743 483	2033.035 174	360

FUTURE VALUE OF
$1 PER PERIOD

MONTHLY
COMPOUNDING

MOS	10.0% ANNUAL RATE	10.5% ANNUAL RATE	11.0% ANNUAL RATE	11.5% ANNUAL RATE	MOS
1	1.000 000	1.000 000	1.000 000	1.000 000	1
2	2.008 333	2.008 750	2.009 167	2.009 583	2
3	3.025 069	3.026 327	3.027 584	3.028 842	3
4	4.050 278	4.052 807	4.055 337	4.057 868	4
5	5.084 031	5.088 269	5.092 511	5.096 756	5
6	6.126 398	6.132 791	6.139 192	6.145 600	6
7	7.177 451	7.186 453	7.195 468	7.204 495	7
8	8.237 263	8.249 335	8.261 427	8.273 538	8
9	9.305 907	9.321 516	9.337 156	9.352 827	9
10	10.383 456	10.403 080	10.422 747	10.442 458	10
11	11.469 985	11.494 107	11.518 289	11.542 531	11
12	12.565 568	12.594 680	12.623 873	12.653 147	12
13	13.670 281	13.704 884	13.739 592	13.774 407	13
14	14.784 200	14.824 801	14.865 538	14.906 411	14
15	15.907 402	15.954 518	16.001 806	16.049 264	15
16	17.039 964	17.094 120	17.148 489	17.203 070	16
17	18.181 963	18.243 694	18.305 683	18.367 933	17
18	19.333 480	19.403 326	19.473 485	19.543 959	18
19	20.494 592	20.573 105	20.651 992	20.731 255	19
20	21.665 380	21.753 120	21.841 302	21.929 929	20
21	22.845 925	22.943 460	23.041 514	23.140 091	21
22	24.036 308	24.144 215	24.252 728	24.361 851	22
23	25.236 610	25.355 477	25.475 045	25.595 318	23

YRS					
2	26.446 915	26.577 337	26.708 566	26.840 607	24
3	41.781 821	42.100 932	42.423 123	42.748 428	36
4	58.722 492	59.335 280	59.956 151	60.585 221	48
5	77.437 072	78.468 912	79.518 080	80.584 891	60
6	98.111 314	99.711 137	101.343 692	103.009 708	72
7	120.950 418	123.294 329	125.694 940	128.153 744	84
8	146.181 076	149.476 469	152.864 085	156.346 728	96
9	174.053 713	178.543 972	183.177 212	187.958 374	108
10	204.844 979	210.814 814	216.998 139	223.403 228	120
11	238.860 493	246.642 013	254.732 784	263.146 100	132
12	276.437 876	286.417 494	296.834 038	307.708 167	144
13	317.950 102	330.576 371	343.807 200	357.673 800	158
14	363.809 201	379.601 707	396.216 042	413.698 232	168
15	414.470 346	434.029 805	454.689 575	476.516 149	180
16	470.436 376	494.456 068	519.929 596	546.951 324	192
17	532.262 780	561.541 512	592.719 117	625.927 421	204
18	600.563 216	636.020 005	673.931 757	714.480 107	216
19	676.015 601	718.706 284	764.542 228	813.770 632	228
20	759.368 836	810.504 876	865.638 038	925.101 060	240
21	851.450 244	912.419 990	978.432 537	1049.931 340	252
22	953.173 779	1025.566 501	1104.279 485	1189.898 456	264
23	1065.549 097	1151.182 148	1244.689 295	1346.837 891	276
24	1189.691 580	1290.641 073	1401.347 165	1522.807 696	288
25	1326.833 403	1445.468 853	1576.133 301	1720.115 481	300
26	1478.335 767	1617.359 188	1771.145 485	1941.348 676	312
27	1645.702 407	1808.192 431	1988.724 252	2189.408 459	324
28	1830.594 523	2020.056 156	2231.480 981	2467.547 806	336
29	2034.847 258	2255.267 995	2502.329 236	2779.414 142	348
30	2260.487 925	2516.400 990	2804.519 736	3129.097 181	360

	12.0% ANNUAL RATE	12.5% ANNUAL RATE	13.0% ANNUAL RATE	13.5% ANNUAL RATE	
MOS					**MOS**
1	1.000 000	1.000 000	1.000 000	1.000 000	1
2	2.010 000	2.010 417	2.010 833	2.011 250	2
3	3.030 100	3.031 359	3.032 617	3.033 877	3
4	4.060 401	4.062 935	4.065 471	4.068 008	4
5	5.101 005	5.105 257	5.109 513	5.113 773	5
6	6.152 015	6.158 437	6.164 866	6.171 303	6
7	7.213 535	7.222 588	7.231 652	7.240 730	7
8	8.285 671	8.297 823	8.309 995	8.322 188	8
9	9.368 527	9.384 258	9.400 020	9.415 813	9
10	10.462 213	10.482 011	10.501 854	10.521 741	10
11	11.566 835	11.591 199	11.615 624	11.640 110	11
12	12.682 503	12.711 940	12.741 460	12.771 061	12
13	13.809 328	13.844 357	13.879 492	13.914 736	13
14	14.947 421	14.988 569	15.029 853	15.071 277	14
15	16.096 896	16.144 699	16.192 677	16.240 828	15
16	17.257 864	17.312 873	17.368 098	17.423 538	16
17	18.430 443	18.493 216	18.556 252	18.619 553	17
18	19.614 748	19.685 854	19.757 278	19.829 023	18
19	20.810 895	20.890 914	20.971 315	21.052 099	19
20	22.019 004	22.108 528	22.198 504	22.288 935	20
21	23.239 194	23.338 825	23.438 988	23.539 686	21
22	24.471 586	24.581 938	24.692 911	24.804 507	22
23	25.716 302	25.838 000	25.960 417	26.083 558	23
YRS					
2	26.973 465	27.107 146	27.241 655	27.376 998	24
3	43.076 878	43.408 507	43.743 348	44.081 434	36
4	61.222 608	61.868 431	62.522 811	63.185 871	48
5	81.669 670	82.772 744	83.894 449	85.035 127	60
6	104.709 931	106.445 124	108.216 068	110.023 563	72
7	130.672 274	133.252 107	135.894 861	138.602 198	84
8	159.927 293	163.608 765	167.394 225	171.286 853	96
9	192.892 579	197.985 131	203.241 525	208.667 457	108
10	230.038 689	236.913 480	244.036 917	251.418 698	120
11	271.895 856	280.996 567	290.463 399	300.312 201	132
12	319.061 559	330.916 961	343.298 242	356.230 450	144
13	372.209 054	387.447 618	403.426 010	420.182 722	156
14	432.096 982	451.463 840	471.853 363	493.323 301	168
15	499.580 198	523.956 837	549.725 914	576.972 311	180
16	575.621 974	606.049 070	638.347 406	672.639 547	192
17	661.307 751	699.011 633	739.201 542	782.051 719	204
18	757.860 630	804.283 930	853.976 825	907.183 624	216
19	866.658 830	923.495 968	984.594 826	1050.293 785	228
20	989.255 365	1058.493 594	1133.242 353	1213.965 218	240
21	1127.400 210	1211.367 071	1302.408 067	1401.152 054	252
22	1283.065 279	1384.483 450	1494.924 144	1615.232 853	264
23	1458.472 574	1580.523 215	1714.013 694	1860.071 591	276
24	1656.125 905	1802.521 791	1963.344 717	2140.087 398	288
25	1878.846 626	2053.916 541	2247.091 520	2460.334 319	300
26	2129.813 909	2338.599 989	2570.004 599	2826.592 538	312
27	2412.610 125	2660.980 094	2937.490 172	3245.472 702	324
28	2731.271 980	3026.048 499	3355.700 690	3724.535 238	336
29	3090.348 134	3439.457 817	3831.637 843	4272.426 817	348
30	3494.964 133	3907.609 164	4373.269 783	4899.036 412	360

MOS	14.0% ANNUAL RATE	14.5% ANNUAL RATE	15.0% ANNUAL RATE	16.0% ANNUAL RATE	MOS
1	1.000 000	1.000 000	1.000 000	1.000 000	1
2	2.011 667	2.012 083	2.012 500	2.013 333	2
3	3.035 136	3.036 396	3.037 656	3.040 178	3
4	4.070 546	4.073 086	4.075 627	4.080 713	4
5	5.118 036	5.122 302	5.126 572	5.135 123	5
6	6.177 746	6.184 197	6.190 654	6.203 591	6
7	7.249 820	7.258 922	7.268 038	7.286 306	7
8	8.334 401	8.346 634	8.358 888	8.383 457	8
9	9.431 636	9.447 490	9.463 374	9.495 236	9
10	10.541 672	10.561 647	10.581 666	10.621 839	10
11	11.664 658	11.689 267	11.713 937	11.763 464	11
12	12.800 745	12.830 512	12.860 361	12.920 310	12
13	13.950 087	13.985 547	14.021 116	14.092 581	13
14	15.112 838	15.154 539	15.196 380	15.280 482	14
15	16.289 155	16.337 657	16.386 335	16.484 221	15
16	17.479 195	17.535 070	17.591 164	17.704 011	16
17	18.683 119	18.746 952	18.811 053	18.940 065	17
18	19.901 089	19.973 478	20.046 192	20.192 599	18
19	21.133 268	21.214 824	21.296 769	21.461 833	19
20	22.379 823	22.471 170	22.562 979	22.747 991	20
21	23.640 921	23.742 696	23.845 016	24.051 298	21
22	24.916 731	25.029 587	25.143 078	25.371 982	22
23	26.207 427	26.332 028	26.457 367	26.710 275	23

YRS					
2	27.513 180	27.650 207	27.788 084	28.066 412	24
3	44.422 800	44.767 478	45.115 505	45.821 745	36
4	63.857 736	64.538 532	65.228 388	66.635 803	48
5	86.195 125	87.374 798	88.574 508	91.035 516	60
6	111.868 425	113.751 493	115.673 621	119.638 587	72
7	141.375 828	144.217 508	147.129 040	153.169 132	84
8	175.289 927	179.406 832	183.641 059	192.476 010	96
9	214.268 826	220.051 745	226.022 551	238.554 316	108
10	259.068 912	266.998 057	275.217 058	292.570 569	120
11	310.559 534	321.222 707	332.319 805	355.892 244	132
12	369.739 871	383.854 095	398.602 077	430.122 395	144
13	437.758 319	456.195 562	475.539 523	517.140 233	156
14	515.934 780	539.752 513	564.845 011	619.148 703	168
15	605.786 272	636.263 747	668.506 759	738.730 255	180
16	709.056 369	747.737 633	788.832 603	878.912 215	192
17	827.749 031	876.493 913	928.501 369	1043.243 434	204
18	964.167 496	1025.211 968	1090.622 520	1235.884 123	216
19	1120.958 972	1196.986 579	1278.805 378	1461.711 177	228
20	1301.166 005	1395.392 327	1497.239 481	1726.441 638	240
21	1508.285 522	1624.557 981	1750.787 854	2036.777 427	252
22	1746.336 688	1889.252 413	2045.095 272	2400.575 011	264
23	2019.938 898	2194.983 839	2386.713 938	2827.044 294	276
24	2334.401 417	2548.114 445	2783.249 347	3326.981 781	288
25	2695.826 407	2955.992 779	3243.529 615	3913.043 898	300
26	3111.227 338	3427.106 674	3777.802 015	4600.067 404	312
27	3588.665 088	3971.259 878	4397.961 118	5405.444 997	324
28	4137.404 359	4599.776 067	5117.813 598	6349.565 632	336
29	4768.093 467	5325.734 484	5953.385 616	7456.330 682	348
30	5492.970 967	6164.242 121	6923.279 611	8753.759 030	360

	17.0% ANNUAL RATE	18.0% ANNUAL RATE	19.0% ANNUAL RATE	20.0% ANNUAL RATE	
MOS					**MOS**
1	1.000 000	1.000 000	1.000 000	1.000 000	1
2	2.014 167	2.015 000	2.015 833	2.016 667	2
3	3.042 701	3.045 225	3.047 751	3.050 278	3
4	4.085 806	4.090 903	4.096 007	4.101 116	4
5	5.143 688	5.152 267	5.160 860	5.169 468	5
6	6.216 557	6.229 551	6.242 574	6.255 625	6
7	7.304 625	7.322 994	7.341 415	7.359 886	7
8	8.408 107	8.432 839	8.457 654	8.482 551	8
9	9.527 222	9.559 332	9.591 566	9.623 926	9
10	10.662 191	10.702 722	10.743 433	10.784 325	10
11	11.813 238	11.863 262	11.913 537	11.964 064	11
12	12.980 593	13.041 211	13.102 168	13.163 465	12
13	14.164 484	14.236 830	14.309 619	14.382 856	13
14	15.365 148	15.450 382	15.536 188	15.622 570	14
15	16.582 821	16.682 138	16.782 178	16.882 947	15
16	17.817 744	17.932 370	18.047 896	18.164 329	16
17	19.070 162	19.201 355	19.333 654	19.467 068	17
18	20.340 323	20.489 376	20.639 770	20.791 519	18
19	21.628 477	21.796 716	21.966 567	22.138 044	19
20	22.934 881	23.123 667	23.314 371	23.507 012	20
21	24.259 792	24.470 522	24.683 515	24.898 795	21
22	25.603 472	25.837 580	26.074 337	26.313 775	22
23	26.966 188	27.225 144	27.487 181	27.752 338	23
YRS					
2	28.348 209	28.633 521	28.922 394	29.214 877	24
3	46.541 802	47.275 969	48.024 542	48.787 826	36
4	68.081 048	69.565 219	71.089 450	72.654 905	48
5	93.581 182	96.214 652	98.939 196	101.758 208	60
6	123.770 579	128.077 197	132.566 399	137.246 517	72
7	159.511 558	166.172 636	173.169 599	180.520 645	84
8	201.825 006	211.720 235	222.195 973	233.288 730	96
9	251.919 548	266.177 771	281.392 918	297.633 662	108
10	311.226 062	331.288 191	352.870 328	376.095 300	120
11	381.438 553	409.135 393	439.175 798	471.770 720	132
12	464.562 540	502.210 922	543.385 424	588.436 476	144
13	562.972 341	613.493 716	669.213 441	730.697 658	156
14	679.478 890	746.545 446	821.144 606	904.169 675	168
15	817.410 030	905.624 513	1004.594 042	1115.699 905	180
16	980.705 566	1095.822 335	1226.100 247	1373.637 983	192
17	1174.029 800	1323.226 308	1493.558 135	1688.165 376	204
18	1402.904 761	1595.114 630	1816.500 430	2071.697 274	216
19	1673.867 935	1920.189 249	2206.437 425	2539.372 652	228
20	1994.698 995	2308.854 370	2677.267 240	3109.651 838	240
21	2374.440 878	2773.549 452	3245.771 169	3805.045 193	252
22	2824.061 507	3329.147 335	3932.211 806	4653.001 652	264
23	3356.363 651	3993.430 261	4761.055 238	5686.992 197	276
24	3986.551 756	4787.658 998	5761.843 068	6947.831 050	288
25	4732.626 240	5737.253 308	6970.245 332	8485.286 707	300
26	5615.897 651	6872.605 521	8429.331 851	10360.046 428	312
27	6661.595 368	8230.053 258	10191.107 326	12646.111 719	324
28	7899.588 246	9853.042 439	12318.364 881	15433.719 354	336
29	9365.237 774	11793.517 795	14886.924 139	18832.903 252	348
30	11100.408 126	14113.585 393	17988.333 579	22977.837 794	360

FUTURE VALUE OF
$1 PER PERIOD

QUARTERLY
COMPOUNDING

QTRS	5.0% ANNUAL RATE	6.0% ANNUAL RATE	7.0% ANNUAL RATE	8.0% ANNUAL RATE	QTRS
1	1.000 000	1.000 000	1.000 000	1.000 000	1
2	2.012 500	2.015 000	2.017 500	2.020 000	2
3	3.037 656	3.045 225	3.052 806	3.060 400	3
4	4.075 627	4.090 903	4.106 230	4.121 608	4
5	5.126 572	5.152 267	5.178 089	5.204 040	5
6	6.190 654	6.229 551	6.268 706	6.308 121	6
7	7.268 038	7.322 994	7.378 408	7.434 283	7
8	8.358 888	8.432 839	8.507 530	8.582 969	8
9	9.463 374	9.559 332	9.656 412	9.754 628	9
10	10.581 666	10.702 722	10.825 399	10.949 721	10
11	11.713 937	11.863 262	12.014 844	12.168 715	11
12	12.860 361	13.041 211	13.225 104	13.412 090	12
13	14.021 116	14.236 830	14.456 543	14.680 332	13
14	15.196 380	15.450 382	15.709 533	15.973 938	14
15	16.386 335	16.682 138	16.984 449	17.293 417	15
16	17.591 164	17.932 370	18.281 677	18.639 285	16
17	18.811 053	19.201 355	19.601 607	20.012 071	17
18	20.046 192	20.489 376	20.944 635	21.412 312	18
19	21.296 769	21.796 716	22.311 166	22.840 559	19

YRS					
5	22.562 979	23.123 667	23.701 611	24.297 370	20
6	27.788 084	28.633 521	29.511 016	30.421 862	24
7	33.279 384	34.481 479	35.737 880	37.051 210	28
8	39.050 441	40.688 288	42.412 200	44.227 030	32
9	45.115 505	47.275 969	49.566 129	51.994 367	36
10	51.489 557	54.267 894	57.234 134	60.401 983	40
11	58.188 337	61.688 868	65.453 154	69.502 657	44
12	65.228 388	69.565 219	74.262 784	79.353 519	48
13	72.627 097	77.924 892	83.705 466	90.016 409	52
14	80.402 736	86.797 543	93.826 816	101.558 264	56
15	88.574 508	96.214 652	104.675 216	114.051 539	60
16	97.162 593	106.209 628	116.303 306	127.574 662	64
17	106.188 201	116.817 931	128.766 979	142.212 525	68
18	115.673 621	128.077 197	142.126 280	158.057 019	72
19	125.642 280	140.027 372	156.445 567	175.207 608	76
20	136.118 795	152.710 852	171.793 824	193.771 958	80
21	147.129 040	166.172 636	188.244 992	213.866 607	84
22	158.700 206	180.460 482	205.878 326	235.617 701	88
23	170.860 868	195.625 082	224.778 773	259.161 785	92
24	183.641 059	211.720 235	245.037 388	284.646 659	96
25	197.072 342	228.803 043	266.751 768	312.232 306	100
26	211.187 886	246.934 114	290.026 522	342.091 897	104
27	226.022 551	266.177 771	314.973 777	374.412 879	108
28	241.612 973	286.602 288	341.713 718	409.398 150	112
29	257.997 654	308.280 125	370.375 165	447.267 331	116
30	275.217 058	331.288 191	401.096 196	488.258 152	120

FUTURE VALUE OF
$1 PER PERIOD

QUARTERLY
COMPOUNDING

QTRS	9.0% ANNUAL RATE	10.0% ANNUAL RATE	11.0% ANNUAL RATE	12.0% ANNUAL RATE	QTRS
1	1.000 000	1.000 000	1.000 000	1.000 000	1
2	2.022 500	2.025 000	2.027 500	2.030 000	2
3	3.068 006	3.075 625	3.083 256	3.090 900	3
4	4.137 036	4.152 516	4.168 046	4.183 627	4
5	5.230 120	5.256 329	5.282 667	5.309 136	5
6	6.347 797	6.387 737	6.427 940	6.468 410	6
7	7.490 623	7.547 430	7.604 709	7.662 462	7
8	8.659 162	8.736 116	8.813 838	8.892 336	8
9	9.853 993	9.954 519	10.056 219	10.159 106	9
10	11.075 708	11.203 382	11.332 765	11.463 879	10
11	12.324 911	12.483 466	12.644 416	12.807 796	11
12	13.602 222	13.795 553	13.992 137	14.192 030	12
13	14.908 272	15.140 442	15.376 921	15.617 790	13
14	16.243 708	16.518 953	16.799 786	17.086 324	14
15	17.609 191	17.931 927	18.261 781	18.598 914	15
16	19.005 398	19.380 225	19.763 979	20.156 881	16
17	20.433 020	20.864 730	21.307 489	21.761 588	17
18	21.892 763	22.386 349	22.893 445	23.414 435	18
19	23.385 350	23.946 007	24.523 015	25.116 868	19
YRS					
5	24.911 520	25.544 658	26.197 398	26.870 374	20
6	31.367 403	32.349 038	33.368 222	34.426 470	24
7	38.424 222	39.859 801	41.360 975	42.930 923	28
8	46.137 912	48.150 278	50.269 868	52.502 759	32
9	54.569 619	57.301 413	60.199 910	63.275 944	36
10	63.786 176	67.402 554	71.268 145	75.401 260	40
11	73.860 642	78.552 323	83.605 035	89.048 409	44
12	84.872 872	90.859 582	97.355 996	104.408 396	48
13	96.910 157	104.444 494	112.683 108	121.696 197	52
14	110.067 912	119.439 694	129.767 034	141.153 768	56
15	124.450 435	135.991 590	148.809 140	163.053 437	60
16	140.171 731	154.261 786	170.033 877	187.701 707	64
17	157.356 417	174.428 663	193.691 420	215.443 551	68
18	176.140 711	196.689 122	220.060 621	246.667 242	72
19	196.673 509	221.260 504	249.452 292	281.809 781	76
20	219.117 569	248.382 713	282.212 873	321.363 019	80
21	243.650 796	278.320 556	318.728 514	365.880 536	84
22	270.467 657	311.366 333	359.429 624	415.985 393	88
23	299.780 720	347.842 687	404.795 946	472.378 852	92
24	331.822 341	388.105 758	455.362 213	535.850 186	96
25	366.846 502	432.548 654	511.724 449	607.287 733	100
26	405.130 828	481.605 296	574.546 995	687.691 320	104
27	446.978 787	535.754 649	644.570 341	778.186 267	108
28	492.722 092	595.525 404	722.619 851	880.039 126	112
29	542.723 336	661.501 133	809.615 495	994.675 416	116
30	597.378 862	734.325 993	906.582 688	1123.699 571	120

QTRS	13.0% ANNUAL RATE	14.0% ANNUAL RATE	15.0% ANNUAL RATE	16.0% ANNUAL RATE	QTRS
1	1.000 000	1.000 000	1.000 000	1.000 000	1
2	2.032 500	2.035 000	2.037 500	2.040 000	2
3	3.098 556	3.106 225	3.113 906	3.121 600	3
4	4.199 259	4.214 943	4.230 678	4.246 464	4
5	5.335 735	5.362 466	5.389 328	5.416 323	5
6	6.509 147	6.550 152	6.591 428	6.632 975	6
7	7.720 694	7.779 408	7.838 607	7.898 294	7
8	8.971 616	9.051 687	9.132 554	9.214 226	8
9	10.263 194	10.368 496	10.475 025	10.582 795	9
10	11.596 748	11.731 393	11.867 838	12.006 107	10
11	12.973 642	13.141 992	13.312 882	13.486 351	11
12	14.395 285	14.601 962	14.812 116	15.025 805	12
13	15.863 132	16.113 030	16.367 570	16.626 838	13
14	17.378 684	17.676 986	17.981 354	18.291 911	14
15	18.943 491	19.295 681	19.655 654	20.023 588	15
16	20.559 155	20.971 030	21.392 742	21.824 531	16
17	22.227 327	22.705 016	23.194 969	23.697 512	17
18	23.949 715	24.499 691	25.064 781	25.645 413	18
19	25.728 081	26.357 180	27.004 710	27.671 229	19

YRS	13.0% ANNUAL RATE	14.0% ANNUAL RATE	15.0% ANNUAL RATE	16.0% ANNUAL RATE	QTRS
5	27.564 244	28.279 682	29.017 387	29.778 079	20
6	35.525 359	36.666 528	37.851 685	39.082 604	24
7	44.572 975	46.290 627	48.087 548	49.967 583	28
8	54.855 372	57.334 502	59.947 335	62.701 469	32
9	66.541 069	70.007 603	73.688 682	77.598 314	36
10	79.821 583	84.550 278	89.610 100	95.025 516	40
11	94.914 566	101.238 331	108.057 458	115.412 877	44
12	112.067 379	120.388 257	129.431 496	139.263 206	48
13	131.561 138	142.363 236	154.196 534	167.164 718	52
14	153.715 326	167.580 031	182.890 556	199.805 540	56
15	178.893 027	196.516 883	216.136 896	237.990 685	60
16	207.506 879	229.722 586	254.657 782	282.661 904	64
17	240.025 832	267.826 894	299.290 023	334.920 912	68
18	276.982 839	311.552 464	351.003 187	396.056 560	72
19	318.983 589	361.728 561	410.920 666	467.576 621	76
20	366.716 429	419.306 787	480.344 078	551.244 977	80
21	420.963 654	485.379 125	560.781 543	649.125 119	84
22	482.614 318	561.198 653	653.980 445	763.631 041	88
23	552.678 815	648.203 305	761.965 392	897.586 774	92
24	632.305 428	748.043 145	887.082 195	1054.296 034	96
25	722.799 158	862.611 657	1032.048 832	1237.623 705	100
26	825.643 103	994.081 659	1200.014 485	1452.091 149	104
27	942.522 771	1144.946 512	1394.627 959	1702.987 724	108
28	1075.353 700	1318.067 399	1620.116 941	1996.501 231	112
29	1226.312 854	1516.727 600	1881.379 844	2339.870 519	116
30	1397.874 298	1744.694 750	2184.092 215	2741.564 020	120

FUTURE VALUE OF $1 PER PERIOD

SEMIANNUAL COMPOUNDING

HALF YRS	5.0% ANNUAL RATE	6.0% ANNUAL RATE	7.0% ANNUAL RATE	8.0% ANNUAL RATE	HALF YRS
1	1.000 000	1.000 000	1.000 000	1.000 000	1
2	2.025 000	2.030 000	2.035 000	2.040 000	2
3	3.075 625	3.090 900	3.106 225	3.121 600	3
4	4.152 516	4.183 627	4.214 943	4.246 464	4
5	5.256 329	5.309 136	5.362 466	5.416 323	5
6	6.387 737	6.468 410	6.550 152	6.632 975	6
7	7.547 430	7.662 462	7.779 408	7.898 294	7
8	8.736 116	8.892 336	9.051 687	9.214 226	8
9	9.954 519	10.159 106	10.368 496	10.582 795	9
10	11.203 382	11.463 879	11.731 393	12.006 107	10
11	12.483 466	12.807 796	13.141 992	13.486 351	11
12	13.795 553	14.192 030	14.601 962	15.025 805	12
13	15.140 442	15.617 790	16.113 030	16.626 838	13
14	16.518 953	17.086 324	17.676 986	18.291 911	14
15	17.931 927	18.598 914	19.295 681	20.023 588	15
16	19.380 225	20.156 881	20.971 030	21.824 531	16
17	20.864 730	21.761 588	22.705 016	23.697 512	17
18	22.386 349	23.414 435	24.499 691	25.645 413	18
19	23.946 007	25.116 868	26.357 180	27.671 229	19
20	25.544 658	26.870 374	28.279 682	29.778 079	20
21	27.183 274	28.676 486	30.269 471	31.969 202	21
22	28.862 856	30.536 780	32.328 902	34.247 970	22
23	30.584 427	32.452 884	34.460 414	36.617 889	23
24	32.349 038	34.426 470	36.666 528	39.082 604	24
25	34.157 764	36.459 264	38.949 857	41.645 908	25
26	36.011 708	38.553 042	41.313 102	44.311 745	26
27	37.912 001	40.709 634	43.759 060	47.084 214	27
28	39.859 801	42.930 923	46.290 627	49.967 583	28
29	41.856 296	45.218 850	48.910 799	52.966 286	29

YRS					
15	43.902 703	47.575 416	51.622 677	56.084 938	30
16	48.150 278	52.502 759	57.334 502	62.701 469	32
17	52.612 885	57.730 177	63.453 152	69.857 909	34
18	57.301 413	63.275 944	70.007 603	77.598 314	36
19	62.227 297	69.159 945	77.028 895	85.970 336	38
20	67.402 554	75.401 260	84.550 278	95.025 516	40
21	72.839 808	82.023 196	92.607 371	104.819 598	42
22	78.552 323	89.048 409	101.238 331	115.412 877	44
23	84.554 034	96.501 457	110.484 031	126.870 568	46
24	90.859 582	104.408 396	120.388 257	139.263 206	48
25	97.484 349	112.796 867	130.997 910	152.667 084	50
26	104.444 494	121.696 197	142.363 236	167.164 718	52
27	111.756 996	131.137 495	154.538 058	182.845 359	54
28	119.439 694	141.153 768	167.580 031	199.805 540	56
29	127.511 329	151.780 033	181.550 919	218.149 672	58
30	135.991 590	163.053 437	196.516 883	237.990 685	60

FUTURE VALUE OF $1 PER PERIOD

SEMIANNUAL COMPOUNDING

	9.0% ANNUAL RATE	10.0% ANNUAL RATE	11.0% ANNUAL RATE	12.0% ANNUAL RATE	
HALF YRS					**HALF YRS**
1	1.000 000	1.000 000	1.000 000	1.000 000	1
2	2.045 000	2.050 000	2.055 000	2.060 000	2
3	3.137 025	3.152 500	3.168 025	3.183 600	3
4	4.278 191	4.310 125	4.342 266	4.374 616	4
5	5.470 710	5.525 631	5.581 091	5.637 093	5
6	6.716 892	6.801 913	6.888 051	6.975 319	6
7	8.019 152	8.142 008	8.266 894	8.393 838	7
8	9.380 014	9.549 109	9.721 573	9.897 468	8
9	10.802 114	11.026 564	11.256 260	11.491 316	9
10	12.288 209	12.577 893	12.875 354	13.180 795	10
11	13.841 179	14.206 787	14.583 498	14.971 643	11
12	15.464 032	15.917 127	16.385 591	16.869 941	12
13	17.159 913	17.712 983	18.286 798	18.882 138	13
14	18.932 109	19.598 632	20.292 572	21.015 066	14
15	20.784 054	21.578 564	22.408 663	23.275 970	15
16	22.719 337	23.657 492	24.641 140	25.672 528	16
17	24.741 707	25.840 366	26.996 403	28.212 880	17
18	26.855 084	28.132 385	29.481 205	30.905 653	18
19	29.063 562	30.539 004	32.102 671	33.759 992	19
20	31.371 423	33.065 954	34.868 318	36.785 591	20
21	33.783 137	35.719 252	37.786 076	39.992 727	21
22	36.303 378	38.505 214	40.864 310	43.392 290	22
23	38.937 030	41.430 475	44.111 847	46.995 828	23
24	41.689 196	44.501 999	47.537 998	50.815 577	24
25	44.565 210	47.727 099	51.152 588	54.864 512	25
26	47.570 645	51.113 454	54.965 981	59.156 383	26
27	50.711 324	54.669 126	58.989 109	63.705 766	27
28	53.993 333	58.402 583	63.233 510	68.528 112	28
29	57.423 033	62.322 712	67.711 354	73.639 798	29
YRS					
15	61.007 070	66.438 848	72.435 478	79.058 186	30
16	68.666 245	75.298 829	82.677 498	90.889 778	32
17	77.030 256	85.066 959	94.077 122	104.183 755	34
18	86.163 966	95.836 323	106.765 189	119.120 867	36
19	96.138 205	107.709 546	120.887 324	135.904 206	38
20	107.030 323	120.799 774	136.605 614	154.761 966	40
21	118.924 789	135.231 751	154.100 464	175.950 545	42
22	131.913 842	151.143 006	173.572 669	199.758 032	44
23	146.098 214	168.685 164	195.245 719	226.508 125	46
24	161.587 902	188.025 393	219.368 367	256.564 529	48
25	178.503 028	209.347 996	246.217 476	290.335 905	50
26	196.974 769	232.856 165	276.101 207	328.281 422	52
27	217.146 373	258.773 922	309.362 546	370.917 006	54
28	239.174 268	287.348 249	346.383 247	418.822 348	56
29	263.229 280	318.851 445	387.588 214	472.648 790	58
30	289.497 954	353.583 718	433.450 372	533.128 181	60

FUTURE VALUE OF $1 PER PERIOD

ANNUAL COMPOUNDING

YRS	5.0% ANNUAL RATE	6.0% ANNUAL RATE	7.0% ANNUAL RATE	7.5% ANNUAL RATE	YRS
1	1.000 000	1.000 000	1.000 000	1.000 000	1
2	2.050 000	2.060 000	2.070 000	2.075 000	2
3	3.152 500	3.183 600	3.214 900	3.230 625	3
4	4.310 125	4.374 616	4.439 943	4.472 922	4
5	5.525 631	5.637 093	5.750 739	5.808 391	5
6	6.801 913	6.975 319	7.153 291	7.244 020	6
7	8.142 008	8.393 838	8.654 021	8.787 322	7
8	9.549 109	9.897 468	10.259 803	10.446 371	8
9	11.026 564	11.491 316	11.977 989	12.229 849	9
10	12.577 893	13.180 795	13.816 448	14.147 087	10
11	14.206 787	14.971 643	15.783 599	16.208 119	11
12	15.917 127	16.869 941	17.888 451	18.423 728	12
13	17.712 983	18.882 138	20.140 643	20.805 508	13
14	19.598 632	21.015 066	22.550 488	23.365 921	14
15	21.578 564	23.275 970	25.129 022	26.118 365	15
16	23.657 492	25.672 528	27.888 054	29.077 242	16
17	25.840 366	28.212 880	30.840 217	32.258 035	17
18	28.132 385	30.905 653	33.999 033	35.677 388	18
19	30.539 004	33.759 992	37.378 965	39.353 192	19
20	33.065 954	36.785 591	40.995 492	43.304 681	20
21	35.719 252	39.992 727	44.865 177	47.552 532	21
22	38.505 214	43.392 290	49.005 739	52.118 972	22
23	41.430 475	46.995 828	53.436 141	57.027 895	23
24	44.501 999	50.815 577	58.176 671	62.304 987	24
25	47.727 099	54.864 512	63.249 038	67.977 862	25
26	51.113 454	59.156 383	68.676 470	74.076 201	26
27	54.669 126	63.705 766	74.483 823	80.631 916	27
28	58.402 583	68.528 112	80.697 691	87.679 310	28
29	62.322 712	73.639 798	87.346 529	95.255 258	29
30	66.438 848	79.058 186	94.460 786	103.399 403	30
31	70.760 790	84.801 677	102.073 041	112.154 358	31
32	75.298 829	90.889 778	110.218 154	121.565 935	32
33	80.063 771	97.343 165	118.933 425	131.683 380	33
34	85.066 959	104.183 755	128.258 765	142.559 633	34
35	90.320 307	111.434 780	138.236 878	154.251 606	35
36	95.836 323	119.120 867	148.913 460	166.820 476	36
37	101.628 139	127.268 119	160.337 402	180.332 012	37
38	107.709 546	135.904 206	172.561 020	194.856 913	38
39	114.095 023	145.058 458	185.640 292	210.471 181	39
40	120.799 774	154.761 966	199.635 112	227.256 520	40
41	127.839 763	165.047 684	214.609 570	245.300 759	41
42	135.231 751	175.950 545	230.632 240	264.698 315	42
43	142.993 339	187.507 577	247.776 496	285.550 689	43
44	151.143 006	199.758 032	266.120 851	307.966 991	44
45	159.700 156	212.743 514	285.749 311	332.064 515	45
46	168.685 164	226.508 125	306.751 763	357.969 354	46
47	178.119 422	241.098 612	329.224 386	385.817 055	47
48	188.025 393	256.564 529	353.270 093	415.753 334	48
49	198.426 663	272.958 401	378.999 000	447.934 835	49
50	209.347 996	290.335 905	406.528 929	482.529 947	50

FUTURE VALUE OF
$1 PER PERIOD

ANNUAL
COMPOUNDING

	8.0%	8.5%	9.0%	9.5%	
	ANNUAL RATE	ANNUAL RATE	ANNUAL RATE	ANNUAL RATE	
YRS					YRS
1	1.000 000	1.000 000	1.000 000	1.000 000	1
2	2.080 000	2.085 000	2.090 000	2.095 000	2
3	3.246 400	3.262 225	3.278 100	3.294 025	3
4	4.506 112	4.539 514	4.573 129	4.606 957	4
5	5.866 601	5.925 373	5.984 711	6.044 618	5
6	7.335 929	7.429 030	7.523 335	7.618 857	6
7	8.922 803	9.060 497	9.200 435	9.342 648	7
8	10.636 628	10.830 639	11.028 474	11.230 200	8
9	12.487 558	12.751 244	13.021 036	13.297 069	9
10	14.486 562	14.835 099	15.192 930	15.560 291	10
11	16.645 487	17.096 083	17.560 293	18.038 518	11
12	18.977 126	19.549 250	20.140 720	20.752 178	12
13	21.495 297	22.210 936	22.953 385	23.723 634	13
14	24.214 920	25.098 866	26.019 189	26.977 380	14
15	27.152 114	28.232 269	29.360 916	30.540 231	15
16	30.324 283	31.632 012	33.003 399	34.441 553	16
17	33.750 226	35.320 733	36.973 705	38.713 500	17
18	37.450 244	39.322 995	41.301 338	43.391 283	18
19	41.446 263	43.665 450	46.018 458	48.513 454	19
20	45.761 964	48.377 013	51.160 120	54.122 233	20
21	50.422 921	53.489 059	56.764 530	60.263 845	21
22	55.456 755	59.035 629	62.873 338	66.988 910	22
23	60.893 296	65.053 658	69.531 939	74.352 856	23
24	66.764 759	71.583 219	76.789 813	82.416 378	24
25	73.105 940	78.667 792	84.700 896	91.245 934	25
26	79.954 415	86.354 555	93.323 977	100.914 297	26
27	87.350 768	94.694 692	102.723 135	111.501 156	27
28	95.338 830	103.743 741	112.968 217	123.093 766	28
29	103.965 936	113.561 959	124.135 356	135.787 673	29
30	113.283 211	124.214 725	136.307 539	149.687 502	30
31	123.345 868	135.772 977	149.575 217	164.907 815	31
32	134.213 537	148.313 680	164.036 987	181.574 057	32
33	145.950 620	161.920 343	179.800 315	199.823 593	33
34	158.626 670	176.683 572	196.982 344	219.806 834	34
35	172.316 804	192.701 675	215.710 755	241.688 483	35
36	187.102 148	210.081 318	236.124 723	265.648 889	36
37	203.070 320	228.938 230	258.375 948	291.885 534	37
38	220.315 945	249.397 979	282.629 783	320.614 659	38
39	238.941 221	271.596 808	309.066 463	352.073 052	39
40	259.056 519	295.682 536	337.882 445	386.519 992	40
41	280.781 040	321.815 552	369.291 865	424.239 391	41
42	304.243 523	350.169 874	403.528 133	465.542 133	42
43	329.583 005	380.934 313	440.845 665	510.768 636	43
44	356.949 646	414.313 730	481.521 775	560.291 656	44
45	386.505 617	450.530 397	525.858 734	614.519 364	45
46	418.426 067	489.825 480	574.186 021	673.898 703	46
47	452.900 152	532.460 646	626.862 762	738.919 080	47
48	490.132 164	578.719 801	684.280 411	810.116 393	48
49	530.342 737	628.910 984	746.865 648	888.077 450	49
50	573.770 156	683.368 418	815.083 556	973.444 808	50

FUTURE VALUE OF
$1 PER PERIOD

ANNUAL
COMPOUNDING

YRS	10.0% ANNUAL RATE	10.5% ANNUAL RATE	11.0% ANNUAL RATE	11.5% ANNUAL RATE	YRS
1	1.000 000	1.000 000	1.000 000	1.000 000	1
2	2.100 000	2.105 000	2.110 000	2.115 000	2
3	3.310 000	3.326 025	3.342 100	3.358 225	3
4	4.641 000	4.675 258	4.709 731	4.744 421	4
5	6.105 100	6.166 160	6.227 801	6.290 029	5
6	7.715 610	7.813 606	7.912 860	8.013 383	6
7	9.487 171	9.634 035	9.783 274	9.934 922	7
8	11.435 888	11.645 609	11.859 434	12.077 438	8
9	13.579 477	13.868 398	14.163 972	14.466 343	9
10	15.937 425	16.324 579	16.722 009	17.129 972	10
11	18.531 167	19.038 660	19.561 430	20.099 919	11
12	21.384 284	22.037 720	22.713 187	23.411 410	12
13	24.522 712	25.351 680	26.211 638	27.103 722	13
14	27.974 983	29.013 607	30.094 918	31.220 650	14
15	31.772 482	33.060 035	34.405 359	35.811 025	15
16	35.949 730	37.531 339	39.189 948	40.929 293	16
17	40.544 703	42.472 130	44.500 843	46.636 161	17
18	45.599 173	47.931 703	50.395 936	52.999 320	18
19	51.159 090	53.964 532	56.939 488	60.094 242	19
20	57.274 999	60.630 808	64.202 832	68.005 080	20
21	64.002 499	67.997 043	72.265 144	76.825 664	21
22	71.402 749	76.136 732	81.214 309	86.660 615	22
23	79.543 024	85.131 089	91.147 884	97.626 586	23
24	88.497 327	95.069 854	102.174 151	109.853 643	24
25	98.347 059	106.052 188	114.413 307	123.486 812	25
26	109.181 765	118.187 668	127.998 771	138.687 796	26
27	121.099 942	131.597 373	143.078 636	155.636 892	27
28	134.209 936	146.415 097	159.817 286	174.535 135	28
29	148.630 930	162.788 683	178.397 187	195.606 675	29
30	164.494 023	180.881 494	199.020 878	219.101 443	30
31	181.943 425	200.874 051	221.913 174	245.298 109	31
32	201.137 767	222.965 827	247.323 624	274.507 391	32
33	222.251 544	247.377 238	275.529 222	307.075 741	33
34	245.476 699	274.351 848	306.837 437	343.389 451	34
35	271.024 368	304.158 792	341.589 555	383.879 238	35
36	299.126 805	337.095 466	380.164 406	429.025 351	36
37	330.039 486	373.490 489	422.982 490	479.363 266	37
38	364.043 434	413.706 991	470.510 564	535.490 042	38
39	401.447 778	458.146 225	523.266 726	598.071 396	39
40	442.592 556	507.251 579	581.826 066	667.849 607	40
41	487.851 811	561.512 994	646.826 934	745.652 312	41
42	537.636 992	621.471 859	718.977 896	832.402 327	42
43	592.400 692	687.726 404	799.065 465	929.128 595	43
44	652.640 761	760.937 676	887.962 666	1036.978 384	44
45	718.904 837	841.836 132	986.638 559	1157.230 898	45
46	791.795 321	931.228 926	1096.168 801	1291.312 451	46
47	871.974 853	1030.007 963	1217.747 369	1440.813 383	47
48	960.172 338	1139.158 800	1352.699 580	1607.506 922	48
49	1057.189 572	1259.770 473	1502.496 533	1793.370 218	49
50	1163.908 529	1393.046 373	1668.771 152	2000.607 793	50

FUTURE VALUE OF
$1 PER PERIOD

YRS	12.0% ANNUAL RATE	12.5% ANNUAL RATE	13.0% ANNUAL RATE	13.5% ANNUAL RATE	YRS
1	1.000 000	1.000 000	1.000 000	1.000 000	1
2	2.120 000	2.125 000	2.130 000	2.135 000	2
3	3.374 400	3.390 625	3.406 900	3.423 225	3
4	4.779 328	4.814 453	4.849 797	4.885 360	4
5	6.352 847	6.416 260	6.480 271	6.544 884	5
6	8.115 189	8.218 292	8.322 706	8.428 443	6
7	10.089 012	10.245 579	10.404 658	10.566 283	7
8	12.299 693	12.526 276	12.757 263	12.992 731	8
9	14.775 656	15.092 061	15.415 707	15.746 750	9
10	17.548 735	17.978 568	18.419 749	18.872 561	10
11	20.654 583	21.225 889	21.814 317	22.420 357	11
12	24.133 133	24.879 125	25.650 178	26.447 106	12
13	28.029 109	28.989 016	29.984 701	31.017 465	13
14	32.392 602	33.612 643	34.882 712	36.204 823	14
15	37.279 715	38.814 223	40.417 464	42.092 474	15
16	42.753 280	44.666 001	46.671 735	48.774 957	16
17	48.883 674	51.249 252	53.739 060	56.359 577	17
18	55.749 715	58.655 408	61.725 138	64.968 120	18
19	63.439 681	66.987 334	70.749 406	74.738 816	19
20	72.052 442	76.360 751	80.946 829	85.828 556	20
21	81.698 736	86.905 845	92.469 917	98.415 411	21
22	92.502 584	98.769 075	105.491 006	112.701 491	22
23	104.602 894	112.115 210	120.204 837	128.916 193	23
24	118.155 241	127.129 611	136.831 465	147.319 879	24
25	133.333 870	144.020 812	155.619 556	168.208 062	25
26	150.333 934	163.023 414	176.850 098	191.916 151	26
27	169.374 007	184.401 340	200.840 611	218.824 831	27
28	190.698 887	208.451 508	227.949 890	249.366 183	28
29	214.582 754	235.507 946	258.583 376	284.030 618	29
30	241.332 684	265.946 440	293.199 215	323.374 752	30
31	271.292 606	300.189 745	332.315 113	368.030 343	31
32	304.847 719	338.713 463	376.516 078	418.714 439	32
33	342.429 446	382.052 645	426.463 168	476.240 889	33
34	384.520 979	430.809 226	482.903 380	541.533 409	34
35	431.663 496	485.660 379	546.680 819	615.640 419	35
36	484.463 116	547.367 927	618.749 325	699.751 875	36
37	543.598 690	616.788 918	700.186 738	795.218 378	37
38	609.830 533	694.887 532	792.211 014	903.572 859	38
39	684.010 197	782.748 474	896.198 445	1026.555 195	39
40	767.091 420	881.592 033	1013.704 243	1166.140 147	40
41	860.142 391	992.791 037	1146.485 795	1324.569 067	41
42	964.359 478	1117.889 917	1296.528 948	1504.385 891	42
43	1081.082 615	1258.626 157	1466.077 712	1708.477 986	43
44	1211.812 529	1416.954 426	1657.667 814	1940.122 514	44
45	1358.230 032	1595.073 729	1874.164 630	2203.039 053	45
46	1522.217 636	1795.457 946	2118.806 032	2501.449 326	46
47	1705.883 752	2020.890 189	2395.250 816	2840.144 984	47
48	1911.589 803	2274.501 462	2707.633 422	3224.564 557	48
49	2141.980 579	2559.814 145	3060.625 767	3660.880 773	49
50	2400.018 249	2880.790 913	3459.507 117	4156.099 677	50

FUTURE VALUE OF
$1 PER PERIOD

ANNUAL
COMPOUNDING

	14.0% ANNUAL RATE	14.5% ANNUAL RATE	15.0% ANNUAL RATE	16.0% ANNUAL RATE	
YRS					YRS
1	1.000 000	1.000 000	1.000 000	1.000 000	1
2	2.140 000	2.145 000	2.150 000	2.160 000	2
3	3.439 600	3.456 025	3.472 500	3.505 600	3
4	4.921 144	4.957 149	4.993 375	5.066 496	4
5	6.610 104	6.675 935	6.742 381	6.877 135	5
6	8.535 519	8.643 946	8.753 738	8.977 477	6
7	10.730 491	10.897 318	11.066 799	11.413 873	7
8	13.232 760	13.477 429	13.726 819	14.240 093	8
9	16.085 347	16.431 656	16.785 842	17.518 508	9
10	19.337 295	19.814 246	20.303 718	21.321 469	10
11	23.044 516	23.687 312	24.349 276	25.732 904	11
12	27.270 749	28.121 972	29.001 667	30.850 169	12
13	32.088 654	33.199 658	34.351 917	36.786 196	13
14	37.581 065	39.013 609	40.504 705	43.671 987	14
15	43.842 414	45.670 582	47.580 411	51.659 505	15
16	50.980 352	53.292 816	55.717 472	60.925 026	16
17	59.117 601	62.020 275	65.075 093	71.673 030	17
18	68.394 066	72.013 215	75.836 357	84.140 715	18
19	78.969 235	83.455 131	88.211 811	98.603 230	19
20	91.024 928	96.556 125	102.443 583	115.379 747	20
21	104.768 418	111.556 763	118.810 120	134.840 506	21
22	120.435 996	128.732 494	137.631 638	157.414 987	22
23	138.297 035	148.398 705	159.276 384	183.601 385	23
24	158.658 620	170.916 517	184.167 841	213.977 607	24
25	181.870 827	196.699 412	212.793 017	249.214 024	25
26	208.332 743	226.220 827	245.711 970	290.088 267	26
27	238.499 327	260.022 847	283.568 766	337.502 390	27
28	272.889 233	298.726 160	327.104 080	392.502 773	28
29	312.093 725	343.041 453	377.169 693	456.303 216	29
30	356.786 847	393.782 464	434.745 146	530.311 731	30
31	407.737 006	451.880 921	500.956 918	616.161 608	31
32	465.820 186	518.403 655	577.100 456	715.747 465	32
33	532.035 012	594.572 185	664.665 524	831.267 059	33
34	607.519 914	681.785 151	765.365 353	965.269 789	34
35	693.572 702	781.643 998	881.170 156	1120.712 955	35
36	791.672 881	895.982 378	1014.345 680	1301.027 028	36
37	903.507 084	1026.899 823	1167.497 532	1510.191 352	37
38	1030.998 076	1176.800 297	1343.622 161	1752.821 968	38
39	1176.337 806	1348.436 340	1546.165 485	2034.273 483	39
40	1342.025 099	1544.959 609	1779.090 308	2360.757 241	40
41	1530.908 613	1769.978 753	2046.953 854	2739.478 399	41
42	1746.235 819	2027.625 672	2354.996 933	3178.794 943	42
43	1991.708 833	2322.631 394	2709.246 473	3688.402 134	43
44	2271.548 070	2660.412 947	3116.633 443	4279.546 475	44
45	2590.564 800	3047.172 824	3585.128 460	4965.273 911	45
46	2954.243 872	3490.012 883	4123.897 729	5760.717 737	46
47	3368.838 014	3997.064 751	4743.482 388	6683.432 575	47
48	3841.475 336	4577.639 140	5456.004 746	7753.781 787	48
49	4380.281 883	5242.396 816	6275.405 458	8995.386 873	49
50	4994.521 346	6003.544 354	7217.716 277	10435.648 773	50

FUTURE VALUE OF
$1 PER PERIOD

ANNUAL
COMPOUNDING

YRS	17.0% ANNUAL RATE	18.0% ANNUAL RATE	19.0% ANNUAL RATE	20.0% ANNUAL RATE	YRS
1	1.000 000	1.000 000	1.000 000	1.000 000	1
2	2.170 000	2.180 000	2.190 000	2.200 000	2
3	3.538 900	3.572 400	3.606 100	3.640 000	3
4	5.140 513	5.215 432	5.291 259	5.368 000	4
5	7.014 400	7.154 210	7.296 598	7.441 600	5
6	9.206 848	9.441 968	9.682 952	9.929 920	6
7	11.772 012	12.141 522	12.522 713	12.915 904	7
8	14.773 255	15.326 996	15.902 028	16.499 085	8
9	18.284 708	19.085 855	19.923 413	20.798 902	9
10	22.393 108	23.521 309	24.708 862	25.958 682	10
11	27.199 937	28.755 144	30.403 546	32.150 419	11
12	32.823 926	34.931 070	37.180 220	39.580 502	12
13	39.403 993	42.218 663	45.244 461	48.496 603	13
14	47.102 672	50.818 022	54.840 909	59.195 923	14
15	56.110 126	60.965 266	66.260 682	72.035 108	15
16	66.648 848	72.939 014	79.850 211	87.442 129	16
17	78.979 152	87.068 036	96.021 751	105.930 555	17
18	93.405 608	103.740 283	115.265 884	128.116 666	18
19	110.284 561	123.413 534	138.166 402	154.740 000	19
20	130.032 936	146.627 970	165.418 018	186.688 000	20
21	153.138 535	174.021 005	197.847 442	225.025 600	21
22	180.172 086	206.344 785	236.438 456	271.030 719	22
23	211.801 341	244.486 847	282.361 762	326.236 863	23
24	248.807 569	289.494 479	337.010 497	392.484 236	24
25	292.104 856	342.603 486	402.042 491	471.981 083	25
26	342.762 681	405.272 113	479.430 565	567.377 300	26
27	402.032 337	479.221 093	571.522 372	681.852 760	27
28	471.377 835	566.480 890	681.111 623	819.223 312	28
29	552.512 066	669.447 450	811.522 831	984.067 974	29
30	647.439 118	790.947 991	966.712 169	1181.881 569	30
31	758.503 768	934.318 630	1151.387 481	1419.257 883	31
32	888.449 408	1103.495 983	1371.151 103	1704.109 459	32
33	1040.485 808	1303.125 260	1632.669 812	2045.931 351	33
34	1218.368 395	1538.687 807	1943.877 077	2456.117 621	34
35	1426.491 022	1816.651 612	2314.213 721	2948.341 146	35
36	1669.994 496	2144.648 902	2754.914 328	3539.009 375	36
37	1954.893 560	2531.685 705	3279.348 051	4247.811 250	37
38	2288.225 465	2988.389 132	3903.424 180	5098.373 500	38
39	2678.223 794	3527.299 175	4646.074 775	6119.048 200	39
40	3134.521 839	4163.213 027	5529.828 982	7343.857 840	40
41	3668.390 552	4913.591 372	6581.496 488	8813.629 408	41
42	4293.016 946	5799.037 819	7832.980 821	10577.355 289	42
43	5023.829 827	6843.864 626	9322.247 177	12693.826 347	43
44	5878.880 897	8076.760 259	11094.474 141	15233.591 617	44
45	6879.290 650	9531.577 105	13203.424 228	18281.309 940	45
46	8049.770 061	11248.260 984	15713.074 831	21938.571 928	46
47	9419.230 971	13273.947 961	18699.559 049	26327.286 314	47
48	11021.500 236	15664.258 594	22253.475 268	31593.743 576	48
49	12896.155 276	18484.825 141	26482.635 569	37913.492 292	49
50	15089.501 673	21813.093 666	31515.336 327	45497.190 750	50

Section 3. Sinking Fund Factors

These factors represent the fixed amount of money that must be invested at a stated rate of interest for a specific interval, i.e., monthly, to accumulate $1. It is also assumed that the regular investment is made at the end of each interval (according to the dictates of convention). These factors are based on the assumption that no funds will be withdrawn at any point during the investment.

In this section, the following four (4) periods are presented in detail: monthly, quarterly, semiannual, and annual.

Monthly:

The factors presented on pages 49 through 54 will indicate the amount of the monthly investment necessary to accumulate $1 in the stated interval. Interest is being earned on each monthly investment, plus interest is being earned on the interest.

Example E

If you want $10,000 at the end of five (5) years, what will the monthly payment be? Assume the annual interest rate of 11.0% and monthly compounding.

Turn to page 51 and locate the 11.0% annual interest rate column. Proceed down that column until you locate the point where the 5 year row intersects the 11.0% interest column. The number is 0.012576. That means that your monthly deposit will be 0.012576 for each $1 you want to accumulate. So, to determine your answer, multiply 0.012576 by $10,000. The correct answer is $125.76. That is, you need to make a monthly payment of $125.76 to accumulate $10,000 in 5 years.

Note: If your investment period is less than two (2) years, we have provided all the monthly payment amounts for each monthly period; over two (2) years, only the annual figures are provided.

Quarterly:

The factors presented on pages 55 through 57 will indicate the amount of the quarterly investment necesssary to accumulate $1 in the stated interval. Interest is being earned on each quarterly investment, plus interest is being earned on the nterest.

Example F

If you want $15,000 in 25 years, what will the quarterly payment be? Assume an annual interest rate of 9.0% and quarterly compounding.

Turn to page 56 and locate the 9.0% column Proceed down that column until you locate the point where the 25 year intersects the 9.0% interest column. The number is 0.002726. That means that your quarterly deposit will be 0.002726 for each $1 you want to accumulate.So, to determine your answer, multiply 0.002726 by $15,000. The correct answer is $40.89. You will need to make a quarterly payment of $40.89 to accumulate $15,000 in 25 years.

Note: For investments of five (5) years and more, only the annual amounts are shown.

Semiannual:

The factors on pages 58 through 59 cover semiannual compounding. The interest is being compounded every six months. They are used the same way as the monthly or quarterly tables.

Annual:

The factors on pages 60 through 65 cover annual compounding (or the interest being compounded every year). They are used the same way as the monthly, quarterly, and semiannual tables.

If you want to do it the hard way, here's the formula. . .

$$\frac{1}{S\overline{n|}} = \frac{i}{(1+i)^n - 1}$$

$S\overline{n|}$ = Future value of \$1 per period

i = interest rate per period

n = number of compounding periods

MOS	5.0% ANNUAL RATE	6.0% ANNUAL RATE	7.0% ANNUAL RATE	7.5% ANNUAL RATE	MOS
1	1.000 000	1.000 000	1.000 000	1.000 000	1
2	0.498 960	0.498 753	0.498 546	0.498 442	2
3	0.331 948	0.331 672	0.331 396	0.331 259	3
4	0.248 443	0.248 133	0.247 823	0.247 668	4
5	0.198 340	0.198 010	0.197 680	0.197 516	5
6	0.164 939	0.164 595	0.164 253	0.164 081	6
7	0.141 081	0.140 729	0.140 377	0.140 201	7
8	0.123 188	0.122 829	0.122 470	0.122 291	8
9	0.109 272	0.108 907	0.108 544	0.108 362	9
10	0.098 139	0.097 771	0.097 403	0.097 220	10
11	0.089 031	0.088 659	0.088 288	0.088 104	11
12	0.081 441	0.081 066	0.080 693	0.080 507	12
13	0.075 019	0.074 642	0.074 267	0.074 080	13
14	0.069 514	0.069 136	0.068 760	0.068 572	14
15	0.064 744	0.064 364	0.063 987	0.063 798	15
16	0.060 570	0.060 189	0.059 811	0.059 622	16
17	0.056 887	0.056 506	0.056 126	0.055 937	17
18	0.053 614	0.053 232	0.052 852	0.052 662	18
19	0.050 685	0.050 303	0.049 922	0.049 733	19
20	0.048 050	0.047 666	0.047 286	0.047 096	20
21	0.045 665	0.045 282	0.044 900	0.044 711	21
22	0.043 498	0.043 114	0.042 733	0.042 543	22
23	0.041 519	0.041 135	0.040 753	0.040 564	23
YRS					
2	0.039 705	0.039 321	0.038 939	0.038 750	24
3	0.025 804	0.025 422	0.025 044	0.024 856	36
4	0.018 863	0.018 485	0.018 113	0.017 929	48
5	0.014 705	0.014 333	0.013 968	0.013 788	60
6	0.011 938	0.011 573	0.011 216	0.011 040	72
7	0.009 967	0.009 609	0.009 259	0.009 088	84
8	0.008 493	0.008 141	0.007 800	0.007 634	96
9	0.007 351	0.007 006	0.006 673	0.006 511	108
10	0.006 440	0.006 102	0.005 778	0.005 620	120
11	0.005 698	0.005 367	0.005 051	0.004 898	132
12	0.005 082	0.004 759	0.004 450	0.004 302	144
13	0.004 564	0.004 247	0.003 947	0.003 804	156
14	0.004 122	0.003 812	0.003 521	0.003 381	168
15	0.003 741	0.003 439	0.003 155	0.003 020	180
16	0.003 410	0.003 114	0.002 839	0.002 708	192
17	0.003 120	0.002 831	0.002 563	0.002 437	204
18	0.002 864	0.002 582	0.002 322	0.002 200	216
19	0.002 636	0.002 361	0.002 109	0.001 991	228
20	0.002 433	0.002 164	0.001 920	0.001 806	240
21	0.002 251	0.001 989	0.001 751	0.001 642	252
22	0.002 086	0.001 831	0.001 601	0.001 495	264
23	0.001 937	0.001 688	0.001 466	0.001 364	276
24	0.001 802	0.001 560	0.001 344	0.001 246	288
25	0.001 679	0.001 443	0.001 234	0.001 140	300
26	0.001 567	0.001 337	0.001 135	0.001 044	312
27	0.001 464	0.001 240	0.001 045	0.000 957	324
28	0.001 369	0.001 151	0.000 963	0.000 879	336
29	0.001 282	0.001 070	0.000 888	0.000 807	348
30	0.001 202	0.000 996	0.000 820	0.000 742	360

SINKING FUND FACTORS

MONTHLY COMPOUNDING

	8.0% ANNUAL RATE	8.5% ANNUAL RATE	9.0% ANNUAL RATE	9.5% ANNUAL RATE	
MOS					MOS
1	1.000 000	1.000 000	1.000 000	1.000 000	1
2	0.498 339	0.498 235	0.498 132	0.498 029	2
3	0.331 121	0.330 983	0.330 846	0.330 708	3
4	0.247 514	0.247 359	0.247 205	0.247 051	4
5	0.197 351	0.197 187	0.197 022	0.196 858	5
6	0.163 910	0.163 740	0.163 569	0.163 398	6
7	0.140 025	0.139 850	0.139 675	0.139 500	7
8	0.122 112	0.121 934	0.121 756	0.121 577	8
9	0.108 181	0.108 000	0.107 819	0.107 639	9
10	0.097 037	0.096 854	0.096 671	0.096 489	10
11	0.087 919	0.087 735	0.087 551	0.087 367	11
12	0.080 322	0.080 136	0.079 951	0.079 767	12
13	0.073 894	0.073 708	0.073 522	0.073 336	13
14	0.068 385	0.068 198	0.068 011	0.067 825	14
15	0.063 611	0.063 423	0.063 236	0.063 050	15
16	0.059 434	0.059 246	0.059 059	0.058 872	16
17	0.055 749	0.055 561	0.055 373	0.055 186	17
18	0.052 474	0.052 285	0.052 098	0.051 910	18
19	0.049 544	0.049 355	0.049 167	0.048 980	19
20	0.046 907	0.046 719	0.046 531	0.046 343	20
21	0.044 522	0.044 333	0.044 145	0.043 958	21
22	0.042 354	0.042 165	0.041 977	0.041 790	22
23	0.040 375	0.040 186	0.039 998	0.039 811	23
YRS					
2	0.038 561	0.038 372	0.038 185	0.037 998	24
3	0.024 670	0.024 484	0.024 300	0.024 116	36
4	0.017 746	0.017 565	0.017 385	0.017 206	48
5	0.013 610	0.013 433	0.013 258	0.013 085	60
6	0.010 867	0.010 695	0.010 526	0.010 358	72
7	0.008 920	0.008 753	0.008 589	0.008 427	84
8	0.007 470	0.007 309	0.007 150	0.006 994	96
9	0.006 352	0.006 196	0.006 043	0.005 893	108
10	0.005 466	0.005 315	0.005 168	0.005 023	120
11	0.004 749	0.004 603	0.004 461	0.004 322	132
12	0.004 158	0.004 017	0.003 880	0.003 747	144
13	0.003 664	0.003 528	0.003 397	0.003 269	156
14	0.003 247	0.003 116	0.002 989	0.002 867	168
15	0.002 890	0.002 764	0.002 643	0.002 526	180
16	0.002 583	0.002 462	0.002 345	0.002 233	192
17	0.002 316	0.002 200	0.002 088	0.001 981	204
18	0.002 083	0.001 971	0.001 864	0.001 762	216
19	0.001 878	0.001 771	0.001 669	0.001 572	228
20	0.001 698	0.001 595	0.001 497	0.001 405	240
21	0.001 538	0.001 439	0.001 346	0.001 258	252
22	0.001 395	0.001 301	0.001 212	0.001 128	264
23	0.001 268	0.001 178	0.001 093	0.001 013	276
24	0.001 154	0.001 067	0.000 987	0.000 911	288
25	0.001 051	0.000 969	0.000 892	0.000 820	300
26	0.000 959	0.000 880	0.000 807	0.000 739	312
27	0.000 876	0.000 801	0.000 731	0.000 667	324
28	0.000 801	0.000 729	0.000 663	0.000 602	336
29	0.000 733	0.000 664	0.000 602	0.000 544	348
30	0.000 671	0.000 606	0.000 546	0.000 492	360

	10.0%	10.5%	11.0%	11.5%	
	ANNUAL RATE	ANNUAL RATE	ANNUAL RATE	ANNUAL RATE	
MOS					MOS
1	1.000 000	1.000 000	1.000 000	1.000 000	1
2	0.497 925	0.497 822	0.497 719	0.497 616	2
3	0.330 571	0.330 434	0.330 296	0.330 159	3
4	0.246 897	0.246 743	0.246 589	0.246 435	4
5	0.196 694	0.196 530	0.196 367	0.196 203	5
6	0.163 228	0.163 058	0.162 888	0.162 718	6
7	0.139 325	0.139 151	0.138 976	0.138 802	7
8	0.121 400	0.121 222	0.121 044	0.120 867	8
9	0.107 459	0.107 279	0.107 099	0.106 920	9
10	0.096 307	0.096 125	0.095 944	0.095 763	10
11	0.087 184	0.087 001	0.086 818	0.086 636	11
12	0.079 583	0.079 399	0.079 215	0.079 032	12
13	0.073 151	0.072 967	0.072 782	0.072 598	13
14	0.067 640	0.067 455	0.067 270	0.067 085	14
15	0.062 864	0.062 678	0.062 493	0.062 308	15
16	0.058 686	0.058 500	0.058 314	0.058 129	16
17	0.055 000	0.054 813	0.054 628	0.054 443	17
18	0.051 724	0.051 538	0.051 352	0.051 167	18
19	0.048 793	0.048 607	0.048 421	0.048 236	19
20	0.046 157	0.045 970	0.045 785	0.045 600	20
21	0.043 771	0.043 585	0.043 400	0.043 215	21
22	0.041 604	0.041 418	0.041 232	0.041 048	22
23	0.039 625	0.039 439	0.039 254	0.039 070	23
YRS					
2	0.037 812	0.037 626	0.037 441	0.037 257	24
3	0.023 934	0.023 752	0.023 572	0.023 393	36
4	0.017 029	0.016 853	0.016 679	0.016 506	48
5	0.012 914	0.012 744	0.012 576	0.012 409	60
6	0.010 193	0.010 029	0.009 867	0.009 708	72
7	0.008 268	0.008 111	0.007 956	0.007 803	84
8	0.006 841	0.006 690	0.006 542	0.006 396	96
9	0.005 745	0.005 601	0.005 459	0.005 320	108
10	0.004 882	0.004 743	0.004 608	0.004 476	120
11	0.004 187	0.004 054	0.003 926	0.003 800	132
12	0.003 617	0.003 491	0.003 369	0.003 250	144
13	0.003 145	0.003 025	0.002 909	0.002 796	156
14	0.002 749	0.002 634	0.002 524	0.002 417	168
15	0.002 413	0.002 304	0.002 199	0.002 099	180
16	0.002 126	0.002 022	0.001 923	0.001 828	192
17	0.001 879	0.001 781	0.001 687	0.001 598	204
18	0.001 665	0.001 572	0.001 484	0.001 400	216
19	0.001 479	0.001 391	0.001 308	0.001 229	228
20	0.001 317	0.001 234	0.001 155	0.001 081	240
21	0.001 174	0.001 096	0.001 022	0.000 952	252
22	0.001 049	0.000 975	0.000 906	0.000 840	264
23	0.000 938	0.000 869	0.000 803	0.000 742	276
24	0.000 841	0.000 775	0.000 714	0.000 657	288
25	0.000 754	0.000 692	0.000 634	0.000 581	300
26	0.000 676	0.000 618	0.000 565	0.000 515	312
27	0.000 608	0.000 553	0.000 503	0.000 457	324
28	0.000 546	0.000 495	0.000 448	0.000 405	336
29	0.000 491	0.000 443	0.000 400	0.000 360	348
30	0.000 442	0.000 397	0.000 357	0.000 320	360

SINKING FUND FACTORS

MOS	12.0% ANNUAL RATE	12.5% ANNUAL RATE	13.0% ANNUAL RATE	13.5% ANNUAL RATE	MOS
1	1.000 000	1.000 000	1.000 000	1.000 000	1
2	0.497 512	0.497 409	0.497 306	0.497 203	2
3	0.330 022	0.329 885	0.329 748	0.329 611	3
4	0.246 281	0.246 127	0.245 974	0.245 821	4
5	0.196 040	0.195 877	0.195 713	0.195 550	5
6	0.162 548	0.162 379	0.162 210	0.162 040	6
7	0.138 628	0.138 455	0.138 281	0.138 108	7
8	0.120 690	0.120 514	0.120 337	0.120 161	8
9	0.106 740	0.106 561	0.106 383	0.106 204	9
10	0.095 582	0.095 402	0.095 221	0.095 041	10
11	0.086 454	0.086 272	0.086 091	0.085 910	11
12	0.078 849	0.078 666	0.078 484	0.078 302	12
13	0.072 415	0.072 232	0.072 049	0.071 866	13
14	0.066 901	0.066 718	0.066 534	0.066 351	14
15	0.062 124	0.061 940	0.061 756	0.061 573	15
16	0.057 945	0.057 760	0.057 577	0.057 394	16
17	0.054 258	0.054 074	0.053 890	0.053 707	17
18	0.050 982	0.050 798	0.050 614	0.050 431	18
19	0.048 052	0.047 868	0.047 684	0.047 501	19
20	0.045 415	0.045 231	0.045 048	0.044 865	20
21	0.043 031	0.042 847	0.042 664	0.042 481	21
22	0.040 864	0.040 680	0.040 497	0.040 315	22
23	0.038 886	0.038 703	0.038 520	0.038 338	23
YRS					
2	0.037 073	0.036 891	0.036 708	0.036 527	24
3	0.023 214	0.023 037	0.022 861	0.022 685	36
4	0.016 334	0.016 163	0.015 994	0.015 826	48
5	0.012 244	0.012 081	0.011 920	0.011 760	60
6	0.009 550	0.009 395	0.009 241	0.009 089	72
7	0.007 653	0.007 505	0.007 359	0.007 215	84
8	0.006 253	0.006 112	0.005 974	0.005 838	96
9	0.005 184	0.005 051	0.004 920	0.004 792	108
10	0.004 347	0.004 221	0.004 098	0.003 977	120
11	0.003 678	0.003 559	0.003 443	0.003 330	132
12	0.003 134	0.003 022	0.002 913	0.002 807	144
13	0.002 687	0.002 581	0.002 479	0.002 380	156
14	0.002 314	0.002 215	0.002 119	0.002 027	168
15	0.002 002	0.001 909	0.001 819	0.001 733	180
16	0.001 737	0.001 650	0.001 567	0.001 487	192
17	0.001 512	0.001 431	0.001 353	0.001 279	204
18	0.001 320	0.001 243	0.001 171	0.001 102	216
19	0.001 154	0.001 083	0.001 016	0.000 952	228
20	0.001 011	0.000 945	0.000 882	0.000 824	240
21	0.000 887	0.000 826	0.000 768	0.000 714	252
22	0.000 779	0.000 722	0.000 669	0.000 619	264
23	0.000 686	0.000 633	0.000 583	0.000 538	276
24	0.000 604	0.000 555	0.000 509	0.000 467	288
25	0.000 532	0.000 487	0.000 445	0.000 406	300
26	0.000 470	0.000 428	0.000 389	0.000 354	312
27	0.000 414	0.000 376	0.000 340	0.000 308	324
28	0.000 366	0.000 330	0.000 298	0.000 268	336
29	0.000 324	0.000 291	0.000 261	0.000 234	348
30	0.000 286	0.000 256	0.000 229	0.000 204	360

MOS	14.0% ANNUAL RATE	14.5% ANNUAL RATE	15.0% ANNUAL RATE	16.0% ANNUAL RATE	MOS
1	1.000 000	1.000 000	1.000 000	1.000 000	1
2	0.497 100	0.496 997	0.496 894	0.496 689	2
3	0.329 475	0.329 338	0.329 201	0.328 928	3
4	0.245 667	0.245 514	0.245 361	0.245 055	4
5	0.195 387	0.195 225	0.195 062	0.194 737	5
6	0.161 871	0.161 702	0.161 534	0.161 197	6
7	0.137 934	0.137 761	0.137 589	0.137 244	7
8	0.119 985	0.119 809	0.119 633	0.119 283	8
9	0.106 026	0.105 848	0.105 671	0.105 316	9
10	0.094 862	0.094 682	0.094 503	0.094 146	10
11	0.085 729	0.085 549	0.085 368	0.085 009	11
12	0.078 120	0.077 939	0.077 758	0.077 398	12
13	0.071 684	0.071 502	0.071 321	0.070 959	13
14	0.066 169	0.065 987	0.065 805	0.065 443	14
15	0.061 391	0.061 208	0.061 026	0.060 664	15
16	0.057 211	0.057 029	0.056 847	0.056 484	16
17	0.053 524	0.053 342	0.053 160	0.052 798	17
18	0.050 249	0.050 066	0.049 885	0.049 523	18
19	0.047 319	0.047 137	0.046 955	0.046 594	19
20	0.044 683	0.044 501	0.044 320	0.043 960	20
21	0.042 300	0.042 118	0.041 937	0.041 578	21
22	0.040 134	0.039 953	0.039 772	0.039 414	22
23	0.038 157	0.037 977	0.037 797	0.037 439	23
YRS					
2	0.036 346	0.036 166	0.035 987	0.035 630	24
3	0.022 511	0.022 338	0.022 165	0.021 824	36
4	0.015 660	0.015 495	0.015 331	0.015 007	48
5	0.011 602	0.011 445	0.011 290	0.010 985	60
6	0.008 939	0.008 791	0.008 645	0.008 359	72
7	0.007 073	0.006 934	0.006 797	0.006 529	84
8	0.005 705	0.005 574	0.005 445	0.005 195	96
9	0.004 667	0.004 544	0.004 424	0.004 192	108
10	0.003 860	0.003 745	0.003 633	0.003 418	120
11	0.003 220	0.003 113	0.003 009	0.002 810	132
12	0.002 705	0.002 605	0.002 509	0.002 325	144
13	0.002 284	0.002 192	0.002 103	0.001 934	156
14	0.001 938	0.001 853	0.001 770	0.001 615	168
15	0.001 651	0.001 572	0.001 496	0.001 354	180
16	0.001 410	0.001 337	0.001 268	0.001 138	192
17	0.001 208	0.001 141	0.001 077	0.000 959	204
18	0.001 037	0.000 975	0.000 917	0.000 809	216
19	0.000 892	0.000 835	0.000 782	0.000 684	228
20	0.000 769	0.000 717	0.000 668	0.000 579	240
21	0.000 663	0.000 616	0.000 571	0.000 491	252
22	0.000 573	0.000 529	0.000 489	0.000 417	264
23	0.000 495	0.000 456	0.000 419	0.000 354	276
24	0.000 428	0.000 392	0.000 359	0.000 301	288
25	0.000 371	0.000 338	0.000 308	0.000 256	300
26	0.000 321	0.000 292	0.000 265	0.000 217	312
27	0.000 279	0.000 252	0.000 227	0.000 185	324
28	0.000 242	0.000 217	0.000 195	0.000 157	336
29	0.000 210	0.000 188	0.000 168	0.000 134	348
30	0.000 182	0.000 162	0.000 144	0.000 114	360

	17.0%	18.0%	19.0%	20.0%	
	ANNUAL RATE	ANNUAL RATE	ANNUAL RATE	ANNUAL RATE	
MOS					MOS
1	1.000 000	1.000 000	1.000 000	1.000 000	1
2	0.496 483	0.496 278	0.496 073	0.495 868	2
3	0.328 655	0.328 383	0.328 111	0.327 839	3
4	0.244 750	0.244 445	0.244 140	0.243 836	4
5	0.194 413	0.194 089	0.193 766	0.193 444	5
6	0.160 861	0.160 525	0.160 190	0.159 856	6
7	0.136 900	0.136 556	0.136 214	0.135 872	7
8	0.118 933	0.118 584	0.118 236	0.117 889	8
9	0.104 962	0.104 610	0.104 258	0.103 908	9
10	0.093 789	0.093 434	0.093 080	0.092 727	10
11	0.084 651	0.084 294	0.083 938	0.083 584	11
12	0.077 038	0.076 680	0.076 323	0.075 968	12
13	0.070 599	0.070 240	0.069 883	0.069 527	13
14	0.065 082	0.064 723	0.064 366	0.064 010	14
15	0.060 303	0.059 944	0.059 587	0.059 231	15
16	0.056 124	0.055 765	0.055 408	0.055 053	16
17	0.052 438	0.052 080	0.051 723	0.051 369	17
18	0.049 163	0.048 806	0.048 450	0.048 097	18
19	0.046 235	0.045 878	0.045 524	0.045 171	19
20	0.043 602	0.043 246	0.042 892	0.042 540	20
21	0.041 220	0.040 865	0.040 513	0.040 163	21
22	0.039 057	0.038 703	0.038 352	0.038 003	22
23	0.037 083	0.036 731	0.036 381	0.036 033	23
YRS					
2	0.035 276	0.034 924	0.034 575	0.034 229	24
3	0.021 486	0.021 152	0.020 823	0.020 497	36
4	0.014 688	0.014 375	0.014 067	0.013 764	48
5	0.010 686	0.010 393	0.010 107	0.009 827	60
6	0.008 079	0.007 808	0.007 543	0.007 286	72
7	0.006 269	0.006 018	0.005 775	0.005 540	84
8	0.004 955	0.004 723	0.004 501	0.004 287	96
9	0.003 970	0.003 757	0.003 554	0.003 360	108
10	0.003 213	0.003 019	0.002 834	0.002 659	120
11	0.002 622	0.002 444	0.002 277	0.002 120	132
12	0.002 153	0.001 991	0.001 840	0.001 699	144
13	0.001 776	0.001 630	0.001 494	0.001 369	156
14	0.001 472	0.001 340	0.001 218	0.001 106	168
15	0.001 223	0.001 104	0.000 995	0.000 896	180
16	0.001 020	0.000 913	0.000 816	0.000 728	192
17	0.000 852	0.000 756	0.000 670	0.000 592	204
18	0.000 713	0.000 627	0.000 551	0.000 483	216
19	0.000 597	0.000 521	0.000 453	0.000 394	228
20	0.000 501	0.000 433	0.000 374	0.000 322	240
21	0.000 421	0.000 361	0.000 308	0.000 263	252
22	0.000 354	0.000 300	0.000 254	0.000 215	264
23	0.000 298	0.000 250	0.000 210	0.000 176	276
24	0.000 251	0.000 209	0.000 174	0.000 144	288
25	0.000 211	0.000 174	0.000 143	0.000 118	300
26	0.000 178	0.000 146	0.000 119	0.000 097	312
27	0.000 150	0.000 122	0.000 098	0.000 079	324
28	0.000 127	0.000 101	0.000 081	0.000 065	336
29	0.000 107	0.000 085	0.000 067	0.000 053	348
30	0.000 090	0.000 071	0.000 056	0.000 044	360

SINKING FUND FACTORS QUARTERLY COMPOUNDING

	5.0%	6.0%	7.0%	8.0%	
	ANNUAL RATE	ANNUAL RATE	ANNUAL RATE	ANNUAL RATE	
QTRS					
1	1.000 000	1.000 000	1.000 000	1.000 000	1
2	0.496 894	0.496 278	0.495 663	0.495 050	2
3	0.329 201	0.328 383	0.327 567	0.326 755	3
4	0.245 361	0.244 445	0.243 532	0.242 624	4
5	0.195 062	0.194 089	0.193 121	0.192 158	5
6	0.161 534	0.160 525	0.159 523	0.158 526	6
7	0.137 589	0.136 556	0.135 531	0.134 512	7
8	0.119 633	0.118 584	0.117 543	0.116 510	8
9	0.105 671	0.104 610	0.103 558	0.102 515	9
10	0.094 503	0.093 434	0.092 375	0.091 327	10
11	0.085 368	0.084 294	0.083 230	0.082 178	11
12	0.077 758	0.076 680	0.075 614	0.074 560	12
13	0.071 321	0.070 240	0.069 173	0.068 118	13
14	0.065 805	0.064 723	0.063 656	0.062 602	14
15	0.061 026	0.059 944	0.058 877	0.057 825	15
16	0.056 847	0.055 765	0.054 700	0.053 650	16
17	0.053 160	0.052 080	0.051 016	0.049 970	17
18	0.049 885	0.048 806	0.047 745	0.046 702	18
19	0.046 955	0.045 878	0.044 821	0.043 782	19
YRS					
5	0.044 320	0.043 246	0.042 191	0.041 157	20
6	0.035 987	0.034 924	0.033 886	0.032 871	24
7	0.030 049	0.029 001	0.027 982	0.026 990	28
8	0.025 608	0.024 577	0.023 578	0.022 611	32
9	0.022 165	0.021 152	0.020 175	0.019 233	36
10	0.019 421	0.018 427	0.017 472	0.016 556	40
11	0.017 186	0.016 210	0.015 278	0.014 388	44
12	0.015 331	0.014 375	0.013 466	0.012 602	48
13	0.013 769	0.012 833	0.011 947	0.011 109	52
14	0.012 437	0.011 521	0.010 658	0.009 847	56
15	0.011 290	0.010 393	0.009 553	0.008 768	60
16	0.010 292	0.009 415	0.008 598	0.007 839	64
17	0.009 417	0.008 560	0.007 766	0.007 032	68
18	0.008 645	0.007 808	0.007 036	0.006 327	72
19	0.007 959	0.007 141	0.006 392	0.005 708	76
20	0.007 347	0.006 548	0.005 821	0.005 161	80
21	0.006 797	0.006 018	0.005 312	0.004 676	84
22	0.006 301	0.005 541	0.004 857	0.004 244	88
23	0.005 853	0.005 112	0.004 449	0.003 859	92
24	0.005 445	0.004 723	0.004 081	0.003 513	96
25	0.005 074	0.004 371	0.003 749	0.003 203	100
26	0.004 735	0.004 050	0.003 448	0.002 923	104
27	0.004 424	0.003 757	0.003 175	0.002 671	108
28	0.004 139	0.003 489	0.002 926	0.002 443	112
29	0.003 876	0.003 244	0.002 700	0.002 236	116
30	0.003 633	0.003 019	0.002 493	0.002 048	120

SINKING FUND FACTORS QUARTERLY COMPOUNDING

	9.0% ANNUAL RATE	10.0% ANNUAL RATE	11.0% ANNUAL RATE	12.0% ANNUAL RATE	
QTRS					QTRS
1	1.000 000	1.000 000	1.000 000	1.000 000	1
2	0.494 438	0.493 827	0.493 218	0.492 611	2
3	0.325 945	0.325 137	0.324 332	0.323 530	3
4	0.241 719	0.240 818	0.239 921	0.239 027	4
5	0.191 200	0.190 247	0.189 298	0.188 355	5
6	0.157 535	0.156 550	0.155 571	0.154 598	6
7	0.133 500	0.132 495	0.131 497	0.130 506	7
8	0.115 485	0.114 467	0.113 458	0.112 456	8
9	0.101 482	0.100 457	0.099 441	0.098 434	9
10	0.090 288	0.089 259	0.088 240	0.087 231	10
11	0.081 136	0.080 106	0.079 086	0.078 077	11
12	0.073 517	0.072 487	0.071 469	0.070 462	12
13	0.067 077	0.066 048	0.065 033	0.064 030	13
14	0.061 562	0.060 537	0.059 525	0.058 526	14
15	0.056 789	0.055 766	0.054 759	0.053 767	15
16	0.052 617	0.051 599	0.050 597	0.049 611	16
17	0.048 940	0.047 928	0.046 932	0.045 953	17
18	0.045 677	0.044 670	0.043 681	0.042 709	18
19	0.042 762	0.041 761	0.040 778	0.039 814	19
YRS					
5	0.040 142	0.039 147	0.038 172	0.037 216	20
6	0.031 880	0.030 913	0.029 969	0.029 047	24
7	0.026 025	0.025 088	0.024 177	0.023 293	28
8	0.021 674	0.020 768	0.019 893	0.019 047	32
9	0.018 325	0.017 452	0.016 611	0.015 804	36
10	0.015 677	0.014 836	0.014 032	0.013 262	40
11	0.013 539	0.012 730	0.011 961	0.011 230	44
12	0.011 782	0.011 006	0.010 272	0.009 578	48
13	0.010 319	0.009 574	0.008 874	0.008 217	52
14	0.009 085	0.008 372	0.007 706	0.007 084	56
15	0.008 035	0.007 353	0.006 720	0.006 133	60
16	0.007 134	0.006 482	0.005 881	0.005 328	64
17	0.006 355	0.005 733	0.005 163	0.004 642	68
18	0.005 677	0.005 084	0.004 544	0.004 054	72
19	0.005 085	0.004 520	0.004 009	0.003 548	76
20	0.004 564	0.004 026	0.003 543	0.003 112	80
21	0.004 104	0.003 593	0.003 137	0.002 733	84
22	0.003 697	0.003 212	0.002 782	0.002 404	88
23	0.003 336	0.002 875	0.002 470	0.002 117	92
24	0.003 014	0.002 577	0.002 196	0.001 866	96
25	0.002 726	0.002 312	0.001 954	0.001 647	100
26	0.002 468	0.002 076	0.001 741	0.001 454	104
27	0.002 237	0.001 867	0.001 551	0.001 285	108
28	0.002 030	0.001 679	0.001 384	0.001 136	112
29	0.001 843	0.001 512	0.001 235	0.001 005	116
30	0.001 674	0.001 362	0.001 103	0.000 890	120

	13.0% ANNUAL RATE	14.0% ANNUAL RATE	15.0% ANNUAL RATE	16.0% ANNUAL RATE	
QTRS					QTRS
1	1.000 000	1.000 000	1.000 000	1.000 000	1
2	0.492 005	0.491 400	0.490 798	0.490 196	2
3	0.322 731	0.321 934	0.321 140	0.320 349	3
4	0.238 137	0.237 251	0.236 369	0.235 490	4
5	0.187 416	0.186 481	0.185 552	0.184 627	5
6	0.153 630	0.152 668	0.151 712	0.150 762	6
7	0.129 522	0.128 544	0.127 574	0.126 610	7
8	0.111 463	0.110 477	0.109 498	0.108 528	8
9	0.097 436	0.096 446	0.095 465	0.094 493	9
10	0.086 231	0.085 241	0.084 261	0.083 291	10
11	0.077 079	0.076 092	0.075 115	0.074 149	11
12	0.069 467	0.068 484	0.067 512	0.066 552	12
13	0.063 039	0.062 062	0.061 096	0.060 144	13
14	0.057 542	0.056 571	0.055 613	0.054 669	14
15	0.052 789	0.051 825	0.050 876	0.049 941	15
16	0.048 640	0.047 685	0.046 745	0.045 820	16
17	0.044 990	0.044 043	0.043 113	0.042 199	17
18	0.041 754	0.040 817	0.039 897	0.038 993	18
19	0.038 868	0.037 940	0.037 031	0.036 139	19
YRS					
5	0.036 279	0.035 361	0.034 462	0.033 582	20
6	0.028 149	0.027 273	0.026 419	0.025 587	24
7	0.022 435	0.021 603	0.020 795	0.020 013	28
8	0.018 230	0.017 442	0.016 681	0.015 949	32
9	0.015 028	0.014 284	0.013 571	0.012 887	36
10	0.012 528	0.011 827	0.011 159	0.010 523	40
11	0.010 536	0.009 878	0.009 254	0.008 665	44
12	0.008 923	0.008 306	0.007 726	0.007 181	48
13	0.007 601	0.007 024	0.006 485	0.005 982	52
14	0.006 506	0.005 967	0.005 468	0.005 005	56
15	0.005 590	0.005 089	0.004 627	0.004 202	60
16	0.004 819	0.004 353	0.003 927	0.003 538	64
17	0.004 166	0.003 734	0.003 341	0.002 986	68
18	0.003 610	0.003 210	0.002 849	0.002 525	72
19	0.003 135	0.002 765	0.002 434	0.002 139	76
20	0.002 727	0.002 385	0.002 082	0.001 814	80
21	0.002 376	0.002 060	0.001 783	0.001 541	84
22	0.002 072	0.001 782	0.001 529	0.001 310	88
23	0.001 809	0.001 543	0.001 312	0.001 114	92
24	0.001 582	0.001 337	0.001 127	0.000 949	96
25	0.001 384	0.001 159	0.000 969	0.000 808	100
26	0.001 211	0.001 006	0.000 833	0.000 689	104
27	0.001 061	0.000 873	0.000 717	0.000 587	108
28	0.000 930	0.000 759	0.000 617	0.000 501	112
29	0.000 815	0.000 659	0.000 532	0.000 427	116
30	0.000 715	0.000 573	0.000 458	0.000 365	120

	5.0% ANNUAL RATE	6.0% ANNUAL RATE	7.0% ANNUAL RATE	8.0% ANNUAL RATE	
HALF YRS					**HALF YRS**
1	1.000 000	1.000 000	1.000 000	1.000 000	1
2	0.493 827	0.492 611	0.491 400	0.490 196	2
3	0.325 137	0.323 530	0.321 934	0.320 349	3
4	0.240 818	0.239 027	0.237 251	0.235 490	4
5	0.190 247	0.188 355	0.186 481	0.184 627	5
6	0.156 550	0.154 598	0.152 668	0.150 762	6
7	0.132 495	0.130 506	0.128 544	0.126 610	7
8	0.114 467	0.112 456	0.110 477	0.108 528	8
9	0.100 457	0.098 434	0.096 446	0.094 493	9
10	0.089 259	0.087 231	0.085 241	0.083 291	10
11	0.080 106	0.078 077	0.076 092	0.074 149	11
12	0.072 487	0.070 462	0.068 484	0.066 552	12
13	0.066 048	0.064 030	0.062 062	0.060 144	13
14	0.060 537	0.058 526	0.056 571	0.054 669	14
15	0.055 766	0.053 767	0.051 825	0.049 941	15
16	0.051 599	0.049 611	0.047 685	0.045 820	16
17	0.047 928	0.045 953	0.044 043	0.042 199	17
18	0.044 670	0.042 709	0.040 817	0.038 993	18
19	0.041 761	0.039 814	0.037 940	0.036 139	19
20	0.039 147	0.037 216	0.035 361	0.033 582	20
21	0.036 787	0.034 872	0.033 037	0.031 280	21
22	0.034 647	0.032 747	0.030 932	0.029 199	22
23	0.032 696	0.030 814	0.029 019	0.027 309	23
24	0.030 913	0.029 047	0.027 273	0.025 587	24
25	0.029 276	0.027 428	0.025 674	0.024 012	25
26	0.027 769	0.025 938	0.024 205	0.022 567	26
27	0.026 377	0.024 564	0.022 852	0.021 239	27
28	0.025 088	0.023 293	0.021 603	0.020 013	28
29	0.023 891	0.022 115	0.020 445	0.018 880	29
YRS					
15	0.022 778	0.021 019	0.019 371	0.017 830	30
16	0.020 768	0.019 047	0.017 442	0.015 949	32
17	0.019 007	0.017 322	0.015 760	0.014 315	34
18	0.017 452	0.015 804	0.014 284	0.012 887	36
19	0.016 070	0.014 459	0.012 982	0.011 632	38
20	0.014 836	0.013 262	0.011 827	0.010 523	40
21	0.013 729	0.012 192	0.010 798	0.009 540	42
22	0.012 730	0.011 230	0.009 878	0.008 665	44
23	0.011 827	0.010 363	0.009 051	0.007 882	46
24	0.011 006	0.009 578	0.008 306	0.007 181	48
25	0.010 258	0.008 865	0.007 634	0.006 550	50
26	0.009 574	0.008 217	0.007 024	0.005 982	52
27	0.008 948	0.007 626	0.006 471	0.005 469	54
28	0.008 372	0.007 084	0.005 967	0.005 005	56
29	0.007 842	0.006 588	0.005 508	0.004 584	58
30	0.007 353	0.006 133	0.005 089	0.004 202	60

	9.0%	10.0%	11.0%	12.0%	
	ANNUAL RATE	ANNUAL RATE	ANNUAL RATE	ANNUAL RATE	
HALF YRS					HALF YRS
1	1.000 000	1.000 000	1.000 000	1.000 000	1
2	0.488 998	0.487 805	0.486 618	0.485 437	2
3	0.318 773	0.317 209	0.315 654	0.314 110	3
4	0.233 744	0.232 012	0.230 294	0.228 591	4
5	0.182 792	0.180 975	0.179 176	0.177 396	5
6	0.148 878	0.147 017	0.145 179	0.143 363	6
7	0.124 701	0.122 820	0.120 964	0.119 135	7
8	0.106 610	0.104 722	0.102 864	0.101 036	8
9	0.092 574	0.090 690	0.088 839	0.087 022	9
10	0.081 379	0.079 505	0.077 668	0.075 868	10
11	0.072 248	0.070 389	0.068 571	0.066 793	11
12	0.064 666	0.062 825	0.061 029	0.059 277	12
13	0.058 275	0.056 456	0.054 684	0.052 960	13
14	0.052 820	0.051 024	0.049 279	0.047 585	14
15	0.048 114	0.046 342	0.044 626	0.042 963	15
16	0.044 015	0.042 270	0.040 583	0.038 952	16
17	0.040 418	0.038 699	0.037 042	0.035 445	17
18	0.037 237	0.035 546	0.033 920	0.032 357	18
19	0.034 407	0.032 745	0.031 150	0.029 621	19
20	0.031 876	0.030 243	0.028 679	0.027 185	20
21	0.029 601	0.027 996	0.026 465	0.025 005	21
22	0.027 546	0.025 971	0.024 471	0.023 046	22
23	0.025 682	0.024 137	0.022 670	0.021 278	23
24	0.023 987	0.022 471	0.021 036	0.019 679	24
25	0.022 439	0.020 952	0.019 549	0.018 227	25
26	0.021 021	0.019 564	0.018 193	0.016 904	26
27	0.019 719	0.018 292	0.016 952	0.015 697	27
28	0.018 521	0.017 123	0.015 814	0.014 593	28
29	0.017 415	0.016 046	0.014 769	0.013 580	29
YRS					
15	0.016 392	0.015 051	0.013 805	0.012 649	30
16	0.014 563	0.013 280	0.012 095	0.011 002	32
17	0.012 982	0.011 755	0.010 630	0.009 598	34
18	0.011 606	0.010 434	0.009 366	0.008 395	36
19	0.010 402	0.009 284	0.008 272	0.007 358	38
20	0.009 343	0.008 278	0.007 320	0.006 462	40
21	0.008 409	0.007 395	0.006 489	0.005 683	42
22	0.007 581	0.006 616	0.005 761	0.005 006	44
23	0.006 845	0.005 928	0.005 122	0.004 415	46
24	0.006 189	0.005 318	0.004 559	0.003 898	48
25	0.005 602	0.004 777	0.004 061	0.003 444	50
26	0.005 077	0.004 294	0.003 622	0.003 046	52
27	0.004 605	0.003 864	0.003 232	0.002 696	54
28	0.004 181	0.003 480	0.002 887	0.002 388	56
29	0.003 799	0.003 136	0.002 580	0.002 116	58
30	0.003 454	0.002 828	0.002 307	0.001 876	60

SINKING FUND FACTORS

YRS	5.0% ANNUAL RATE	6.0% ANNUAL RATE	7.0% ANNUAL RATE	7.5% ANNUAL RATE	YRS
1	1.000 000	1.000 000	1.000 000	1.000 000	1
2	0.487 805	0.485 437	0.483 092	0.481 928	2
3	0.317 209	0.314 110	0.311 052	0.309 538	3
4	0.232 012	0.228 591	0.225 228	0.223 568	4
5	0.180 975	0.177 396	0.173 891	0.172 165	5
6	0.147 017	0.143 363	0.139 796	0.138 045	6
7	0.122 820	0.119 135	0.115 553	0.113 800	7
8	0.104 722	0.101 036	0.097 468	0.095 727	8
9	0.090 690	0.087 022	0.083 486	0.081 767	9
10	0.079 505	0.075 868	0.072 378	0.070 686	10
11	0.070 389	0.066 793	0.063 357	0.061 697	11
12	0.062 825	0.059 277	0.055 902	0.054 278	12
13	0.056 456	0.052 960	0.049 651	0.048 064	13
14	0.051 024	0.047 585	0.044 345	0.042 797	14
15	0.046 342	0.042 963	0.039 795	0.038 287	15
16	0.042 270	0.038 952	0.035 858	0.034 391	16
17	0.038 699	0.035 445	0.032 425	0.031 000	17
18	0.035 546	0.032 357	0.029 413	0.028 029	18
19	0.032 745	0.029 621	0.026 753	0.025 411	19
20	0.030 243	0.027 185	0.024 393	0.023 092	20
21	0.027 996	0.025 005	0.022 289	0.021 029	21
22	0.025 971	0.023 046	0.020 406	0.019 187	22
23	0.024 137	0.021 278	0.018 714	0.017 535	23
24	0.022 471	0.019 679	0.017 189	0.016 050	24
25	0.020 952	0.018 227	0.015 811	0.014 711	25
26	0.019 564	0.016 904	0.014 561	0.013 500	26
27	0.018 292	0.015 697	0.013 426	0.012 402	27
28	0.017 123	0.014 593	0.012 392	0.011 405	28
29	0.016 046	0.013 580	0.011 449	0.010 498	29
30	0.015 051	0.012 649	0.010 586	0.009 671	30
31	0.014 132	0.011 792	0.009 797	0.008 916	31
32	0.013 280	0.011 002	0.009 073	0.008 226	32
33	0.012 490	0.010 273	0.008 408	0.007 594	33
34	0.011 755	0.009 598	0.007 797	0.007 015	34
35	0.011 072	0.008 974	0.007 234	0.006 483	35
36	0.010 434	0.008 395	0.006 715	0.005 994	36
37	0.009 840	0.007 857	0.006 237	0.005 545	37
38	0.009 284	0.007 358	0.005 795	0.005 132	38
39	0.008 765	0.006 894	0.005 387	0.004 751	39
40	0.008 278	0.006 462	0.005 009	0.004 400	40
41	0.007 822	0.006 059	0.004 660	0.004 077	41
42	0.007 395	0.005 683	0.004 336	0.003 778	42
43	0.006 993	0.005 333	0.004 036	0.003 502	43
44	0.006 616	0.005 006	0.003 758	0.003 247	44
45	0.006 262	0.004 700	0.003 500	0.003 011	45
46	0.005 928	0.004 415	0.003 260	0.002 794	46
47	0.005 614	0.004 148	0.003 037	0.002 592	47
48	0.005 318	0.003 898	0.002 831	0.002 405	48
49	0.005 040	0.003 664	0.002 639	0.002 232	49
50	0.004 777	0.003 444	0.002 460	0.002 072	50

SINKING FUND FACTORS

ANNUAL
COMPOUNDING

	8.0%	8.5%	9.0%	9.5%	
	ANNUAL RATE	ANNUAL RATE	ANNUAL RATE	ANNUAL RATE	
YRS					YRS
1	1.000 000	1.000 000	1.000 000	1.000 000	1
2	0.480 769	0.479 616	0.478 469	0.477 327	2
3	0.308 034	0.306 539	0.305 055	0.303 580	3
4	0.221 921	0.220 288	0.218 669	0.217 063	4
5	0.170 456	0.168 766	0.167 092	0.165 436	5
6	0.136 315	0.134 607	0.132 920	0.131 253	6
7	0.112 072	0.110 369	0.108 691	0.107 036	7
8	0.094 015	0.092 331	0.090 674	0.089 046	8
9	0.080 080	0.078 424	0.076 799	0.075 205	9
10	0.069 029	0.067 408	0.065 820	0.064 266	10
11	0.060 076	0.058 493	0.056 947	0.055 437	11
12	0.052 695	0.051 153	0.049 651	0.048 188	12
13	0.046 522	0.045 023	0.043 567	0.042 152	13
14	0.041 297	0.039 842	0.038 433	0.037 068	14
15	0.036 830	0.035 420	0.034 059	0.032 744	15
16	0.032 977	0.031 614	0.030 300	0.029 035	16
17	0.029 629	0.028 312	0.027 046	0.025 831	17
18	0.026 702	0.025 430	0.024 212	0.023 046	18
19	0.024 128	0.022 901	0.021 730	0.020 613	19
20	0.021 852	0.020 671	0.019 546	0.018 477	20
21	0.019 832	0.018 695	0.017 617	0.016 594	21
22	0.018 032	0.016 939	0.015 905	0.014 928	22
23	0.016 422	0.015 372	0.014 382	0.013 449	23
24	0.014 978	0.013 970	0.013 023	0.012 134	24
25	0.013 679	0.012 712	0.011 806	0.010 959	25
26	0.012 507	0.011 580	0.010 715	0.009 909	26
27	0.011 448	0.010 560	0.009 735	0.008 969	27
28	0.010 489	0.009 639	0.008 852	0.008 124	28
29	0.009 619	0.008 806	0.008 056	0.007 364	29
30	0.008 827	0.008 051	0.007 336	0.006 681	30
31	0.008 107	0.007 365	0.006 686	0.006 064	31
32	0.007 451	0.006 742	0.006 096	0.005 507	32
33	0.006 852	0.006 176	0.005 562	0.005 004	33
34	0.006 304	0.005 660	0.005 077	0.004 549	34
35	0.005 803	0.005 189	0.004 636	0.004 138	35
36	0.005 345	0.004 760	0.004 235	0.003 764	36
37	0.004 924	0.004 368	0.003 870	0.003 426	37
38	0.004 539	0.004 010	0.003 538	0.003 119	38
39	0.004 185	0.003 682	0.003 236	0.002 840	39
40	0.003 860	0.003 382	0.002 960	0.002 587	40
41	0.003 561	0.003 107	0.002 708	0.002 357	41
42	0.003 287	0.002 856	0.002 478	0.002 148	42
43	0.003 034	0.002 625	0.002 268	0.001 958	43
44	0.002 802	0.002 414	0.002 077	0.001 785	44
45	0.002 587	0.002 220	0.001 902	0.001 627	45
46	0.002 390	0.002 042	0.001 742	0.001 484	46
47	0.002 208	0.001 878	0.001 595	0.001 353	47
48	0.002 040	0.001 728	0.001 461	0.001 234	48
49	0.001 886	0.001 590	0.001 339	0.001 126	49
50	0.001 743	0.001 463	0.001 227	0.001 027	50

YRS	10.0% ANNUAL RATE	10.5% ANNUAL RATE	11.0% ANNUAL RATE	11.5% ANNUAL RATE	YRS
1	1.000 000	1.000 000	1.000 000	1.000 000	1
2	0.476 190	0.475 059	0.473 934	0.472 813	2
3	0.302 115	0.300 659	0.299 213	0.297 776	3
4	0.215 471	0.213 892	0.212 326	0.210 774	4
5	0.163 797	0.162 175	0.160 570	0.158 982	5
6	0.129 607	0.127 982	0.126 377	0.124 791	6
7	0.105 405	0.103 799	0.102 215	0.100 655	7
8	0.087 444	0.085 869	0.084 321	0.082 799	8
9	0.073 641	0.072 106	0.070 602	0.069 126	9
10	0.062 745	0.061 257	0.059 801	0.058 377	10
11	0.053 963	0.052 525	0.051 121	0.049 751	11
12	0.046 763	0.045 377	0.044 027	0.042 714	12
13	0.040 779	0.039 445	0.038 151	0.036 895	13
14	0.035 746	0.034 467	0.033 228	0.032 030	14
15	0.031 474	0.030 248	0.029 065	0.027 924	15
16	0.027 817	0.026 644	0.025 517	0.024 432	16
17	0.024 664	0.023 545	0.022 471	0.021 443	17
18	0.021 930	0.020 863	0.019 843	0.018 868	18
19	0.019 547	0.018 531	0.017 563	0.016 641	19
20	0.017 460	0.016 493	0.015 576	0.014 705	20
21	0.015 624	0.014 707	0.013 838	0.013 016	21
22	0.014 005	0.013 134	0.012 313	0.011 539	22
23	0.012 572	0.011 747	0.010 971	0.010 243	23
24	0.011 300	0.010 519	0.009 787	0.009 103	24
25	0.010 168	0.009 429	0.008 740	0.008 098	25
26	0.009 159	0.008 461	0.007 813	0.007 210	26
27	0.008 258	0.007 599	0.006 989	0.006 425	27
28	0.007 451	0.006 830	0.006 257	0.005 730	28
29	0.006 728	0.006 143	0.005 605	0.005 112	29
30	0.006 079	0.005 528	0.005 025	0.004 564	30
31	0.005 496	0.004 978	0.004 506	0.004 077	31
32	0.004 972	0.004 485	0.004 043	0.003 643	32
33	0.004 499	0.004 042	0.003 629	0.003 257	33
34	0.004 074	0.003 645	0.003 259	0.002 912	34
35	0.003 690	0.003 288	0.002 927	0.002 605	35
36	0.003 343	0.002 967	0.002 630	0.002 331	36
37	0.003 030	0.002 677	0.002 364	0.002 086	37
38	0.002 747	0.002 417	0.002 125	0.001 867	38
39	0.002 491	0.002 183	0.001 911	0.001 672	39
40	0.002 259	0.001 971	0.001 719	0.001 497	40
41	0.002 050	0.001 781	0.001 546	0.001 341	41
42	0.001 860	0.001 609	0.001 391	0.001 201	42
43	0.001 688	0.001 454	0.001 251	0.001 076	43
44	0.001 532	0.001 314	0.001 126	0.000 964	44
45	0.001 391	0.001 188	0.001 014	0.000 864	45
46	0.001 263	0.001 074	0.000 912	0.000 774	46
47	0.001 147	0.000 971	0.000 821	0.000 694	47
48	0.001 041	0.000 878	0.000 739	0.000 622	48
49	0.000 946	0.000 794	0.000 666	0.000 558	49
50	0.000 859	0.000 718	0.000 599	0.000 500	50

	12.0%	12.5%	13.0%	13.5%	
	ANNUAL RATE	ANNUAL RATE	ANNUAL RATE	ANNUAL RATE	
YRS					
1	1.000 000	1.000 000	1.000 000	1.000 000	1
2	0.471 698	0.470 588	0.469 484	0.468 384	2
3	0.296 349	0.294 931	0.293 522	0.292 122	3
4	0.209 234	0.207 708	0.206 194	0.204 693	4
5	0.157 410	0.155 854	0.154 315	0.152 791	5
6	0.123 226	0.121 680	0.120 153	0.118 646	6
7	0.099 118	0.097 603	0.096 111	0.094 641	7
8	0.081 303	0.079 832	0.078 387	0.076 966	8
9	0.067 679	0.066 260	0.064 869	0.063 505	9
10	0.056 984	0.055 622	0.054 290	0.052 987	10
11	0.048 415	0.047 112	0.045 841	0.044 602	11
12	0.041 437	0.040 194	0.038 986	0.037 811	12
13	0.035 677	0.034 496	0.033 350	0.032 240	13
14	0.030 871	0.029 751	0.028 667	0.027 621	14
15	0.026 824	0.025 764	0.024 742	0.023 757	15
16	0.023 390	0.022 388	0.021 426	0.020 502	16
17	0.020 457	0.019 512	0.018 608	0.017 743	17
18	0.017 937	0.017 049	0.016 201	0.015 392	18
19	0.015 763	0.014 928	0.014 134	0.013 380	19
20	0.013 879	0.013 096	0.012 354	0.011 651	20
21	0.012 240	0.011 507	0.010 814	0.010 161	21
22	0.010 811	0.010 125	0.009 479	0.008 873	22
23	0.009 560	0.008 919	0.008 319	0.007 757	23
24	0.008 463	0.007 866	0.007 308	0.006 788	24
25	0.007 500	0.006 943	0.006 426	0.005 945	25
26	0.006 652	0.006 134	0.005 655	0.005 211	26
27	0.005 904	0.005 423	0.004 979	0.004 570	27
28	0.005 244	0.004 797	0.004 387	0.004 010	28
29	0.004 660	0.004 246	0.003 867	0.003 521	29
30	0.004 144	0.003 760	0.003 411	0.003 092	30
31	0.003 686	0.003 331	0.003 009	0.002 717	31
32	0.003 280	0.002 952	0.002 656	0.002 388	32
33	0.002 920	0.002 617	0.002 345	0.002 100	33
34	0.002 601	0.002 321	0.002 071	0.001 847	34
35	0.002 317	0.002 059	0.001 829	0.001 624	35
36	0.002 064	0.001 827	0.001 616	0.001 429	36
37	0.001 840	0.001 621	0.001 428	0.001 258	37
38	0.001 640	0.001 439	0.001 262	0.001 107	38
39	0.001 462	0.001 278	0.001 116	0.000 974	39
40	0.001 304	0.001 134	0.000 986	0.000 858	40
41	0.001 163	0.001 007	0.000 872	0.000 755	41
42	0.001 037	0.000 895	0.000 771	0.000 665	42
43	0.000 925	0.000 795	0.000 682	0.000 585	43
44	0.000 825	0.000 706	0.000 603	0.000 515	44
45	0.000 736	0.000 627	0.000 534	0.000 454	45
46	0.000 657	0.000 557	0.000 472	0.000 400	46
47	0.000 586	0.000 495	0.000 417	0.000 352	47
48	0.000 523	0.000 440	0.000 369	0.000 310	48
49	0.000 467	0.000 391	0.000 327	0.000 273	49
50	0.000 417	0.000 347	0.000 289	0.000 241	50

YRS	14.0% ANNUAL RATE	14.5% ANNUAL RATE	15.0% ANNUAL RATE	16.0% ANNUAL RATE	YRS
1	1.000 000	1.000 000	1.000 000	1.000 000	1
2	0.467 290	0.466 200	0.465 116	0.462 963	2
3	0.290 731	0.289 350	0.287 977	0.285 258	3
4	0.203 205	0.201 729	0.200 265	0.197 375	4
5	0.151 284	0.149 792	0.148 316	0.145 409	5
6	0.117 157	0.115 688	0.114 237	0.111 390	6
7	0.093 192	0.091 766	0.090 360	0.087 613	7
8	0.075 570	0.074 198	0.072 850	0.070 224	8
9	0.062 168	0.060 858	0.059 574	0.057 082	9
10	0.051 714	0.050 469	0.049 252	0.046 901	10
11	0.043 394	0.042 217	0.041 069	0.038 861	11
12	0.036 669	0.035 559	0.034 481	0.032 415	12
13	0.031 164	0.030 121	0.029 110	0.027 184	13
14	0.026 609	0.025 632	0.024 688	0.022 898	14
15	0.022 809	0.021 896	0.021 017	0.019 358	15
16	0.019 615	0.018 764	0.017 948	0.016 414	16
17	0.016 915	0.016 124	0.015 367	0.013 952	17
18	0.014 621	0.013 886	0.013 186	0.011 885	18
19	0.012 663	0.011 982	0.011 336	0.010 142	19
20	0.010 986	0.010 357	0.009 761	0.008 667	20
21	0.009 545	0.008 964	0.008 417	0.007 416	21
22	0.008 303	0.007 768	0.007 266	0.006 353	22
23	0.007 231	0.006 739	0.006 278	0.005 447	23
24	0.006 303	0.005 851	0.005 430	0.004 673	24
25	0.005 498	0.005 084	0.004 699	0.004 013	25
26	0.004 800	0.004 420	0.004 070	0.003 447	26
27	0.004 193	0.003 846	0.003 526	0.002 963	27
28	0.003 664	0.003 348	0.003 057	0.002 548	28
29	0.003 204	0.002 915	0.002 651	0.002 192	29
30	0.002 803	0.002 539	0.002 300	0.001 886	30
31	0.002 453	0.002 213	0.001 996	0.001 623	31
32	0.002 147	0.001 929	0.001 733	0.001 397	32
33	0.001 880	0.001 682	0.001 505	0.001 203	33
34	0.001 646	0.001 467	0.001 307	0.001 036	34
35	0.001 442	0.001 279	0.001 135	0.000 892	35
36	0.001 263	0.001 116	0.000 986	0.000 769	36
37	0.001 107	0.000 974	0.000 857	0.000 662	37
38	0.000 970	0.000 850	0.000 744	0.000 571	38
39	0.000 850	0.000 742	0.000 647	0.000 492	39
40	0.000 745	0.000 647	0.000 562	0.000 424	40
41	0.000 653	0.000 565	0.000 489	0.000 365	41
42	0.000 573	0.000 493	0.000 425	0.000 315	42
43	0.000 502	0.000 431	0.000 369	0.000 271	43
44	0.000 440	0.000 376	0.000 321	0.000 234	44
45	0.000 386	0.000 328	0.000 279	0.000 201	45
46	0.000 338	0.000 287	0.000 242	0.000 174	46
47	0.000 297	0.000 250	0.000 211	0.000 150	47
48	0.000 260	0.000 218	0.000 183	0.000 129	48
49	0.000 228	0.000 191	0.000 159	0.000 111	49
50	0.000 200	0.000 167	0.000 139	0.000 096	50

	17.0%	18.0%	19.0%	20.0%	
	ANNUAL RATE	ANNUAL RATE	ANNUAL RATE	ANNUAL RATE	
YRS					
1	1.000 000	1.000 000	1.000 000	1.000 000	1
2	0.460 829	0.458 716	0.456 621	0.454 545	2
3	0.282 574	0.279 924	0.277 308	0.274 725	3
4	0.194 533	0.191 739	0.188 991	0.186 289	4
5	0.142 564	0.139 778	0.137 050	0.134 380	5
6	0.108 615	0.105 910	0.103 274	0.100 706	6
7	0.084 947	0.082 362	0.079 855	0.077 424	7
8	0.067 690	0.065 244	0.062 885	0.060 609	8
9	0.054 691	0.052 395	0.050 192	0.048 079	9
10	0.044 657	0.042 515	0.040 471	0.038 523	10
11	0.036 765	0.034 776	0.032 891	0.031 104	11
12	0.030 466	0.028 628	0.026 896	0.025 265	12
13	0.025 378	0.023 686	0.022 102	0.020 620	13
14	0.021 230	0.019 678	0.018 235	0.016 893	14
15	0.017 822	0.016 403	0.015 092	0.013 882	15
16	0.015 004	0.013 710	0.012 523	0.011 436	16
17	0.012 662	0.011 485	0.010 414	0.009 440	17
18	0.010 706	0.009 639	0.008 676	0.007 805	18
19	0.009 067	0.008 103	0.007 238	0.006 462	19
20	0.007 690	0.006 820	0.006 045	0.005 357	20
21	0.006 530	0.005 746	0.005 054	0.004 444	21
22	0.005 550	0.004 846	0.004 229	0.003 690	22
23	0.004 721	0.004 090	0.003 542	0.003 065	23
24	0.004 019	0.003 454	0.002 967	0.002 548	24
25	0.003 423	0.002 919	0.002 487	0.002 119	25
26	0.002 917	0.002 467	0.002 086	0.001 762	26
27	0.002 487	0.002 087	0.001 750	0.001 467	27
28	0.002 121	0.001 765	0.001 468	0.001 221	28
29	0 001 810	0.001 494	0.001 232	0.001 016	29
30	0.001 545	0.001 264	0.001 034	0.000 846	30
31	0.001 318	0.001 070	0.000 869	0.000 705	31
32	0.001 126	0.000 906	0.000 729	0.000 587	32
33	0.000 961	0.000 767	0.000 612	0.000 489	33
34	0.000 821	0.000 650	0.000 514	0.000 407	34
35	0.000 701	0.000 550	0.000 432	0.000 339	35
36	0.000 599	0.000 466	0.000 363	0.000 283	36
37	0.000 512	0.000 395	0.000 305	0.000 235	37
38	0.000 437	0.000 335	0.000 256	0.000 196	38
39	0.000 373	0.000 284	0.000 215	0.000 163	39
40	0.000 319	0.000 240	0.000 181	0.000 136	40
41	0.000 273	0.000 204	0.000 152	0.000 113	41
42	0.000 233	0.000 172	0.000 128	0.000 095	42
43	0.000 199	0.000 146	0.000 107	0.000 079	43
44	0.000 170	0.000 124	0.000 090	0.000 066	44
45	0.000 145	0.000 105	0.000 076	0.000 055	45
46	0.000 124	0.000 089	0.000 064	0.000 046	46
47	0.000 106	0.000 075	0.000 053	0.000 038	47
48	0.000 091	0.000 064	0.000 045	0.000 032	48
49	0.000 078	0.000 054	0.000 038	0.000 026	49
50	0.000 066	0.000 046	0.000 032	0.000 022	50

Section 4. Present Value of $1.00:

These tables indicate what amount of money must be invested today in order to accumulate $1 at a given time in the future. In this section it is important to understand that investment of the initial amount of money will begin the investment period. The factors are also based on the fact that no additional investments may be made, and that the future growth of this fund depends upon the interest paid. No funds may be withdrawn at any point in the duration of the investment.

In this section the following four (4) periods are presented in detail: monthly, quarterly, semiannual, and annual.

Monthly:

The factors presented on pages 69 through 74 will indicate the amount of money needed to invest today to receive $1 at the end of the stated period. These factors are based on the condition that interest is earned at the end of each monthly period during the term of the investment. Therefore, the interest is compounding monthly. This is interest earned on interest.

Example G

You will need $1,000.00 in 1 year, and you should estimate how much money to invest now to achieve your monetary goal. You can predict an annual interest rate of 6.0%, and interest will compound at the end of each monthly period.

Turn to page 69 and locate the 6.0% column. Proceed down that column until you locate the point where the 12 month (or 1 year) row intersects with the 6.0% column. The number is 0.941905 for each $1 you need to accumulate. So, to determine your answer, multiply 0.941905 by $1,000.00 The correct answer is $941.91. That is, you will need to invest $941.91 today to accumulate $1,000.00 in 12 months or 1 year.

Note: If your investment is less than 2 years, we have provided all the $1 amounts for each monthly period. For two years and over, the annual figures are provided.

Quarterly:

The factors presented on pages 75 through 77, will indicate the amount of money needed to invest today to receive $1 at the end of the stated period. These factors are based on the condition that interest is earned at the end of each quarterly period during the term of the investment. Therefore, the interest is compounding quarterly, i.e., interest earned on interest.

Example H

You need to open a savings account today that will produce $10,000.00 in 10 years. Your credit union compounds interest at the end of every quarter, and pays 8.0% annual interest. How much do you deposit today?

Turn to page 75 and locate the 8.0% column. Proceed down that column until you locate the point where the 10 years row intersects the 8% interest column. The answer is 0.452890 for every $1 you need to accumulate. So, to determine your answer, multiply 0.452890 by $10,000. The correct answer is $4528.90. Just deposit this $4528.90 today and you will have $10,000.00 in ten (10) years.

Note: For investment of 5 years and more, only the annual amounts are shown.

Semiannual:

The factors on pages 78 through 79 cover semiannual compounding (or the interest being compounded every six (6) months).

Annual:

The factors of pages 80 through 85 cover annual compounding (or the interest being compounded every year).

Both the semiannual and annual tables are used the same way as the monthly and quarterly tables.

Just in case you need to know, here is the formula.

$$V^n = \frac{1}{(1 + i)^n}$$

V^n = Present value of $1
i = interest rate per period
n = number of compounding periods

PRESENT VALUE OF $1

MOS	5.0% ANNUAL RATE	6.0% ANNUAL RATE	7.0% ANNUAL RATE	7.5% ANNUAL RATE	MOS
1	0.995 851	0.995 025	0.994 200	0.993 789	1
2	0.991 718	0.990 075	0.988 435	0.987 616	2
3	0.987 603	0.985 149	0.982 702	0.981 482	3
4	0.983 506	0.980 248	0.977 003	0.975 386	4
5	0.979 425	0.975 371	0.971 337	0.969 327	5
6	0.975 361	0.970 518	0.965 704	0.963 307	6
7	0.971 313	0.965 690	0.960 103	0.957 324	7
8	0.967 283	0.960 885	0.954 535	0.951 377	8
9	0.963 269	0.956 105	0.948 999	0.945 468	9
10	0.959 272	0.951 348	0.943 495	0.939 596	10
11	0.955 292	0.946 615	0.938 024	0.933 760	11
12	0.951 328	0.941 905	0.932 583	0.927 960	12
13	0.947 381	0.937 219	0.927 175	0.922 196	13
14	0.943 450	0.932 556	0.921 798	0.916 468	14
15	0.939 535	0.927 917	0.916 452	0.910 776	15
16	0.935 637	0.923 300	0.911 137	0.905 119	16
17	0.931 754	0.918 707	0.905 853	0.899 497	17
18	0.927 888	0.914 136	0.900 599	0.893 910	18
19	0.924 038	0.909 588	0.895 376	0.888 358	19
20	0.920 204	0.905 063	0.890 183	0.882 840	20
21	0.916 385	0.900 560	0.885 021	0.877 357	21
22	0.912 583	0.896 080	0.879 888	0.871 907	22
23	0.908 796	0.891 622	0.874 785	0.866 492	23
YRS					
2	0.905 025	0.887 186	0.869 712	0.861 110	24
3	0.860 976	0.835 645	0.811 079	0.799 076	36
4	0.819 071	0.787 098	0.756 399	0.741 510	48
5	0.779 205	0.741 372	0.705 405	0.688 092	60
6	0.741 280	0.698 302	0.657 849	0.638 522	72
7	0.705 201	0.657 735	0.613 499	0.592 523	84
8	0.670 877	0.619 524	0.572 139	0.549 837	96
9	0.638 225	0.583 533	0.533 568	0.510 227	108
10	0.607 161	0.549 633	0.497 596	0.473 470	120
11	0.577 609	0.517 702	0.464 050	0.439 362	132
12	0.549 496	0.487 626	0.432 765	0.407 710	144
13	0.522 751	0.459 298	0.403 590	0.378 339	156
14	0.497 308	0.432 615	0.376 381	0.351 083	168
15	0.473 103	0.407 482	0.351 007	0.325 791	180
16	0.450 076	0.383 810	0.327 343	0.302 321	192
17	0.428 170	0.361 513	0.305 275	0.280 542	204
18	0.407 331	0.340 511	0.284 694	0.260 332	216
19	0.387 505	0.320 729	0.265 501	0.241 577	228
20	0.368 645	0.302 096	0.247 602	0.224 174	240
21	0.350 702	0.284 546	0.230 910	0.208 025	252
22	0.333 633	0.268 015	0.215 342	0.193 039	264
23	0.317 394	0.252 445	0.200 825	0.179 132	276
24	0.301 946	0.237 779	0.187 286	0.166 227	288
25	0.287 250	0.223 966	0.174 660	0.154 252	300
26	0.273 269	0.210 954	0.162 885	0.143 140	312
27	0.259 968	0.198 699	0.151 904	0.132 828	324
28	0.247 315	0.187 156	0.141 663	0.123 259	336
29	0.235 278	0.176 283	0.132 112	0.114 380	348
30	0.223 827	0.166 042	0.123 206	0.106 140	360

	8.0%		8.5%		9.0%		9.5%		
	ANNUAL RATE		ANNUAL RATE		ANNUAL RATE		ANNUAL RATE			
MOS										
1	0.993 377		0.992 966		0.992 556		0.992 146			1
2	0.986 799		0.985 982		0.985 167		0.984 353			2
3	0.980 264		0.979 048		0.977 833		0.976 621			3
4	0.973 772		0.972 161		0.970 554		0.968 950			4
5	0.967 323		0.965 324		0.963 329		0.961 340			5
6	0.960 917		0.958 534		0.956 158		0.953 789			6
7	0.954 553		0.951 792		0.949 040		0.946 297			7
8	0.948 232		0.945 098		0.941 975		0.938 865			8
9	0.941 952		0.938 450		0.934 963		0.931 490			9
10	0.935 714		0.931 850		0.928 003		0.924 174			10
11	0.929 517		0.925 296		0.921 095		0.916 915			11
12	0.923 361		0.918 788		0.914 238		0.909 713			12
13	0.917 246		0.912 325		0.907 432		0.902 568			13
14	0.911 172		0.905 908		0.900 677		0.895 479			14
15	0.905 138		0.899 537		0.893 973		0.888 445			15
16	0.899 143		0.893 210		0.887 318		0.881 467			16
17	0.893 189		0.886 927		0.880 712		0.874 543			17
18	0.887 274		0.880 689		0.874 156		0.867 674			18
19	0.881 398		0.874 495		0.867 649		0.860 859			9
20	0.875 561		0.868 344		0.861 190		0.854 098			20
21	0.869 762		0.862 237		0.854 779		0.847 389			21
22	0.864 002		0.856 172		0.848 416		0.840 733			22
23	0.858 280		0.850 150		0.842 100		0.834 130			23
YRS										
2	0.852 596		0.844 171		0.835 831		0.827 578			24
3	0.787 255		0.775 613		0.764 149		0.752 859			36
4	0.726 921		0.712 624		0.698 614		0.684 885			48
5	0.671 210		0.654 750		0.638 700		0.623 049			60
6	0.619 770		0.601 576		0.583 924		0.566 796			72
7	0.572 272		0.552 721		0.533 845		0.515 622			84
8	0.528 414		0.507 833		0.488 062		0.469 068			96
9	0.487 917		0.466 590		0.446 205		0.426 717			108
10	0.450 523		0.428 698		0.407 937		0.388 190			120
11	0.415 996		0.393 882		0.372 952		0.353 142			132
12	0.384 115		0.361 894		0.340 967		0.321 258			144
13	0.354 677		0.332 504		0.311 725		0.292 253			156
14	0.327 495		0.305 500		0.284 991		0.265 866			168
15	0.302 396		0.280 690		0.260 549		0.241 862			180
16	0.279 221		0.257 894		0.238 204		0.220 025			192
17	0.257 822		0.236 950		0.217 775		0.200 159			204
18	0.238 063		0.217 707		0.199 099		0.182 088			216
19	0.219 818		0.200 026		0.182 024		0.165 648			228
20	0.202 971		0.183 782		0.166 413		0.150 692			240
21	0.187 416		0.168 856		0.152 141		0.137 086			252
22	0.173 053		0.155 143		0.139 093		0.124 709			264
23	0.159 790		0.142 543		0.127 164		0.113 450			276
24	0.147 544		0.130 967		0.116 258		0.103 207			288
25	0.136 237		0.120 331		0.106 288		0.093 888			300
26	0.125 796		0.110 559		0.097 172		0.085 412			312
27	0.116 155		0.101 580		0.088 839		0.077 700			324
28	0.107 253		0.093 330		0.081 220		0.070 685			336
29	0.099 033		0.085 751		0.074 254		0.064 303			348
30	0.091 443		0.078 787		0.067 886		0.058 497			360

	10.0%	10.5%	11.0%	11.5%	
	ANNUAL RATE	ANNUAL RATE	ANNUAL RATE	ANNUAL RATE	
MOS					MOS
1	0.991 736	0.991 326	0.990 917	0.990 508	1
2	0.983 539	0.982 727	0.981 916	0.981 105	2
3	0.975 411	0.974 203	0.972 997	0.971 792	3
4	0.967 350	0.965 752	0.964 158	0.962 568	4
5	0.959 355	0.957 375	0.955 401	0.953 431	5
6	0.951 427	0.949 071	0.946 722	0.944 380	6
7	0.943 563	0.940 839	0.938 123	0.935 416	7
8	0.935 765	0.932 678	0.929 602	0.926 537	8
9	0.928 032	0.924 588	0.921 158	0.917 742	9
10	0.920 362	0.916 568	0.912 790	0.909 030	10
11	0.912 756	0.908 617	0.904 499	0.900 401	11
12	0.905 212	0.900 736	0.896 283	0.891 854	12
13	0.897 731	0.892 923	0.888 142	0.883 389	13
14	0.890 312	0.885 177	0.880 075	0.875 003	14
15	0.882 954	0.877 499	0.872 080	0.866 697	15
16	0.875 657	0.869 888	0.864 159	0.858 470	16
17	0.868 420	0.862 342	0.856 309	0.850 321	17
18	0.861 243	0.854 862	0.848 531	0.842 250	18
19	0.854 125	0.847 447	0.840 824	0.834 255	19
20	0.847 067	0.840 096	0.833 186	0.826 336	20
21	0.840 066	0.832 809	0.825 618	0.818 492	21
22	0.833 123	0.825 585	0.818 119	0.810 722	22
23	0.826 238	0.818 424	0.810 687	0.803 027	23
YRS					
2	0.819 410	0.811 325	0.803 323	0.795 404	24
3	0.741 740	0.730 789	0.720 005	0.709 385	36
4	0.671 432	0.658 248	0.645 329	0.632 668	48
5	0.607 789	0.592 908	0.578 397	0.564 248	60
6	0.550 178	0.534 053	0.518 408	0.503 227	72
7	0.498 028	0.481 041	0.464 640	0.448 805	84
8	0.450 821	0.433 291	0.416 449	0.400 269	96
9	0.408 089	0.390 280	0.373 256	0.356 981	108
10	0.369 407	0.351 540	0.334 543	0.318 375	120
11	0.334 392	0.316 644	0.299 846	0.283 944	132
12	0.302 696	0.285 213	0.268 747	0.253 237	144
13	0.274 004	0.256 901	0.240 873	0.225 851	156
14	0.248 032	0.231 400	0.215 890	0.201 426	168
15	0.224 521	0.208 431	0.193 499	0.179 642	180
16	0.203 240	0.187 741	0.173 430	0.160 215	192
17	0.183 975	0.169 105	0.155 442	0.142 888	204
18	0.166 536	0.152 319	0.139 320	0.127 436	216
19	0.150 751	0.137 199	0.124 870	0.113 654	228
20	0.136 462	0.123 580	0.111 919	0.101 363	240
21	0.123 527	0.111 313	0.100 311	0.090 401	252
22	0.111 818	0.100 264	0.089 907	0.080 624	264
23	0.101 219	0.090 311	0.080 582	0.071 905	276
24	0.091 625	0.081 346	0.072 225	0.064 129	288
25	0.082 940	0.073 272	0.064 734	0.057 194	300
26	0.075 078	0.065 998	0.058 020	0.051 008	312
27	0.067 962	0.059 447	0.052 002	0.045 492	324
28	0.061 520	0.053 546	0.046 609	0.040 572	336
29	0.055 688	0.048 231	0.041 775	0.036 185	348
30	0.050 410	0.043 443	0.037 442	0.032 271	360

SECTION 4

	12.0%	12.5%	13.0%	13.5%	
	ANNUAL RATE	ANNUAL RATE	ANNUAL RATE	ANNUAL RATE	
MOS					MOS
1	0.990 099	0.989 691	0.989 283	0.988 875	1
2	0.980 296	0.979 488	0.978 680	0.977 874	2
3	0.970 590	0.969 390	0.968 192	0.966 995	3
4	0.960 980	0.959 396	0.957 815	0.956 238	4
5	0.951 466	0.949 506	0.947 550	0.945 600	5
6	0.942 045	0.939 717	0.937 395	0.935 080	6
7	0.932 718	0.930 029	0.927 349	0.924 677	7
8	0.923 483	0.920 441	0.917 410	0.914 391	8
9	0.914 340	0.910 952	0.907 578	0.904 218	9
10	0.905 287	0.901 561	0.897 851	0.894 159	10
11	0.896 324	0.892 266	0.888 229	0.884 211	11
12	0.887 449	0.883 068	0.878 710	0.874 375	12
13	0.878 663	0.873 964	0.869 292	0.864 647	13
14	0.869 963	0.864 954	0.859 976	0.855 028	14
15	0.861 349	0.856 037	0.850 759	0.845 516	15
16	0.852 821	0.847 212	0.841 641	0.836 110	16
17	0.844 377	0.838 478	0.832 621	0.826 808	17
18	0.836 017	0.829 834	0.823 698	0.817 610	18
19	0.827 740	0.821 279	0.814 870	0.808 515	19
20	0.819 544	0.812 812	0.806 137	0.799 520	20
21	0.811 430	0.804 432	0.797 498	0.790 625	21
22	0.803 396	0.796 139	0.788 951	0.781 830	22
23	0.795 442	0.787 932	0.780 495	0.773 132	23
YRS					
2	0.787 566	0.779 809	0.772 130	0.764 531	24
3	0.698 925	0.688 624	0.678 478	0.668 487	36
4	0.620 260	0.608 101	0.596 185	0.584 508	48
5	0.550 450	0.536 995	0.523 874	0.511 079	60
6	0.488 496	0.474 203	0.460 333	0.446 874	72
7	0.433 515	0.418 753	0.404 499	0.390 736	84
8	0.384 723	0.369 787	0.355 437	0.341 649	96
9	0.341 422	0.326 547	0.312 326	0.298 730	108
10	0.302 995	0.288 363	0.274 444	0.261 202	120
11	0.268 892	0.254 644	0.241 156	0.228 388	132
12	0.238 628	0.224 868	0.211 906	0.199 697	144
13	0.211 771	0.198 574	0.186 204	0.174 610	156
14	0.187 936	0.175 354	0.163 619	0.152 674	168
15	0.166 783	0.154 849	0.143 774	0.133 495	180
16	0.148 012	0.136 743	0.126 336	0.116 724	192
17	0.131 353	0.120 753	0.111 012	0.102 061	204
18	0.116 569	0.106 633	0.097 548	0.089 239	216
19	0.103 449	0.094 164	0.085 716	0.078 029	228
20	0.091 806	0.083 153	0.075 319	0.068 226	240
21	0.081 473	0.073 430	0.066 184	0.059 655	252
22	0.072 303	0.064 844	0.058 156	0.052 161	264
23	0.064 165	0.057 261	0.051 103	0.045 608	276
24	0.056 944	0.050 566	0.044 904	0.039 879	288
25	0.050 534	0.044 653	0.039 458	0.034 869	300
26	0.044 847	0.039 432	0.034 672	0.030 489	312
27	0.039 799	0.034 821	0.030 467	0.026 658	324
28	0.035 320	0.030 749	0.026 771	0.023 309	336
29	0.031 345	0.027 153	0.023 524	0.020 381	348
30	0.027 817	0.023 978	0.020 671	0.017 821	360

MOS	14.0% ANNUAL RATE	14.5% ANNUAL RATE	15.0% ANNUAL RATE	16.0% ANNUAL RATE	MOS
1	0.988 468	0.988 061	0.987 654	0.986 842	1
2	0.977 069	0.976 264	0.975 461	0.973 857	2
3	0.965 801	0.964 609	0.963 418	0.961 043	3
4	0.954 663	0.953 092	0.951 524	0.948 398	4
5	0.943 654	0.941 713	0.939 777	0.935 919	5
6	0.932 772	0.930 470	0.928 175	0.923 604	6
7	0.922 015	0.919 361	0.916 716	0.911 452	7
8	0.911 382	0.908 385	0.905 398	0.899 459	8
9	0.900 872	0.897 539	0.894 221	0.887 624	9
10	0.890 483	0.886 824	0.883 181	0.875 945	10
11	0.880 214	0.876 236	0.872 277	0.864 419	11
12	0.870 063	0.865 774	0.861 509	0.853 045	12
13	0.860 029	0.855 438	0.850 873	0.841 821	13
14	0.850 111	0.845 225	0.840 368	0.830 744	14
15	0.840 308	0.835 133	0.829 993	0.819 814	15
16	0.830 617	0.825 163	0.819 746	0.809 026	16
17	0.821 038	0.815 311	0.809 626	0.798 381	17
18	0.811 570	0.805 577	0.799 631	0.787 876	18
19	0.802 211	0.795 959	0.789 759	0.777 510	19
20	0.792 960	0.786 456	0.780 009	0.767 279	20
21	0.783 815	0.777 067	0.770 379	0.757 183	21
22	0.774 776	0.767 789	0.760 868	0.747 220	22
23	0.765 841	0.758 622	0.751 475	0.737 389	23

YRS					
2	0.757 010	0.749 565	0.742 197	0.727 686	24
3	0.658 646	0.648 954	0.639 409	0.620 749	36
4	0.573 064	0.561 848	0.550 856	0.529 527	48
5	0.498 601	0.486 434	0.474 568	0.451 711	60
6	0.433 815	0.421 142	0.408 844	0.385 330	72
7	0.377 446	0.364 614	0.352 223	0.328 704	84
8	0.328 402	0.315 673	0.303 443	0.280 399	96
9	0.285 730	0.273 302	0.261 419	0.239 193	108
10	0.248 603	0.236 618	0.225 214	0.204 042	120
11	0.216 301	0.204 858	0.194 024	0.174 057	132
12	0.188 195	0.177 360	0.167 153	0.148 479	144
13	0.163 742	0.153 554	0.144 004	0.126 659	156
14	0.142 466	0.132 943	0.124 061	0.108 046	168
15	0.123 954	0.115 099	0.106 879	0.092 168	180
16	0.107 848	0.099 650	0.092 078	0.078 624	192
17	0.093 834	0.086 274	0.079 326	0.067 069	204
18	0.081 642	0.074 694	0.068 340	0.057 213	216
19	0.071 034	0.064 668	0.058 875	0.048 806	228
20	0.061 804	0.055 988	0.050 722	0.041 633	240
21	0.053 773	0.048 473	0.043 697	0.035 515	252
22	0.046 786	0.041 967	0.037 645	0.030 296	264
23	0.040 707	0.036 334	0.032 432	0.025 844	276
24	0.035 417	0.031 457	0.027 940	0.022 046	288
25	0.030 815	0.027 234	0.024 071	0.018 806	300
26	0.026 811	0.023 579	0.020 737	0.016 043	312
27	0.023 328	0.020 414	0.017 865	0.013 685	324
28	0.020 296	0.017 674	0.015 391	0.011 674	336
29	0.017 659	0.015 302	0.013 260	0.009 958	348
30	0.015 365	0.013 248	0.011 423	0.008 495	360

	17.0%	18.0%	19.0%	20.0%	
	ANNUAL RATE	ANNUAL RATE	ANNUAL RATE	ANNUAL RATE	
MOS					
1	0.986 031	0.985 222	0.984 413	0.983 607	1
2	0.972 258	0.970 662	0.969 070	0.967 482	2
3	0.958 676	0.956 317	0.953 965	0.951 622	3
4	0.945 285	0.942 184	0.939 096	0.936 021	4
5	0.932 080	0.928 260	0.924 459	0.920 677	5
6	0.919 060	0.914 542	0.910 050	0.905 583	6
7	0.906 222	0.901 027	0.895 865	0.890 738	7
8	0.893 563	0.887 711	0.881 902	0.876 136	8
9	0.881 081	0.874 592	0.868 156	0.861 773	9
10	0.868 774	0.861 667	0.854 625	0.847 645	10
11	0.856 638	0.848 933	0.841 304	0.833 749	11
12	0.844 672	0.836 387	0.828 191	0.820 081	12
13	0.832 873	0.824 027	0.815 282	0.806 637	13
14	0.821 239	0.811 849	0.802 575	0.793 414	14
15	0.809 767	0.799 852	0.790 066	0.780 407	15
16	0.798 455	0.788 031	0.777 751	0.767 614	16
17	0.787 302	0.776 385	0.765 629	0.755 030	17
18	0.776 304	0.764 912	0.753 695	0.742 652	18
19	0.765 460	0.753 607	0.741 948	0.730 478	19
20	0.754 768	0.742 470	0.730 383	0.718 503	20
21	0.744 225	0.731 498	0.718 999	0.706 724	21
22	0.733 829	0.720 688	0.707 792	0.695 138	22
23	0.723 578	0.710 037	0.696 760	0.683 742	23
YRS					
2	0.713 471	0.699 544	0.685 900	0.672 534	24
3	0.602 648	0.585 090	0.568 056	0.551 532	36
4	0.509 040	0.489 362	0.470 459	0.452 301	48
5	0.429 972	0.409 296	0.389 630	0.370 924	60
6	0.363 185	0.342 330	0.322 688	0.304 188	72
7	0.306 772	0.286 321	0.267 247	0.249 459	84
8	0.259 122	0.239 475	0.221 332	0.204 577	96
9	0.218 873	0.200 294	0.183 305	0.167 769	108
10	0.184 876	0.167 523	0.151 812	0.137 585	120
11	0.156 159	0.140 114	0.125 729	0.112 831	132
12	0.131 903	0.117 190	0.104 128	0.092 530	144
13	0.111 415	0.098 016	0.086 238	0.075 882	156
14	0.094 109	0.081 979	0.071 421	0.062 230	168
15	0.079 491	0.068 567	0.059 150	0.051 033	180
16	0.067 144	0.057 348	0.048 988	0.041 852	192
17	0.056 715	0.047 965	0.040 571	0.034 322	204
18	0.047 905	0.040 118	0.033 601	0.028 147	216
19	0.040 464	0.033 554	0.027 828	0.023 082	228
20	0.034 179	0.028 064	0.023 047	0.018 930	240
21	0.028 870	0.023 472	0.019 087	0.015 524	252
22	0.024 386	0.019 632	0.015 808	0.012 731	264
23	0.020 598	0.016 420	0.013 092	0.010 440	276
24	0.017 399	0.013 733	0.010 843	0.008 562	288
25	0.014 696	0.011 486	0.008 980	0.007 021	300
26	0.012 413	0.009 607	0.007 437	0.005 758	312
27	0.010 485	0.008 035	0.006 159	0.004 722	324
28	0.008 857	0.006 721	0.005 101	0.003 873	336
29	0.007 481	0.005 621	0.004 225	0.003 176	348
30	0.006 319	0.004 701	0.003 499	0.002 604	360

74

	5.0%	6.0%	7.0%	8.0%	
	ANNUAL RATE	ANNUAL RATE	ANNUAL RATE	ANNUAL RATE	
QTRS					
1	0.987 654	0.985 222	0.982 801	0.980 392	1
2	0.975 461	0.970 662	0.965 898	0.961 169	2
3	0.963 418	0.956 317	0.949 285	0.942 322	3
4	0.951 524	0.942 184	0.932 959	0.923 845	4
5	0.939 777	0.928 260	0.916 913	0.905 731	5
6	0.928 175	0.914 542	0.901 143	0.887 971	6
7	0.916 716	0.901 027	0.885 644	0.870 560	7
8	0.905 398	0.887 711	0.870 412	0.853 490	8
9	0.894 221	0.874 592	0.855 441	0.836 755	9
10	0.883 181	0.861 667	0.840 729	0.820 348	10
11	0.872 277	0.848 933	0.826 269	0.804 263	11
12	0.861 509	0.836 387	0.812 058	0.788 493	12
13	0.850 873	0.824 027	0.798 091	0.773 033	13
14	0.840 368	0.811 849	0.784 365	0.757 875	14
15	0.829 993	0.799 852	0.770 875	0.743 015	15
16	0.819 746	0.788 031	0.757 616	0.728 446	16
17	0.809 626	0.776 385	0.744 586	0.714 163	17
18	0.799 631	0.764 912	0.731 780	0.700 159	18
19	0.789 759	0.753 607	0.719 194	0.686 431	19
YRS					
5	0.780 009	0.742 470	0.706 825	0.672 971	20
6	0.742 197	0.699 544	0.659 438	0.621 721	24
7	0.706 219	0.659 099	0.615 228	0.574 375	28
8	0.671 984	0.620 993	0.573 982	0.530 633	32
9	0.639 409	0.585 090	0.535 502	0.490 223	36
10	0.608 413	0.551 262	0.499 601	0.452 890	40
11	0.578 920	0.519 391	0.466 107	0.418 401	44
12	0.550 856	0.489 362	0.434 858	0.386 538	48
13	0.524 153	0.461 069	0.405 705	0.357 101	52
14	0.498 745	0.434 412	0.378 506	0 329 906	56
15	0.474 568	0.409 296	0.353 130	0.304 782	60
16	0.451 563	0.385 632	0.329 456	0.281 572	64
17	0.429 673	0.363 337	0.307 369	0.260 129	68
18	0.408 844	0.342 330	0.286 762	0.240 319	72
19	0.389 025	0.322 538	0.267 537	0.222 017	76
20	0.370 167	0.303 890	0.249 601	0.205 110	80
21	0.352 223	0.286 321	0.232 868	0.189 490	84
22	0.335 148	0.269 767	0.217 256	0.175 059	88
23	0.318 902	0.254 170	0.202 691	0.161 728	92
24	0.303 443	0.239 475	0.189 102	0.149 411	96
25	0.288 733	0.225 629	0.176 424	0.138 033	100
26	0.274 737	0.212 585	0.164 596	0.127 521	104
27	0.261 419	0.200 294	0.153 562	0.117 810	108
28	0.248 746	0.188 714	0.143 267	0.108 838	112
29	0.236 688	0.177 803	0.133 662	0.100 550	116
30	0.225 214	0.167 523	0.124 701	0.092 892	120

	9.0%	10.0%	11.0%	12.0%	
	ANNUAL RATE	ANNUAL RATE	ANNUAL RATE	ANNUAL RATE	
QTRS					QTRS
1	0.977 995	0.975 610	0.973 236	0.970 874	1
2	0.956 474	0.951 814	0.947 188	0.942 596	2
3	0.935 427	0.928 599	0.921 838	0.915 142	3
4	0.914 843	0.905 951	0.897 166	0.888 487	4
5	0.894 712	0.883 854	0.873 154	0.862 609	5
6	0.875 024	0.862 297	0.849 785	0.837 484	6
7	0.855 769	0.841 265	0.827 041	0.813 092	7
8	0.836 938	0.820 747	0.804 906	0.789 409	8
9	0.818 522	0.800 728	0.783 364	0.766 417	9
10	0.800 510	0.781 198	0.762 398	0.744 094	10
11	0.782 895	0.762 145	0.741 993	0.722 421	11
12	0.765 667	0.743 556	0.722 134	0.701 380	12
13	0.748 819	0.725 420	0.702 807	0.680 951	13
14	0.732 341	0.707 727	0.683 997	0.661 118	14
15	0.716 226	0.690 466	0.665 691	0.641 862	15
16	0.700 466	0.673 625	0.647 874	0.623 167	16
17	0.685 052	0.657 195	0.630 535	0.605 016	17
18	0.669 978	0.641 166	0.613 659	0.587 395	18
19	0.655 235	0.625 528	0.597 235	0.570 286	19
YRS					
5	0.640 816	0.610 271	0.581 251	0.553 676	20
6	0.586 247	0.552 875	0.521 478	0.491 934	24
7	0.536 324	0.500 878	0.467 852	0.437 077	28
8	0.490 652	0.453 771	0.419 741	0.388 337	32
9	0.448 870	0.411 094	0.376 577	0.345 032	36
10	0.410 646	0.372 431	0.337 852	0.306 557	40
11	0.375 677	0.337 404	0.303 109	0.272 372	44
12	0.343 685	0.305 671	0.271 939	0.241 999	48
13	0.314 418	0.276 923	0.243 975	0.215 013	52
14	0.287 643	0.250 879	0.218 886	0.191 036	56
15	0.263 149	0.227 284	0.196 377	0.169 733	60
16	0.240 740	0.205 908	0.176 183	0.150 806	64
17	0.220 239	0.186 542	0.158 065	0.133 989	68
18	0.201 484	0.168 998	0.141 810	0.119 047	72
19	0.184 327	0.153 104	0.127 227	0.105 772	76
20	0.168 630	0.138 705	0.114 144	0.093 977	80
21	0.154 270	0.125 659	0.102 406	0.083 497	84
22	0.141 133	0.113 841	0.091 875	0.074 186	88
23	0.129 114	0.103 135	0.082 427	0.065 914	92
24	0.118 119	0.093 435	0.073 951	0.058 563	96
25	0.108 061	0.084 647	0.066 346	0.052 033	100
26	0.098 859	0.076 686	0.059 524	0.046 231	104
27	0.090 440	0.069 474	0.053 403	0.041 075	108
28	0.082 739	0.062 940	0.047 911	0.036 495	112
29	0.075 693	0.057 021	0.042 984	0.032 425	116
30	0.069 247	0.051 658	0.038 564	0.028 809	120

	13.0%	14.0%	15.0%	16.0%	
	ANNUAL RATE	ANNUAL RATE	ANNUAL RATE	ANNUAL RATE	
QTRS					QTRS
1	0.968 523	0.966 184	0.963 855	0.961 538	1
2	0.938 037	0.933 511	0.929 017	0.924 556	2
3	0.908 510	0.901 943	0.895 438	0.888 996	3
4	0.879 913	0.871 442	0.863 073	0.854 804	4
5	0.852 216	0.841 973	0.831 878	0.821 927	5
6	0.825 391	0.813 501	0.801 810	0.790 315	6
7	0.799 410	0.785 991	0.772 829	0.759 918	7
8	0.774 247	0.759 412	0.744 895	0.730 690	8
9	0.749 876	0.733 731	0.717 971	0.702 587	9
10	0.726 272	0.708 919	0.692 020	0.675 564	10
11	0.703 411	0.684 946	0.667 008	0.649 581	11
12	0.681 270	0.661 783	0.642 899	0.624 597	12
13	0.659 826	0.639 404	0.619 662	0.600 574	13
14	0.639 056	0.617 782	0.597 264	0.577 475	14
15	0.618 941	0.596 891	0.575 676	0.555 265	15
16	0.599 458	0.576 706	0.554 869	0.533 908	16
17	0.580 589	0.557 204	0.534 813	0.513 373	17
18	0.562 314	0.538 361	0.515 483	0.493 628	18
19	0.544 614	0.520 156	0.496 851	0.474 642	19
YRS					
5	0.527 471	0.502 566	0.478 892	0.456 387	20
6	0.464 129	0.437 957	0.413 319	0.390 121	24
7	0.408 393	0.381 654	0.356 725	0.333 477	28
8	0.359 350	0.332 590	0.307 879	0.285 058	32
9	0.316 197	0.289 833	0.265 722	0.243 669	36
10	0.278 226	0.252 572	0.229 338	0.208 289	40
11	0.244 815	0.220 102	0.197 935	0.178 046	44
12	0.215 416	0.191 806	0.170 833	0.152 195	48
13	0.189 547	0.167 148	0.147 441	0.130 097	52
14	0.166 785	0.145 660	0.127 252	0.111 207	56
15	0.146 756	0.126 934	0.109 828	0.095 060	60
16	0.129 133	0.110 616	0.094 790	0.081 258	64
17	0.113 626	0.096 395	0.081 810	0.069 460	68
18	0.099 981	0.084 003	0.070 608	0.059 374	72
19	0.087 974	0.073 204	0.060 940	0.050 754	76
20	0.077 410	0.063 793	0.052 596	0.043 384	80
21	0.068 114	0.055 592	0.045 394	0.037 085	84
22	0.059 934	0.048 445	0.039 178	0.031 701	88
23	0.052 737	0.042 217	0.033 814	0.027 098	92
24	0.046 404	0.036 790	0.029 184	0.023 163	96
25	0.040 831	0.032 060	0.025 188	0.019 800	100
26	0.035 928	0.027 939	0.021 739	0.016 925	104
27	0.031 614	0.024 347	0.018 762	0.014 468	108
28	0.027 817	0.021 217	0.016 193	0.012 367	112
29	0.024 477	0.018 489	0.013 976	0.010 571	116
30	0.021 537	0.016 112	0.012 062	0.009 036	120

	5.0%	6.0%	7.0%	8.0%	
	ANNUAL RATE	ANNUAL RATE	ANNUAL RATE	ANNUAL RATE	
HALF YRS					HALF YRS
1	0.975 610	0.970 874	0.966 184	0.961 538	1
2	0.951 814	0.942 596	0.933 511	0.924 556	2
3	0.928 599	0.915 142	0.901 943	0.888 996	3
4	0.905 951	0.888 487	0.871 442	0.854 804	4
5	0.883 854	0.862 609	0.841 973	0.821 927	5
6	0.862 297	0.837 484	0.813 501	0.790 315	6
7	0.841 265	0.813 092	0.785 991	0.759 918	7
8	0.820 747	0.789 409	0.759 412	0.730 690	8
9	0.800 728	0.766 417	0.733 731	0.702 587	9
10	0.781 198	0.744 094	0.708 919	0.675 564	10
11	0.762 145	0.722 421	0.684 946	0.649 581	11
12	0.743 556	0.701 380	0.661 783	0.624 597	12
13	0.725 420	0.680 951	0.639 404	0.600 574	13
14	0.707 727	0.661 118	0.617 782	0.577 475	14
15	0.690 466	0.641 862	0.596 891	0.555 265	15
16	0.673 625	0.623 167	0.576 706	0.533 908	16
17	0.657 195	0.605 016	0.557 204	0.513 373	17
18	0.641 166	0.587 395	0.538 361	0.493 628	18
19	0.625 528	0.570 286	0.520 156	0.474 642	19
20	0.610 271	0.553 676	0.502 566	0.456 387	20
21	0.595 386	0.537 549	0.485 571	0.438 834	21
22	0.580 865	0.521 893	0.469 151	0.421 955	22
23	0.566 697	0.506 692	0.453 286	0 405 726	23
24	0.552 875	0.491 934	0.437 957	0.390 121	24
25	0.539 391	0.477 606	0.423 147	0.375 117	25
26	0.526 235	0.463 695	0.408 838	0.360 689	26
27	0.513 400	0.450 189	0.395 012	0.346 817	27
28	0.500 878	0.437 077	0.381 654	0.333 477	28
29	0.488 661	0.424 346	0.368 748	0.320 651	29
YRS					
15	0.476 743	0.411 987	0.356 278	0.308 319	30
16	0.453 771	0.388 337	0.332 590	0.285 058	32
17	0.431 905	0.366 045	0.310 476	0.263 552	34
18	0.411 094	0.345 032	0.289 833	0.243 669	36
19	0.391 285	0.325 226	0.270 562	0.225 285	38
20	0.372 431	0.306 557	0.252 572	0.208 289	40
21	0.354 485	0.288 959	0.235 779	0.192 575	42
22	0.337 404	0.272 372	0.220 102	0.178 046	44
23	0.321 146	0.256 737	0.205 468	0.164 614	46
24	0.305 671	0.241 999	0.191 806	0.152 195	48
25	0.290 942	0.228 107	0.179 053	0.140 713	50
26	0.276 923	0.215 013	0.167 148	0.130 097	52
27	0.263 579	0.202 670	0.156 035	0.120 282	54
28	0.250 879	0.191 036	0.145 660	0.111 207	56
29	0.238 790	0.180 070	0.135 975	0.102 817	58
30	0.227 284	0.169 733	0.126 934	0.095 060	60

HALF YRS	9.0% ANNUAL RATE	10.0% ANNUAL RATE	11.0% ANNUAL RATE	12.0% ANNUAL RATE	HALF YRS
1	0.956 938	0.952 381	0.947 867	0.943 396	1
2	0.915 730	0.907 029	0.898 452	0.889 996	2
3	0.876 297	0.863 838	0.851 614	0.839 619	3
4	0.838 561	0.822 702	0.807 217	0.792 094	4
5	0.802 451	0.783 526	0.765 134	0.747 258	5
6	0.767 896	0.746 215	0.725 246	0.704 961	6
7	0.734 828	0.710 681	0.687 437	0.665 057	7
8	0.703 185	0.676 839	0.651 599	0.627 412	8
9	0.672 904	0.644 609	0.617 629	0.591 898	9
10	0.643 928	0.613 913	0.585 431	0.558 395	10
11	0.616 199	0.584 679	0.554 911	0.526 788	11
12	0.589 664	0.556 837	0.525 982	0.496 969	12
13	0.564 272	0.530 321	0.498 561	0.468 839	13
14	0.539 973	0.505 068	0.472 569	0.442 301	14
15	0.516 720	0.481 017	0.447 933	0.417 265	15
16	0.494 469	0.458 112	0.424 581	0.393 646	16
17	0.473 176	0.436 297	0.402 447	0.371 364	17
18	0.452 800	0.415 521	0.381 466	0.350 344	18
19	0.433 302	0.395 734	0.361 579	0.330 513	19
20	0.414 643	0.376 889	0.342 729	0.311 805	20
21	0.396 787	0.358 942	0.324 862	0.294 155	21
22	0.379 701	0.341 850	0.307 926	0.277 505	22
23	0.363 350	0.325 571	0.291 873	0.261 797	23
24	0.347 703	0.310 068	0.276 657	0.246 979	24
25	0.332 731	0.295 303	0.262 234	0.232 999	25
26	0.318 402	0.281 241	0.248 563	0.219 810	26
27	0.304 691	0.267 848	0.235 605	0.207 368	27
28	0.291 571	0.255 094	0.223 322	0.195 630	28
29	0.279 015	0.242 946	0.211 679	0.184 557	29

YRS	9.0% ANNUAL RATE	10.0% ANNUAL RATE	11.0% ANNUAL RATE	12.0% ANNUAL RATE	
15	0.267 000	0.231 377	0.200 644	0.174 110	30
16	0.244 500	0.209 866	0.180 269	0.154 957	32
17	0.223 896	0.190 355	0.161 963	0.137 912	34
18	0.205 028	0.172 657	0.145 516	0.122 741	36
19	0.187 750	0.156 605	0.130 739	0.109 239	38
20	0.171 929	0.142 046	0.117 463	0.097 222	40
21	0.157 440	0.128 840	0.105 535	0.086 527	42
22	0.144 173	0.116 861	0.094 818	0.077 009	44
23	0.132 023	0.105 997	0.085 190	0.068 538	46
24	0.120 898	0.096 142	0.076 539	0.060 998	48
25	0.110 710	0.087 204	0.068 767	0.054 288	50
26	0.101 380	0.079 096	0.061 783	0.048 316	52
27	0.092 837	0.071 743	0.055 509	0.043 001	54
28	0.085 013	0.065 073	0.049 873	0.038 271	56
29	0.077 849	0.059 023	0.044 808	0.034 061	58
30	0.071 289	0.053 536	0.040 258	0.030 314	60

	5.0%	6.0%	7.0%	7.5%	
	ANNUAL RATE	ANNUAL RATE	ANNUAL RATE	ANNUAL RATE	
YRS					YRS
1	0.952 381	0.943 396	0.934 579	0.930 233	1
2	0.907 029	0.889 996	0.873 439	0.865 333	2
3	0.863 838	0.839 619	0.816 298	0.804 961	3
4	0.822 702	0.792 094	0.762 895	0.748 801	4
5	0.783 526	0.747 258	0.712 986	0.696 559	5
6	0.746 215	0.704 961	0.666 342	0.647 962	6
7	0.710 681	0.665 057	0.622 750	0.602 755	7
8	0.676 839	0.627 412	0.582 009	0.560 702	8
9	0.644 609	0.591 898	0.543 934	0.521 583	9
10	0.613 913	0.558 395	0.508 349	0.485 194	10
11	0.584 679	0.526 788	0.475 093	0.451 343	11
12	0.556 837	0.496 969	0.444 012	0.419 854	12
13	0.530 321	0.468 839	0.414 964	0.390 562	13
14	0.505 068	0.442 301	0.387 817	0.363 313	14
15	0.481 017	0.417 265	0.362 446	0.337 966	15
16	0.458 112	0.393 646	0.338 735	0.314 387	16
17	0.436 297	0.371 364	0.316 574	0.292 453	17
18	0.415 521	0.350 344	0.295 864	0.272 049	18
19	0.395 734	0.330 513	0.276 508	0.253 069	19
20	0.376 889	0.311 805	0.258 419	0.235 413	20
21	0.358 942	0.294 155	0.241 513	0.218 989	21
22	0.341 850	0.277 505	0.225 713	0.203 711	22
23	0.325 571	0.261 797	0.210 947	0.189 498	23
24	0.310 068	0.246 979	0.197 147	0.176 277	24
25	0.295 303	0.232 999	0.184 249	0.163 979	25
26	0.281 241	0.219 810	0.172 195	0.152 539	26
27	0.267 848	0.207 368	0.160 930	0.141 896	27
28	0.255 094	0.195 630	0.150 402	0.131 997	28
29	0.242 946	0.184 557	0.140 563	0.122 788	29
30	0.231 377	0.174 110	0.131 367	0.114 221	30
31	0.220 359	0.164 255	0.122 773	0.106 252	31
32	0.209 866	0.154 957	0.114 741	0.098 839	32
33	0.199 873	0.146 186	0.107 235	0.091 943	33
34	0.190 355	0.137 912	0.100 219	0.085 529	34
35	0.181 290	0.130 105	0.093 663	0.079 562	35
36	0.172 657	0.122 741	0.087 535	0.074 011	36
37	0.164 436	0.115 793	0.081 809	0.068 847	37
38	0.156 605	0.109 239	0.076 457	0.064 044	38
39	0.149 148	0.103 056	0.071 455	0.059 576	39
40	0.142 046	0.097 222	0.066 780	0.055 419	40
41	0.135 282	0.091 719	0.062 412	0.051 553	41
42	0.128 840	0.086 527	0.058 329	0.047 956	42
43	0.122 704	0.081 630	0.054 513	0.044 610	43
44	0.116 861	0.077 009	0.050 946	0.041 498	44
45	0.111 297	0.072 650	0.047 613	0.038 603	45
46	0.105 997	0.068 538	0.044 499	0.035 910	46
47	0.100 949	0.064 658	0.041 587	0.033 404	47
48	0.096 142	0.060 998	0.038 867	0.031 074	48
49	0.091 564	0.057 546	0.036 324	0.028 906	49
50	0.087 204	0.054 288	0.033 948	0.026 889	50

ANNUAL COMPOUNDING

YRS	8.0% ANNUAL RATE	8.5% ANNUAL RATE	9.0% ANNUAL RATE	9.5% ANNUAL RATE	YRS
1	0.925 926	0.921 659	0.917 431	0.913 242	1
2	0.857 339	0.849 455	0.841 680	0.834 011	2
3	0.793 832	0.782 908	0.772 183	0.761 654	3
4	0.735 030	0.721 574	0.708 425	0.695 574	4
5	0.680 583	0.665 045	0.649 931	0.635 228	5
6	0.630 170	0.612 945	0.596 267	0.580 117	6
7	0.583 490	0.564 926	0.547 034	0.529 787	7
8	0.540 269	0.520 669	0.501 866	0.483 824	8
9	0.500 249	0.479 880	0.460 428	0.441 848	9
10	0.463 193	0.442 285	0.422 411	0.403 514	10
11	0.428 883	0.407 636	0.387 533	0.368 506	11
12	0.397 114	0.375 702	0.355 535	0.336 535	12
13	0.367 698	0.346 269	0.326 179	0.307 338	13
14	0.340 461	0.319 142	0.299 246	0.280 674	14
15	0.315 242	0.294 140	0.274 538	0.256 323	15
16	0.291 890	0.271 097	0.251 870	0.234 085	16
17	0.270 269	0.249 859	0.231 073	0.213 777	17
18	0.250 249	0.230 285	0.211 994	0.195 230	18
19	0.231 712	0.212 244	0.194 490	0.178 292	19
20	0.214 548	0.195 616	0.178 431	0.162 824	20
21	0.198 656	0.180 292	0.163 698	0.148 697	21
22	0.183 941	0.166 167	0.150 182	0.135 797	22
23	0.170 315	0.153 150	0.137 781	0.124 015	23
24	0.157 699	0.141 152	0.126 405	0.113 256	24
25	0.146 018	0.130 094	0.115 968	0.103 430	25
26	0.135 202	0.119 902	0.106 393	0.094 457	26
27	0.125 187	0.110 509	0.097 608	0.086 262	27
28	0.115 914	0.101 851	0.089 548	0.078 778	28
29	0.107 328	0.093 872	0.082 155	0.071 943	29
30	0.099 377	0.086 518	0.075 371	0.065 702	30
31	0.092 016	0.079 740	0.069 148	0.060 002	31
32	0.085 200	0.073 493	0.063 438	0.054 796	32
33	0.078 889	0.067 736	0.058 200	0.050 042	33
34	0.073 045	0.062 429	0.053 395	0.045 700	34
35	0.067 635	0.057 539	0.048 986	0.041 736	35
36	0.062 625	0.053 031	0.044 941	0.038 115	36
37	0.057 986	0.048 876	0.041 231	0.034 808	37
38	0.053 690	0.045 047	0.037 826	0.031 788	38
39	0.049 713	0.041 518	0.034 703	0.029 030	39
40	0.046 031	0.038 266	0.031 838	0.026 512	40
41	0.042 621	0.035 268	0.029 209	0.024 211	41
42	0.039 464	0.032 505	0.026 797	0.022 111	42
43	0.036 541	0.029 959	0.024 584	0.020 193	43
44	0.033 834	0.027 612	0.022 555	0.018 441	44
45	0.031 328	0.025 448	0.020 692	0.016 841	45
46	0.029 007	0.023 455	0.018 984	0.015 380	46
47	0.026 859	0.021 617	0.017 416	0.014 045	47
48	0.024 869	0.019 924	0.015 978	0.012 827	48
49	0.023 027	0.018 363	0.014 659	0.011 714	49
50	0.021 321	0.016 924	0.013 449	0.010 698	50

YRS	10.0% ANNUAL RATE	10.5% ANNUAL RATE	11.0% ANNUAL RATE	11.5% ANNUAL RATE	YRS
1	0.909 091	0.904 977	0.900 901	0.896 861	1
2	0.826 446	0.818 984	0.811 622	0.804 360	2
3	0.751 315	0.741 162	0.731 191	0.721 399	3
4	0.683 013	0.670 735	0.658 731	0.646 994	4
5	0.620 921	0.607 000	0.593 451	0.580 264	5
6	0.564 474	0.549 321	0.534 641	0.520 416	6
7	0.513 158	0.497 123	0.481 658	0.466 741	7
8	0.466 507	0.449 885	0.433 926	0.418 602	8
9	0.424 098	0.407 136	0.390 925	0.375 428	9
10	0.385 543	0.368 449	0.352 184	0.336 706	10
11	0.350 494	0.333 438	0.317 283	0.301 979	11
12	0.318 631	0.301 754	0.285 841	0.270 833	12
13	0.289 664	0.273 080	0.257 514	0.242 900	13
14	0.263 331	0.247 132	0.231 995	0.217 847	14
15	0.239 392	0.223 648	0.209 004	0.195 379	15
16	0.217 629	0.202 397	0.188 292	0.175 227	16
17	0.197 845	0.183 164	0.169 633	0.157 155	17
18	0.179 859	0.165 760	0.152 822	0.140 946	18
19	0.163 508	0.150 009	0.137 678	0.126 409	19
20	0.148 644	0.135 755	0.124 034	0.113 371	20
21	0.135 131	0.122 855	0.111 742	0.101 678	21
22	0.122 846	0.111 181	0.100 669	0.091 191	22
23	0.111 678	0.100 616	0.090 693	0.081 786	23
24	0.101 526	0.091 055	0.081 705	0.073 351	24
25	0.092 296	0.082 403	0.073 608	0.065 785	25
26	0.083 905	0.074 573	0.066 314	0.059 000	26
27	0.076 278	0.067 487	0.059 742	0.052 915	27
28	0.069 343	0.061 074	0.053 822	0.047 457	28
29	0.063 039	0.055 271	0.048 488	0.042 563	29
30	0.057 309	0.050 019	0.043 683	0.038 173	30
31	0.052 099	0.045 266	0.039 354	0.034 236	31
32	0.047 362	0.040 964	0.035 454	0.030 705	32
33	0.043 057	0.037 072	0.031 940	0.027 538	33
34	0.039 143	0.033 549	0.028 775	0.024 698	34
35	0.035 584	0.030 361	0.025 924	0.022 150	35
36	0.032 349	0.027 476	0.023 355	0.019 866	36
37	0.029 408	0.024 865	0.021 040	0.017 817	37
38	0.026 735	0.022 503	0.018 955	0.015 979	38
39	0.024 304	0.020 364	0.017 077	0.014 331	39
40	0.022 095	0.018 429	0.015 384	0.012 853	40
41	0.020 086	0.016 678	0.013 860	0.011 527	41
42	0.018 260	0.015 093	0.012 486	0.010 338	42
43	0.016 600	0.013 659	0.011 249	0.009 272	43
44	0.015 091	0.012 361	0.010 134	0.008 316	44
45	0.013 719	0.011 187	0.009 130	0.007 458	45
46	0.012 472	0.010 124	0.008 225	0.006 689	46
47	0.011 338	0.009 162	0.007 410	0.005 999	47
48	0.010 307	0.008 291	0.006 676	0.005 380	48
49	0.009 370	0.007 503	0.006 014	0.004 825	49
50	0.008 519	0.006 790	0.005 418	0.004 328	50

	12.0%	12.5%	13.0%	13.5%	
	ANNUAL RATE	ANNUAL RATE	ANNUAL RATE	ANNUAL RATE	
YRS					YRS
1	0.892 857	0.888 889	0.884 956	0.881 057	1
2	0.797 194	0.790 123	0.783 147	0.776 262	2
3	0.711 780	0.702 332	0.693 050	0.683 931	3
4	0.635 518	0.624 295	0.613 319	0.602 583	4
5	0.567 427	0.554 929	0.542 760	0.530 910	5
6	0.506 631	0.493 270	0.480 319	0.467 762	6
7	0.452 349	0.438 462	0.425 061	0.412 125	7
8	0.403 883	0.389 744	0.376 160	0.363 106	8
9	0.360 610	0.346 439	0.332 885	0.319 917	9
10	0.321 973	0.307 946	0.294 588	0.281 865	10
11	0.287 476	0.273 730	0.260 698	0.248 339	11
12	0.256 675	0.243 315	0.230 706	0.218 801	12
13	0.229 174	0.216 280	0.204 165	0.192 776	13
14	0.204 620	0.192 249	0.180 677	0.169 847	14
15	0.182 696	0.170 888	0.159 891	0.149 645	15
16	0.163 122	0.151 901	0.141 496	0.131 846	16
17	0.145 644	0.135 023	0.125 218	0.116 164	17
18	0.130 040	0.120 020	0.110 812	0.102 347	18
19	0.116 107	0.106 685	0.098 064	0.090 173	19
20	0.103 667	0.094 831	0.086 782	0.079 448	20
21	0.092 560	0.084 294	0.076 798	0.069 998	21
22	0.082 643	0.074 928	0.067 963	0.061 672	22
23	0.073 788	0.066 603	0.060 144	0.054 337	23
24	0.065 882	0.059 202	0.053 225	0.047 874	24
25	0.058 823	0.052 624	0.047 102	0.042 180	25
26	0.052 521	0.046 777	0.041 683	0.037 163	26
27	0.046 894	0.041 580	0.036 888	0.032 742	27
28	0.041 869	0.036 960	0.032 644	0.028 848	28
29	0.037 383	0.032 853	0.028 889	0.025 417	29
30	0.033 378	0.029 203	0.025 565	0.022 394	30
31	0.029 802	0.025 958	0.022 624	0.019 730	31
32	0.026 609	0.023 074	0.020 021	0.017 383	32
33	0.023 758	0.020 510	0.017 718	0.015 316	33
34	0.021 212	0.018 231	0.015 680	0.013 494	34
35	0.018 940	0.016 205	0.013 876	0.011 889	35
36	0.016 910	0.014 405	0.012 279	0.010 475	36
37	0.015 098	0.012 804	0.010 867	0.009 229	37
38	0.013 481	0.011 382	0.009 617	0.008 131	38
39	0.012 036	0.010 117	0.008 510	0.007 164	39
40	0.010 747	0.008 993	0.007 531	0.006 312	40
41	0.009 595	0.007 994	0.006 665	0.005 561	41
42	0.008 567	0.007 105	0.005 898	0.004 900	42
43	0.007 649	0.006 316	0.005 219	0.004 317	43
44	0.006 830	0.005 614	0.004 619	0.003 803	44
45	0.006 098	0.004 990	0.004 088	0.003 351	45
46	0.005 445	0.004 436	0.003 617	0.002 953	46
47	0.004 861	0.003 943	0.003 201	0.002 601	47
48	0.004 340	0.003 505	0.002 833	0.002 292	48
49	0.003 875	0.003 115	0.002 507	0.002 019	49
50	0.003 460	0.002 769	0.002 219	0.001 779	50

YRS	14.0% ANNUAL RATE	14.5% ANNUAL RATE	15.0% ANNUAL RATE	16.0% ANNUAL RATE	YRS
1	0.877 193	0.873 362	0.869 565	0.862 069	1
2	0.769 468	0.762 762	0.756 144	0.743 163	2
3	0.674 972	0.666 168	0.657 516	0.640 658	3
4	0.592 080	0.581 806	0.571 753	0.552 291	4
5	0.519 369	0.508 127	0.497 177	0.476 113	5
6	0.455 587	0.443 779	0.432 328	0.410 442	6
7	0.399 637	0.387 580	0.375 937	0.353 830	7
8	0.350 559	0.338 498	0.326 902	0.305 025	8
9	0.307 508	0.295 631	0.284 262	0.262 953	9
10	0.269 744	0.258 193	0.247 185	0.226 684	10
11	0.236 617	0.225 496	0.214 943	0.195 417	11
12	0.207 559	0.196 940	0.186 907	0.168 463	12
13	0.182 069	0.172 000	0.162 528	0.145 227	13
14	0.159 710	0.150 218	0.141 329	0.125 195	14
15	0.140 096	0.131 195	0.122 894	0.107 927	15
16	0.122 892	0.114 581	0.106 865	0.093 041	16
17	0.107 800	0.100 071	0.092 926	0.080 207	17
18	0.094 561	0.087 398	0.080 805	0.069 144	18
19	0.082 948	0.076 330	0.070 265	0.059 607	19
20	0.072 762	0.066 664	0.061 100	0.051 385	20
21	0.063 826	0.058 222	0.053 131	0.044 298	21
22	0.055 988	0.050 849	0.046 201	0.038 188	22
23	0.049 112	0.044 409	0.040 174	0.032 920	23
24	0.043 081	0.038 785	0.034 934	0.028 380	24
25	0.037 790	0.033 874	0.030 378	0.024 465	25
26	0.033 149	0.029 584	0.026 415	0.021 091	26
27	0.029 078	0.025 838	0.022 970	0.018 182	27
28	0.025 507	0.022 566	0.019 974	0.015 674	28
29	0.022 375	0.019 708	0.017 369	0.013 512	29
30	0.019 627	0.017 212	0.015 103	0.011 648	30
31	0.017 217	0.015 032	0.013 133	0.010 042	31
32	0.015 102	0.013 129	0.011 420	0.008 657	32
33	0.013 248	0.011 466	0.009 931	0.007 463	33
34	0.011 621	0.010 014	0.008 635	0.006 433	34
35	0.010 194	0.008 746	0.007 509	0.005 546	35
36	0.008 942	0.007 638	0.006 529	0.004 781	36
37	0.007 844	0.006 671	0.005 678	0.004 121	37
38	0.006 880	0.005 826	0.004 937	0.003 553	38
39	0.006 035	0.005 088	0.004 293	0.003 063	39
40	0.005 294	0.004 444	0.003 733	0.002 640	40
41	0.004 644	0.003 881	0.003 246	0.002 276	41
42	0.004 074	0.003 390	0.002 823	0.001 962	42
43	0.003 573	0.002 960	0.002 455	0.001 692	43
44	0.003 135	0.002 586	0.002 134	0.001 458	44
45	0.002 750	0.002 258	0.001 856	0.001 257	45
46	0.002 412	0.001 972	0.001 614	0.001 084	46
47	0.002 116	0.001 722	0.001 403	0.000 934	47
48	0.001 856	0.001 504	0.001 220	0.000 805	48
49	0.001 628	0.001 314	0.001 061	0.000 694	49
50	0.001 428	0.001 147	0.000 923	0.000 599	50

YRS	17.0% ANNUAL RATE	18.0% ANNUAL RATE	19.0% ANNUAL RATE	20.0% ANNUAL RATE	YRS
1	0.854 701	0.847 458	0.840 336	0.833 333	1
2	0.730 514	0.718 184	0.706 165	0.694 444	2
3	0.624 371	0.608 631	0.593 416	0.578 704	3
4	0.533 650	0.515 789	0.498 669	0.482 253	4
5	0.456 111	0.437 109	0.419 049	0.401 878	5
6	0.389 839	0.370 432	0.352 142	0.334 898	6
7	0.333 195	0.313 925	0.295 918	0.279 082	7
8	0.284 782	0.266 038	0.248 671	0.232 568	8
9	0.243 404	0.225 456	0.208 967	0.193 807	9
10	0.208 037	0.191 064	0.175 602	0.161 506	10
11	0.177 810	0.161 919	0.147 565	0.134 588	11
12	0.151 974	0.137 220	0.124 004	0.112 157	12
13	0.129 892	0.116 288	0.104 205	0.093 464	13
14	0.111 019	0.098 549	0.087 567	0.077 887	14
15	0.094 888	0.083 516	0.073 586	0.064 905	15
16	0.081 101	0.070 776	0.061 837	0.054 088	16
17	0.069 317	0.059 980	0.051 964	0.045 073	17
18	0.059 245	0.050 830	0.043 667	0.037 561	18
19	0.050 637	0.043 077	0.036 695	0.031 301	19
20	0.043 280	0.036 506	0.030 836	0.026 084	20
21	0.036 991	0.030 937	0.025 913	0.021 737	21
22	0.031 616	0.026 218	0.021 775	0.018 114	22
23	0.027 022	0.022 218	0.018 299	0.015 095	23
24	0.023 096	0.018 829	0.015 377	0.012 579	24
25	0.019 740	0.015 957	0.012 922	0.010 483	25
26	0.016 872	0.013 523	0.010 859	0.008 735	26
27	0.014 421	0.011 460	0.009 125	0.007 280	27
28	0.012 325	0.009 712	0.007 668	0.006 066	28
29	0.010 534	0.008 230	0.006 444	0.005 055	29
30	0.009 004	0.006 975	0.005 415	0.004 213	30
31	0.007 696	0.005 911	0.004 550	0.003 511	31
32	0.006 577	0.005 009	0.003 824	0.002 926	32
33	0.005 622	0.004 245	0.003 213	0.002 438	33
34	0.004 805	0.003 598	0.002 700	0.002 032	34
35	0.004 107	0.003 049	0.002 269	0.001 693	35
36	0.003 510	0.002 584	0.001 907	0.001 411	36
37	0.003 000	0.002 190	0.001 602	0.001 176	37
38	0.002 564	0.001 856	0.001 347	0.000 980	38
39	0.002 192	0.001 573	0.001 132	0.000 816	39
40	0.001 873	0.001 333	0.000 951	0.000 680	40
41	0.001 601	0.001 129	0.000 799	0.000 567	41
42	0.001 368	0.000 957	0.000 671	0.000 472	42
43	0.001 170	0.000 811	0.000 564	0.000 394	43
44	0.001 000	0.000 687	0.000 474	0.000 328	44
45	0.000 854	0.000 583	0.000 398	0.000 273	45
46	0.000 730	0.000 494	0.000 335	0.000 228	46
47	0.000 624	0.000 418	0.000 281	0.000 190	47
48	0.000 533	0.000 355	0.000 236	0.000 158	48
49	0.000 456	0.000 300	0.000 199	0.000 132	49
50	0.000 390	0.000 255	0.000 167	0.000 110	50

Section 5. Present Value of $1.00 Per Period:

These tables indicate the amount of money you must invest today to receive an income of $1 per period for a specific term. The initial investment will begin the investment period. These factors depend upon the same equal income per period. No additional withdrawals or investments can be made during the stated period.

In this section the following four (4) periods are presented in detail: monthly, quarterly, semiannual, and annual.

Monthly:

The factors presented on pages 89 through 94 indicate the amount of money you will need to invest today to receive a monthly income at the end of each month for a stated period of time. These factors are based on the condition that interest is earned at the end of each monthly period for the stated period of months. Therefore, the interest is compounded monthly. This is interest earned on interest.

Example I

You would like to establish a monthly retirement income for yourself. The desired income is $1,000.00 per month, and you want that income for 10 years, or 120 months. The interest is compounded monthly and the annual interst rate is 8.0%.

Turn to page 90 and locate the 8.0% column. Proceed down that column until you locate the part where the 10 years row intersects the 8.0% column.

The answer is 82.421481 for every monthly income of $1 needed. So, to determine your answer, multiply 82.421481 by $1,000.00. The correct answer is $82,421.48. That means you must deposit or invest $82,421.48 today to receive a monthly income of $1,000.00 for 120 months.

Note: If your investment period is less than 2 years, we have provided all the factors for each monthly period. The annual figures are provided for two (2) years and over.

Quarterly:

The factors presented on pages 95 through 97 indicate the amount of money you need to invest today to receive an income of $1 at the end of each quarter for a stated period of time. The interest is earned at the end of each quarter and is also compounded quarterly. This is interest earned on interest.

Example J

You are offered a choice of investments: $12,000.00 cash today or $1,000.00 at the end of each quarterly period for five (5) years or twenty (20) quarters. In order to evaluate these two options, you will need to know today's value of the $1,000.00 per quarter, stream of income.

Let's assume an interest rate of 10.0% and quarterly compounding. Turn to page 96 and locate the 10.0% column. Proceed down that column until you locate the point where the five (5) years or twenty (20) quarter row intersects the 10.0% interest column. The number is 15.589162 for every $1 of quarterly income So, to determine your answer, multiply 15.589162 by $1,000.00 and you arrive at the solution of $15,589.16. This means today's value of that stream of income is $15,589.16, which is $3,589.16 greater than the $12,000.00 cash. Therefore, unless you need the money, the $1,000.00 per quarter is a better investment.

Note: For investment of five (5) years and more, only the annual amounts are shown.

Semiannual:

The factors on pages 98 through 99 cover semiannual compounding (or the interest being compounded every 6 months).

Annual:

The factors on pages 100 through 105 cover annual compounding (or the interest being compounded every year).

Both the semiannual and annual tables are used the same way as the monthly and quarterly tables.

Just in case you want to do it the hard way, here's the formula . . .

$$a_{\overline{n}|} = \frac{1 - V^n}{i}$$

V^n = Present value of $1
i = interest rate per period
$a_{\overline{n}|}$ = Present value of $1 per period

PRESENT VALUE OF
$1 PER PERIOD

MONTHLY
COMPOUNDING

	5.0%	6.0%	7.0%	7.5%	
	ANNUAL RATE	ANNUAL RATE	ANNUAL RATE	ANNUAL RATE	
MOS					MOS
1	0.995 851	0.995 025	0.994 200	0.993 789	1
2	1.987 569	1.985 099	1.982 635	1.981 405	2
3	2.975 173	2.970 248	2.965 337	2.962 887	3
4	3.958 678	3.950 496	3.942 340	3.938 273	4
5	4.938 103	4.925 866	4.913 677	4.907 600	5
6	5.913 463	5.896 384	5.879 381	5.870 907	6
7	6.884 777	6.862 074	6.839 484	6.828 231	7
8	7.852 060	7.822 959	7.794 019	7.779 608	8
9	8.815 329	8.779 064	8.743 018	8.725 076	9
10	9.774 602	9.730 412	9.686 513	9.664 672	10
11	10.729 894	10.677 027	10.624 537	10.598 432	11
12	11.681 222	11.618 932	11.557 120	11.526 392	12
13	12.628 603	12.556 151	12.484 295	12.448 588	13
14	13.572 053	13.488 708	13.406 093	13.365 057	14
15	14.511 588	14.416 625	14.322 545	14.275 833	15
16	15.447 224	15.339 925	15.233 682	15.180 952	16
17	16.378 978	16.258 632	16.139 534	16.080 892	17
18	17.306 867	17.172 768	17.040 133	16.974 359	18
19	18.230 904	18.082 356	17.935 510	17.862 717	19
20	19.151 108	18.987 419	18.825 693	18.745 558	20
21	20.067 494	19.887 979	19.710 714	19.622 914	21
22	20.980 077	20.784 059	20.590 602	20.494 822	22
23	21.888 873	21.675 681	21.465 387	21.361 314	23
YRS					
2	22.793 898	22.562 866	22.335 099	22.222 423	24
3	33.365 701	32.871 016	32.386 464	32.147 913	36
4	43.422 956	42.580 318	41.760 201	41.358 371	48
5	52.990 706	51.725 561	50.501 994	49.905 308	60
6	62.092 777	60.339 514	58.654 444	57.836 508	72
7	70.751 835	68.453 042	66.257 285	65.196 376	84
8	78.989 441	76.095 218	73.347 569	72.026 024	96
9	86.826 108	83.293 424	79.959 850	78.363 665	108
10	94.281 350	90.073 453	86.126 354	84.244 743	120
11	101.373 733	96.459 599	91.877 134	89.702 148	132
12	108.120 917	102.474 743	97.240 216	94.766 401	144
13	114.539 704	108.140 440	102.241 738	99.465 827	156
14	120.646 077	113.476 990	106.906 074	103.826 706	168
15	126.455 243	118.503 515	111.255 958	107.873 427	180
16	131.981 666	123.238 025	115.312 587	111.628 623	192
17	137.239 108	127.697 486	119.095 732	115.113 294	204
18	142.240 661	131.897 876	122.623 831	118.346 930	216
19	146.998 780	135.854 246	125.914 077	121.347 615	228
20	151.525 313	139.580 772	128.982 506	124.132 131	240
21	155.831 532	143.090 806	131.844 073	126.716 051	252
22	159.928 159	146.396 927	134.512 723	129.113 825	264
23	163.825 396	149.510 979	137.001 461	131.338 863	276
24	167.532 948	152.444 121	139.322 418	133.403 610	288
25	171.060 047	155.206 864	141.486 903	135.319 613	300
26	174.415 476	157.809 106	143.505 467	137.097 587	312
27	177.607 590	160.260 172	145.387 946	138.747 475	324
28	180.644 338	162.568 844	147.143 515	140.278 506	336
29	183.533 283	164.743 394	148.780 729	141.699 242	348
30	186.281 617	166.791 614	150.307 568	143.017 627	360

MOS	8.0% ANNUAL RATE	8.5% ANNUAL RATE	9.0% ANNUAL RATE	9.5% ANNUAL RATE	MOS
1	0.993 377	0.992 966	0.992 556	0.992 146	1
2	1.980 176	1.978 949	1.977 723	1.976 498	2
3	2.960 440	2.957 996	2.955 556	2.953 119	3
4	3.934 212	3.930 158	3.926 110	3.922 070	4
5	4.901 535	4.895 482	4.889 440	4.883 409	5
6	5.862 452	5.854 016	5.845 598	5.837 198	6
7	6.817 005	6.805 808	6.794 638	6.783 496	7
8	7.765 237	7.750 906	7.736 613	7.722 360	8
9	8.707 189	8.689 356	8.671 576	8.653 851	9
10	9.642 903	9.621 206	9.599 580	9.578 024	10
11	10.572 420	10.546 501	10.520 675	10.494 940	11
12	11.495 782	11.465 289	11.434 913	11.404 653	12
13	12.413 028	12.377 614	12.342 345	12.307 221	13
14	13.324 200	13.283 522	13.243 022	13.202 699	14
15	14.229 338	14.183 059	14.136 995	14.091 144	15
16	15.128 481	15.076 269	15.024 313	14.972 611	16
17	16.021 670	15.963 196	15.905 025	15.847 154	17
18	16.908 944	16.843 885	16.779 181	16.714 829	18
19	17.790 342	17.718 380	17.646 830	17.575 688	19
20	18.665 902	18.586 724	18.508 020	18.429 785	20
21	19.535 665	19.448 961	19.362 799	19.277 174	21
22	20.399 667	20.305 133	20.211 215	20.117 908	22
23	21.257 947	21.155 283	21.053 315	20.952 037	23
YRS					
2	22.110 544	21.999 453	21.889 146	21.779 615	24
3	31.911 806	31.678 112	31.446 805	31.217 856	36
4	40.961 913	40.570 744	40.184 782	39.803 947	48
5	49.318 433	48.741 183	48.171 374	47.614 827	60
6	57.034 522	56.248 080	55.476 849	54.720 488	72
7	64.159 261	63.145 324	62.153 965	61.184 601	84
8	70.737 970	69.482 425	68.258 439	67.065 090	96
9	76.812 497	75.304 875	73.839 382	72.414 648	108
10	82.421 481	80.654 470	78.941 693	77.281 211	120
11	87.600 600	85.569 611	83.606 420	81.708 388	132
12	92.382 800	90.085 581	87.871 092	85.735 849	144
13	96.798 498	94.234 798	91.770 018	89.399 684	156
14	100.875 784	98.047 046	95.334 564	92.732 722	168
15	104.640 592	101.549 693	98.593 409	95.764 831	180
16	108.116 871	104.767 881	101.572 769	98.523 180	192
17	111.326 733	107.724 713	104.296 613	101.032 487	204
18	114.290 596	110.441 412	106.786 856	103.315 236	216
19	117.027 313	112.937 482	109.063 531	105.391 883	228
20	119.554 292	115.230 840	111.144 954	107.281 037	240
21	121.887 606	117.337 948	113.047 870	108.999 624	252
22	124.042 099	119.273 933	114.787 589	110.563 046	264
23	126.031 475	121.052 692	116.378 106	111.985 311	276
24	127.868 388	122.686 994	117.832 218	113.279 165	288
25	129.564 523	124.188 570	119.161 622	114.456 200	300
26	131.130 668	125.568 199	120.377 014	115.526 965	312
27	132.576 786	126.835 785	121.488 172	116.501 054	324
28	133.912 076	128.000 428	122.504 035	117.387 195	336
29	135.145 031	129.070 487	123.432 776	118.193 330	348
30	136.283 494	130.053 643	124.281 866	118.926 681	360

PRESENT VALUE OF $1 PER PERIOD

MONTHLY COMPOUNDING

MOS	10.0% ANNUAL RATE	10.5% ANNUAL RATE	11.0% ANNUAL RATE	11.5% ANNUAL RATE	MOS
1	0.991 736	0.991 326	0.990 917	0.990 508	1
2	1.975 275	1.974 053	1.972 832	1.971 613	2
3	2.950 686	2.948 256	2.945 829	2.943 405	3
4	3.918 036	3.914 008	3.909 987	3.905 973	4
5	4.877 391	4.871 384	4.865 388	4.859 404	5
6	5.828 817	5.820 455	5.812 110	5.803 784	6
7	6.772 381	6.761 293	6.750 233	6.739 200	7
8	7.708 146	7.693 971	7.679 835	7.665 737	8
9	8.636 178	8.618 559	8.600 992	8.583 479	9
10	9.556 540	9.535 126	9.513 783	9.492 509	10
11	10.469 296	10.443 743	10.418 282	10.392 910	11
12	11.374 508	11.344 479	11.314 565	11.284 764	12
13	12.272 240	12.237 402	12.202 707	12.168 153	13
14	13.162 550	13.122 579	13.082 781	13.043 156	14
15	14.045 506	14.000 079	13.954 862	13.909 853	15
16	14.921 163	14.869 967	14.819 021	14.768 323	16
17	15.789 583	15.732 309	15.675 330	15.618 645	17
18	16.650 826	16.587 171	16.523 861	16.460 895	18
19	17.504 952	17.434 618	17.364 685	17.295 149	19
20	18.352 018	18.274 914	18.197 843	18.121 485	20
21	19.192 084	19.107 524	19.023 489	18.939 977	21
22	20.025 207	19.933 109	19.841 608	19.750 699	22
23	20.851 445	20.751 533	20.652 295	20.553 726	23

YRS					
2	21.670 855	21.562 858	21.455 619	21.349 130	24
3	30.991 236	30.766 918	30.544 874	30.325 079	36
4	39.428 160	39.057 344	38.691 421	38.330 318	48
5	47.065 369	46.524 827	45.993 034	45.469 825	60
6	53.978 665	53.251 057	52.537 346	51.837 225	72
7	60.236 667	59.309 613	58.402 903	57.516 018	84
8	65.901 488	64.766 771	63.660 103	62.580 675	96
9	71.029 355	69.682 229	68.372 043	67.097 611	108
10	75.671 163	74.109 758	72.595 275	71.126 060	120
11	79.872 986	78.097 992	76.380 487	74.718 850	132
12	83.676 528	81.689 957	79.773 109	77.923 095	144
13	87.119 542	84.925 549	82.813 859	80.780 815	156
14	90.236 201	87.839 962	85.539 231	83.329 485	168
15	93.057 439	90.465 078	87.981 937	85.602 527	180
16	95.611 259	92.829 614	90.171 293	87.629 750	192
17	97.923 008	94.959 437	92.133 576	89.437 737	204
18	100.015 633	96.877 844	93.892 337	91.050 199	216
19	101.909 902	98.605 822	95.468 685	92.488 279	228
20	103.624 619	100.162 274	96.881 539	93.770 838	240
21	105.176 801	101.564 226	98.147 856	94.914 693	252
22	106.581 856	102.827 014	99.282 835	95.934 846	264
23	107.853 730	103.964 453	100.300 098	96.844 673	276
24	109.005 045	104.988 985	101.211 853	97.656 106	288
25	110.047 230	105.911 817	102.029 044	98.379 787	300
26	110.990 629	106.743 045	102.761 478	99.025 204	312
27	111.844 605	107.491 762	103.417 947	99.600 823	324
28	112.617 635	108.166 158	104.006 328	100.114 191	336
29	113.317 392	108.773 611	104.533 685	100.572 040	348
30	113.950 820	109.320 766	105.006 346	100.980 375	360

PRESENT VALUE OF
$1 PER PERIOD

MONTHLY COMPOUNDING

	12.0%	12.5%	13.0%	13.5%	
	ANNUAL RATE	ANNUAL RATE	ANNUAL RATE	ANNUAL RATE	
MOS					MOS
1	0.990 099	0.989 691	0.989 283	0.988 875	1
2	1.970 395	1.969 178	1.967 963	1.966 749	2
3	2.940 985	2.938 568	2.936 155	2.933 745	3
4	3.901 966	3.897 965	3.893 970	3.889 982	4
5	4.853 431	4.847 470	4.841 520	4.835 582	5
6	5.795 476	5.787 187	5.778 915	5.770 662	6
7	6.728 195	6.717 216	6.706 264	6.695 339	7
8	7.651 678	7.637 657	7.623 674	7.609 730	8
9	8.566 018	8.548 609	8.531 253	8.513 948	9
10	9.471 305	9.450 170	9.429 104	9.408 107	10
11	10.367 628	10.342 436	10.317 333	10.292 318	11
12	11.255 077	11.225 504	11.196 042	11.166 693	12
13	12.133 740	12.099 468	12.065 335	12.031 340	13
14	13.003 703	12.964 421	12.925 310	12.886 369	14
15	13.865 053	13.820 458	13.776 070	13.731 885	15
16	14.717 874	14.667 670	14.617 711	14.567 995	16
17	15.562 251	15.506 148	15.450 332	15.394 804	17
18	16.398 269	16.335 981	16.274 030	16.212 414	18
19	17.226 008	17.157 260	17.088 901	17.020 928	19
20	18.045 553	17.970 072	17.895 038	17.820 448	20
21	18.856 983	18.774 504	18.692 535	18.611 074	21
22	19.660 379	19.570 643	19.481 486	19.392 904	22
23	20.455 821	20.358 574	20.261 981	20.166 036	23
YRS					
2	21.243 387	21.138 383	21.034 112	20.930 567	24
3	30.107 505	29.892 126	29.678 917	29.467 851	36
4	37.973 959	37.622 274	37.275 190	36.932 637	48
5	44.955 038	44.448 517	43.950 107	43.459 656	60
6	51.150 391	50.476 552	49.815 421	49.166 717	72
7	56.648 453	55.799 715	54.969 328	54.156 827	84
8	61.527 703	60.500 428	59.498 115	58.520 052	96
9	65.857 790	64.651 476	63.477 604	62.335 146	108
10	69.700 522	68.317 132	66.974 419	65.670 968	120
11	73.110 752	71.554 164	70.047 103	68.587 726	132
12	76.137 157	74.412 664	72.747 100	71.138 066	144
13	78.822 939	76.936 921	75.119 613	73.368 018	156
14	81.206 434	79.166 011	77.204 363	75.317 832	168
15	83.321 664	81.134 449	79.036 253	77.022 700	180
16	85.198 824	82.872 712	80.645 952	78.513 394	192
17	86.864 707	84.407 717	82.060 410	79.816 818	204
18	88.343 095	85.763 229	83.303 307	80.956 500	216
19	89.655 089	86.960 239	84.395 453	81.953 009	228
20	90.819 416	88.017 279	85.355 132	82.824 331	240
21	91.852 698	88.950 717	86.198 412	83.586 193	252
22	92.769 683	89.775 006	86.939 409	84.252 345	264
23	93.583 461	90.502 909	87.590 531	84.834 813	276
24	94.305 647	91.145 697	88.162 677	85.344 107	288
25	94.946 551	91.713 322	88.665 428	85.789 421	300
26	95.515 321	92.214 573	89.107 200	86.178 793	312
27	96.020 075	92.657 212	89.495 389	86.519 249	324
28	96.468 019	93.048 092	89.836 495	86.816 936	336
29	96.865 546	93.393 265	90.136 227	87.077 226	348
30	97.218 331	93.698 077	90.399 605	87.304 817	360

PRESENT VALUE OF $1 PER PERIOD

MONTHLY COMPOUNDING

MOS	14.0% ANNUAL RATE	14.5% ANNUAL RATE	15.0% ANNUAL RATE	16.0% ANNUAL RATE	MOS
1	0.988 468	0.988 061	0.987 654	0.986 842	1
2	1.965 537	1.964 325	1.963 115	1.960 699	2
3	2.931 338	2.928 934	2.926 534	2.921 743	3
4	3.886 001	3.882 026	3.878 058	3.870 141	4
5	4.829 655	4.823 739	4.817 835	4.806 060	5
6	5.762 427	5.754 209	5.746 010	5.729 665	6
7	6.684 442	6.673 570	6.662 726	6.641 116	7
8	7.595 824	7.581 955	7.568 124	7.540 575	8
9	8.496 696	8.479 495	8.462 345	8.428 199	9
10	9.387 178	9.366 318	9.345 526	9.304 144	10
11	10.267 392	10.242 554	10.217 803	10.168 563	11
12	11.137 455	11.108 328	11.079 312	11.021 609	12
13	11.997 485	11.963 766	11.930 185	11.863 430	13
14	12.847 596	12.808 991	12.770 553	12.694 174	14
15	13.687 904	13.644 124	13.600 546	13.513 987	15
16	14.518 521	14.469 287	14.420 292	14.323 014	16
17	15.339 559	15.284 598	15.229 918	15.121 395	17
18	16.151 130	16.090 175	16.029 549	15.909 272	18
19	16.953 341	16.886 135	16.819 308	16.686 781	19
20	17.746 300	17.672 591	17.599 316	17.454 060	20
21	18.530 116	18.449 657	18.369 695	18.211 244	21
22	19.304 892	19.217 447	19.130 563	18.958 464	22
23	20.070 733	19.976 069	19.882 037	19.695 853	23

YRS					
2	20.827 743	20.725 634	20.624 235	20.423 539	24
3	29.258 904	29.052 051	28.847 267	28.443 811	36
4	36.594 546	36.260 850	35.931 481	35.285 465	48
5	42.977 016	42.502 042	42.034 592	41.121 706	60
6	48.530 168	47.905 507	47.292 474	46.100 283	72
7	53.361 760	52.583 688	51.822 185	50.347 235	84
8	57.565 549	56.633 938	55.724 570	53.970 077	96
9	61.223 111	60.140 540	59.086 509	57.060 524	108
10	64.405 420	63.176 466	61.982 847	59.696 816	120
11	67.174 230	65.804 893	64.478 068	61.945 692	132
12	69.583 269	68.080 518	66.627 722	63.864 085	144
13	71.679 284	70.050 696	68.479 668	65.500 561	156
14	73.502 930	71.756 425	70.075 134	66.896 549	168
15	75.089 654	73.233 202	71.449 643	68.087 390	180
16	76.470 187	74.511 757	72.633 794	69.103 231	192
17	77.671 337	75.618 698	73.653 950	69.969 789	204
18	78.716 413	76.577 058	74.532 823	70.709 003	216
19	79.625 696	77.406 782	75.289 980	71.339 585	228
20	80.416 829	78.125 136	75.942 278	71.877 501	240
21	81.105 164	78.747 069	76.504 237	72.336 367	252
22	81.704 060	79.285 522	76.988 370	72.727 801	264
23	82.225 136	79.751 701	77.405 455	73.061 711	276
24	82.678 506	80.155 306	77.764 777	73.346 552	288
25	83.072 966	80.504 738	78.074 336	73.589 534	300
26	83.416 171	80.807 267	78.341 024	73.796 809	312
27	83.714 781	81.069 189	78.570 778	73.973 623	324
28	83.974 591	81.295 954	78.768 713	74.124 454	336
29	84.200 641	81.492 281	78.939 236	74.253 120	348
30	84.397 320	81.662 256	79.086 142	74.362 878	360

PRESENT VALUE OF
$1 PER PERIOD

MONTHLY
COMPOUNDING

	17.0%	18.0%	19.0%	20.0%	
	ANNUAL RATE	ANNUAL RATE	ANNUAL RATE	ANNUAL RATE	
MOS					MOS
1	0.986 031	0.985 222	0.984 413	0.983 607	1
2	1.958 289	1.955 883	1.953 483	1.951 088	2
3	2.916 965	2.912 200	2.907 449	2.902 710	3
4	3.862 250	3.854 385	3.846 545	3.838 731	4
5	4.794 330	4.782 645	4.771 004	4.759 408	5
6	5.713 391	5.697 187	5.681 054	5.664 991	6
7	6.619 613	6.598 214	6.576 920	6.555 729	7
8	7.513 176	7.485 925	7.458 822	7.431 865	8
9	8.394 257	8.360 517	8.326 978	8.293 637	9
10	9.263 031	9.222 185	9.181 602	9.141 283	10
11	10.119 669	10.071 118	10.022 906	9.975 032	11
12	10.964 341	10.907 505	10.851 097	10.795 113	12
13	11.797 214	11.731 532	11.666 380	11.601 751	13
14	12.618 452	12.543 382	12.468 955	12.395 165	14
15	13.428 219	13.343 233	13.259 020	13.175 572	15
16	14.226 675	14.131 264	14.036 771	13.943 186	16
17	15.013 977	14.907 649	14.802 400	14.698 215	17
18	15.790 281	15.672 561	15.556 095	15.440 868	18
19	16.555 741	16.426 168	16.298 043	16.171 345	19
20	17.310 509	17.168 639	17.028 426	16.889 848	20
21	18.054 734	17.900 137	17.747 425	17.596 571	21
22	18.788 562	18.620 824	18.455 217	18.291 710	22
23	19.512 140	19.330 861	19.151 978	18.975 452	23
YRS					
2	20.225 611	20.030 405	19.837 878	19.647 986	24
3	28.048 345	27.660 684	27.280 649	26.908 062	36
4	34.655 988	34.042 554	33.444 684	32.861 916	48
5	40.237 278	39.380 269	38.549 682	37.744 561	60
6	44.951 636	43.844 667	42.777 596	41.748 727	72
7	48.933 722	47.578 633	46.279 115	45.032 470	84
8	52.297 278	50.701 675	49.179 042	47.725 406	96
9	55.138 379	53.313 749	51.580 735	49.933 833	108
10	57.538 177	55.498 454	53.569 796	51.744 924	120
11	59.565 218	57.325 714	55.217 118	53.230 165	132
12	61.277 403	58.854 011	56.581 415	54.448 184	144
13	62.723 638	60.132 260	57.711 314	55.447 059	156
14	63.945 231	61.201 371	58.647 086	56.266 217	168
15	64.977 077	62.095 562	59.422 084	56.937 994	180
16	65.848 648	62.843 452	60.063 930	57.488 906	192
17	66.584 839	63.468 978	60.595 501	57.940 698	204
18	67.206 679	63.992 160	61.035 743	58.311 205	216
19	67.731 930	64.429 743	61.400 348	58.615 050	228
20	68.175 595	64.795 732	61.702 310	58.864 229	240
21	68.550 346	65.101 841	61.952 393	59.068 575	252
22	68.866 887	65.357 866	62.159 509	59.236 156	264
23	69.134 261	65.572 002	62.331 041	59.373 585	276
24	69.360 104	65.751 103	62.473 102	59.486 289	288
25	69.550 868	65.900 901	62.590 755	59.578 715	300
26	69.712 000	66.026 190	62.688 195	59.654 512	312
27	69.848 104	66.130 980	62.768 894	59.716 672	324
28	69.963 067	66.218 625	62.835 728	59.767 648	336
29	70.060 174	66.291 930	62.891 079	59.809 452	348
30	70.142 196	66.353 242	62.936 920	59.843 735	360

PRESENT VALUE OF $1 PER PERIOD

QUARTERLY COMPOUNDING

QTRS	5.0% ANNUAL RATE	6.0% ANNUAL RATE	7.0% ANNUAL RATE	8.0% ANNUAL RATE	QTRS
1	0.987 654	0.985 222	0.982 801	0.980 392	1
2	1.963 115	1.955 883	1.948 699	1.941 561	2
3	2.926 534	2.912 200	2.897 984	2.883 883	3
4	3.878 058	3.854 385	3.830 943	3.807 729	4
5	4.817 835	4.782 645	4.747 855	4.713 460	5
6	5.746 010	5.697 187	5.648 998	5.601 431	6
7	6.662 726	6.598 214	6.534 641	6.471 991	7
8	7.568 124	7.485 925	7.405 053	7.325 481	8
9	8.462 345	8.360 517	8.260 494	8.162 237	9
10	9.345 526	9.222 185	9.101 223	8.982 585	10
11	10.217 803	10.071 118	9.927 492	9.786 848	11
12	11.079 312	10.907 505	10.739 550	10.575 341	12
13	11.930 185	11.731 532	11.537 641	11.348 374	13
14	12.770 553	12.543 382	12.322 006	12.106 249	14
15	13.600 546	13.343 233	13.092 880	12.849 264	15
16	14.420 292	14.131 264	13.850 497	13.577 709	16
17	15.229 918	14.907 649	14.595 083	14.291 872	17
18	16.029 549	15.672 561	15.326 863	14.992 031	18
19	16.819 308	16.426 168	16.046 057	15.678 462	19

YRS					
5	17.599 316	17.168 639	16.752 881	16.351 433	20
6	20.624 235	20.030 405	19.460 686	18.913 926	24
7	23.502 518	22.726 717	21.986 955	21.281 272	28
8	26.241 274	25.267 139	24.343 859	23.468 335	32
9	28.847 267	27.660 684	26.542 753	25.488 842	36
10	31.326 933	29.915 845	28.594 230	27.355 479	40
11	33.686 395	32.040 622	30.508 172	29.079 963	44
12	35.931 481	34.042 554	32.293 801	30.673 120	48
13	38.067 734	35.928 742	33.959 719	32.144 950	52
14	40.100 431	37.705 879	35.513 951	33.504 694	56
15	42.034 592	39.380 269	36.963 986	34.760 887	60
16	43.874 992	40.957 853	38.316 807	35.921 415	64
17	45.626 178	42.444 228	39.578 934	36.993 564	68
18	47.292 474	43.844 667	40.756 445	37.984 063	72
19	48.877 995	45.164 138	41.855 015	38.899 132	76
20	50.386 657	46.407 323	42.879 935	39.744 514	80
21	51.822 185	47.578 633	43.836 142	40.525 516	84
22	53.188 125	48.682 222	44.728 244	41.247 041	88
23	54.487 850	49.722 007	45.560 539	41.913 619	92
24	55.724 570	50.701 675	46.337 035	42.529 434	96
25	56.901 339	51.624 704	47.061 473	43.098 352	100
26	58.021 064	52.494 366	47.737 344	43.623 944	104
27	59.086 509	53.313 749	48.367 904	44.109 510	108
28	60.100 305	54.085 758	48.956 190	44.558 097	112
29	61.064 957	54.813 133	49.505 036	44.972 523	116
30	61.982 847	55.498 454	50.017 087	45.355 389	120

QTRS	9.0% ANNUAL RATE	10.0% ANNUAL RATE	11.0% ANNUAL RATE	12.0% ANNUAL RATE	QTRS
1	0.977 995	0.975 610	0.973 236	0.970 874	1
2	1.934 470	1.927 424	1.920 424	1.913 470	2
3	2.869 897	2.856 024	2.842 262	2.828 611	3
4	3.784 740	3.761 974	3.739 428	3.717 098	4
5	4.679 453	4.645 828	4.612 582	4.579 707	5
6	5.554 477	5.508 125	5.462 367	5.417 191	6
7	6.410 246	6.349 391	6.289 408	6.230 283	7
8	7.247 185	7.170 137	7.094 314	7.019 692	8
9	8.065 706	7.970 866	7.877 678	7.786 109	9
10	8.866 216	8.752 064	8.640 076	8.530 203	10
11	9.649 111	9.514 209	9.382 069	9.252 624	11
12	10.414 779	10.257 765	10.104 204	9.954 004	12
13	11.163 598	10.983 185	10.807 011	10.634 955	13
14	11.895 939	11.690 912	11.491 008	11.296 073	14
15	12.612 166	12.381 378	12.156 699	11.937 935	15
16	13.312 631	13.055 003	12.804 573	12.561 102	16
17	13.997 683	13.712 198	13.435 108	13.166 118	17
18	14.667 661	14.353 364	14.048 767	13.753 513	18
19	15.322 896	14.978 891	14.646 002	14.323 799	19
YRS					
5	15.963 712	15.589 162	15.227 252	14.877 475	20
6	18.389 036	17.884 986	17.400 797	16.935 542	24
7	20.607 828	19.964 889	19.350 826	18.764 108	28
8	22.637 674	21.849 178	21.100 326	20.388 766	32
9	24.494 666	23.556 251	22.669 918	21.832 252	36
10	26.193 522	25.102 775	24.078 101	23.114 772	40
11	27.747 710	26.503 849	25.341 475	24.254 274	44
12	29.169 548	27.773 154	26.474 931	25.266 707	48
13	30.470 307	28.923 081	27.491 829	26.116 240	52
14	31.660 298	29.964 858	28.404 155	26.965 464	56
15	32.748 953	30.908 656	29.222 662	27.675 564	60
16	33.744 902	31.763 691	29.956 999	28.306 478	64
17	34.656 039	32.538 311	30.615 821	28.867 038	68
18	35.489 587	33.240 078	31.206 893	29.365 088	72
19	36.252 153	33.875 844	31.737 183	29.807 598	76
20	36.949 781	34.451 817	32.212 941	30.200 763	80
21	37.588 001	34.973 620	32.639 775	30.550 086	84
22	38.171 873	35.446 348	33.022 715	30.860 454	88
23	38.706 024	35.874 616	33.366 276	31.136 212	92
24	39.194 689	36.262 606	33.674 508	31.381 219	96
25	39.641 741	36.614 105	33.951 042	31.598 905	100
26	40.050 723	36.932 546	34.199 140	31.792 317	104
27	40.424 877	37.221 039	34.421 724	31.964 160	108
28	40.767 170	37.482 398	34.621 419	32.116 840	112
29	41.080 315	37.719 177	34.800 579	32.252 495	116
30	41.366 793	37.933 687	34.961 315	32.373 023	120

	13.0%	14.0%	15.0%	16.0%	
	ANNUAL RATE	ANNUAL RATE	ANNUAL RATE	ANNUAL RATE	
QTRS					QTRS
1	0.968 523	0.966 184	0.963 855	0.961 538	1
2	1.906 560	1.899 694	1.892 873	1.886 095	2
3	2.815 070	2.801 637	2.788 311	2.775 091	3
4	3.694 983	3.673 079	3.651 384	3.629 895	4
5	4.547 199	4.515 052	4.483 262	4.451 822	5
6	5.372 590	5.328 553	5.285 072	5.242 137	6
7	6.172 000	6.114 544	6.057 900	6.002 055	7
8	6.946 247	6.873 956	6.802 796	6.732 745	8
9	7.696 123	7.607 687	7.520 767	7.435 332	9
10	8.422 395	8.316 605	8.212 787	8.110 896	10
11	9.125 806	9.001 551	8.879 795	8.760 477	11
12	9.807 076	9.663 334	9.522 694	9.385 074	12
13	10.466 902	10.302 738	10.142 356	9.985 648	13
14	11.105 958	10.920 520	10.739 620	10.563 123	14
15	11.724 899	11.517 411	11.315 296	11.118 387	15
16	12.324 358	12.094 117	11.870 165	11.652 296	16
17	12.904 947	12.651 321	12.404 978	12.165 669	17
18	13.467 261	13.189 682	12.920 461	12.659 297	18
19	14.011 875	13.709 837	13.417 312	13.133 939	19
YRS					
5	14.539 346	14.212 403	13.896 204	13.590 326	20
6	16.488 343	16.058 368	15.644 824	15.246 963	24
7	18.203 292	17.667 019	17.154 011	16.663 063	28
8	19.712 297	19.068 865	18.456 549	17.873 551	32
9	21.040 090	20.290 494	19.580 735	18.908 282	36
10	22.208 433	21.355 072	20.550 990	19.792 774	40
11	23.236 473	22.282 791	21.388 391	20.548 841	44
12	24.141 059	23.091 244	22.111 129	21.195 131	48
13	24.937 016	23.795 765	22.734 904	21.747 582	52
14	25.637 389	24.409 713	23.273 268	22.219 819	56
15	26.253 656	24.944 734	23.737 916	22.623 490	60
16	26.795 918	25.410 974	24.138 941	22.968 549	64
17	27.273 061	25.817 275	24.485 054	23.263 507	68
18	27.692 905	26.171 343	24.783 776	23.515 639	72
19	28.062 332	26.479 892	25.041 594	23.731 162	76
20	28.387 395	26.748 776	25.264 110	23.915 392	80
21	28.673 422	26.983 092	25.456 158	24.072 872	84
22	28.925 102	27.187 285	25.621 909	24.207 487	88
23	29.146 505	27.365 227	25.764 965	24.322 557	92
24	29.341 419	27.520 294	25.888 432	24.420 919	96
25	29.512 881	27.655 425	25.994 993	24.504 999	100
26	29.663 752	27.773 185	26.086 963	24.576 871	104
27	29.796 506	27.875 805	26.166 340	24.638 308	108
28	29.913 317	27.965 233	26.234 848	24.690 824	112
29	30.016 101	28.043 164	26.293 976	24.735 715	116
30	30.106 542	28.111 077	26.345 007	24.774 088	120

	5.0%	6.0%	7.0%	8.0%	
	ANNUAL RATE	ANNUAL RATE	ANNUAL RATE	ANNUAL RATE	
HALF YRS					HALF YRS
1	0.975 610	0.970 874	0.966 184	0.961 538	1
2	1.927 424	1.913 470	1.899 694	1.886 095	2
3	2.856 024	2.828 611	2.801 637	2.775 091	3
4	3.761 974	3.717 098	3.673 079	3.629 895	4
5	4.645 828	4.579 707	4.515 052	4.451 822	5
6	5.508 125	5.417 191	5.328 553	5.242 137	6
7	6.349 391	6.230 283	6.114 544	6.002 055	7
8	7.170 137	7.019 692	6.873 956	6.732 745	8
9	7.970 866	7.786 109	7.607 687	7.435 332	9
10	8.752 064	8.530 203	8.316 605	8.110 896	10
11	9.514 209	9.252 624	9.001 551	8.760 477	11
12	10.257 765	9.954 004	9.663 334	9.385 074	12
13	10.983 185	10.634 955	10.302 738	9.985 648	13
14	11.690 912	11.296 073	10.920 520	10.563 123	14
15	12.381 378	11.937 935	11.517 411	11.118 387	15
16	13.055 003	12.561 102	12.094 117	11.652 296	16
17	13.712 198	13.166 118	12.651 321	12.165 669	17
18	14.353 364	13.753 513	13.189 682	12.659 297	18
19	14.978 891	14.323 799	13.709 837	13.133 939	19
20	15.589 162	14.877 475	14.212 403	13.590 326	20
21	16.184 549	15.415 024	14.697 974	14.029 160	21
22	16.765 413	15.936 917	15.167 125	14.451 115	22
23	17.332 110	16.443 608	15.620 410	14.856 842	23
24	17.884 986	16.935 542	16.058 368	15.246 963	24
25	18.424 376	17.413 148	16.481 515	15.622 080	25
26	18.950 611	17.876 842	16.890 352	15.982 769	26
27	19.464 011	18.327 031	17.285 365	16.329 586	27
28	19.964 889	18.764 108	17.667 019	16.663 063	28
29	20.453 550	19.188 455	18.035 767	16.983 715	29
YRS					
15	20.930 293	19.600 441	18.392 045	17.292 033	30
16	21.849 178	20.388 766	19.068 865	17.873 551	32
17	22.723 786	21.131 837	19.700 684	18.411 198	34
18	23.556 251	21.832 252	20.290 494	18.908 282	36
19	24.348 603	22.492 462	20.841 087	19.367 864	38
20	25.102 775	23.114 772	21.355 072	19.792 774	40
21	25.820 607	23.701 359	21.834 883	20.185 627	42
22	26.503 849	24.254 274	22.282 791	20.548 841	44
23	27.154 170	24.775 449	22.700 918	20.884 654	46
24	27.773 154	25.266 707	23.091 244	21.195 131	48
25	28.362 312	25.729 764	23.455 618	21.482 185	50
26	28.923 081	26.166 240	23.795 765	21.747 582	52
27	29.456 829	26.577 660	24.113 295	21.992 957	54
28	29.964 858	26.965 464	24.409 713	22.219 819	56
29	30.448 407	27.331 005	24.686 423	22.429 567	58
30	30.908 656	27.675 564	24.944 734	22.623 490	60

PRESENT VALUE OF $1 PER PERIOD — SEMIANNUAL COMPOUNDING

HALF YRS	9.0% ANNUAL RATE	10.0% ANNUAL RATE	11.0% ANNUAL RATE	12.0% ANNUAL RATE	HALF YRS
1	0.956 938	0.952 381	0.947 867	0.943 396	1
2	1.872 668	1.859 410	1.846 320	1.833 393	2
3	2.748 964	2.723 248	2.697 933	2.673 012	3
4	3.587 526	3.545 951	3.505 150	3.465 106	4
5	4.389 977	4.329 477	4.270 284	4.212 364	5
6	5.157 872	5.075 692	4.995 530	4.917 324	6
7	5.892 701	5.786 373	5.682 967	5.582 381	7
8	6.595 886	6.463 213	6.334 566	6.209 794	8
9	7.268 790	7.107 822	6.952 195	6.801 692	9
10	7.912 718	7.721 735	7.537 626	7.360 087	10
11	8.528 917	8.306 414	8.092 536	7.886 875	11
12	9.118 581	8.863 252	8.618 518	8.383 844	12
13	9.682 852	9.393 573	9.117 079	8.852 683	13
14	10.222 825	9.898 641	9.589 648	9.294 984	14
15	10.739 546	10.379 658	10.037 581	9.712 249	15
16	11.234 015	10.837 770	10.462 162	10.105 895	16
17	11.707 191	11.274 066	10.864 609	10.477 260	17
18	12.159 992	11.689 587	11.246 074	10.827 603	18
19	12.593 294	12.085 321	11.607 654	11.158 116	19
20	13.007 936	12.462 210	11.950 382	11.469 921	20
21	13.404 724	12.821 153	12.275 244	11.764 077	21
22	13.784 425	13.163 003	12.583 170	12.041 582	22
23	14.147 775	13.488 574	12.875 042	12.303 379	23
24	14.495 478	13.798 642	13.151 699	12.550 358	24
25	14.828 209	14.093 945	13.413 933	12.783 356	25
26	15.146 611	14.375 185	13.662 495	13.003 166	26
27	15.451 303	14.643 034	13.898 100	13.210 534	27
28	15.742 874	14.898 127	14.121 422	13.406 164	28
29	16.021 889	15.141 074	14.333 101	13.590 721	29

YRS					
15	16.288 889	15.372 451	14.533 745	13.764 831	30
16	16.788 891	15.802 677	14.904 198	14.084 043	32
17	17.246 758	16.192 904	15.237 033	14.368 141	34
18	17.666 041	16.546 852	15.536 068	14.620 987	36
19	18.049 990	16.867 893	15.804 738	14.846 019	38
20	18.401 584	17.159 086	16.046 125	15.046 297	40
21	18.723 550	17.423 208	16.262 999	15.224 543	42
22	19.018 383	17.662 773	16.457 851	15.383 182	44
23	19.288 371	17.880 066	16.632 915	15.524 370	46
24	19.535 607	18.077 158	16.790 203	15.650 027	48
25	19.762 008	18.255 925	16.931 518	15.761 861	50
26	19.969 330	18.418 073	17.058 483	15.861 393	52
27	20.159 181	18.565 146	17.172 555	15.949 976	54
28	20.333 034	18.698 545	17.275 043	16.028 814	56
29	20.492 236	18.819 542	17.367 124	16.098 980	58
30	20.638 022	18.929 290	17.449 854	16.161 428	60

YRS	5.0% ANNUAL RATE	6.0% ANNUAL RATE	7.0% ANNUAL RATE	7.5% ANNUAL RATE	YRS
1	0.952 381	0.943 396	0.934 579	0.930 233	1
2	1.859 410	1.833 393	1.808 018	1.795 565	2
3	2.723 248	2.673 012	2.624 316	2.600 526	3
4	3.545 951	3.465 106	3.387 211	3.349 326	4
5	4.329 477	4.212 364	4.100 197	4.045 885	5
6	5.075 692	4.917 324	4.766 540	4.693 846	6
7	5.786 373	5.582 381	5.389 289	5.296 601	7
8	6.463 213	6.209 794	5.971 299	5.857 304	8
9	7.107 822	6.801 692	6.515 232	6.378 887	9
10	7.721 735	7.360 087	7.023 582	6.864 081	10
11	8.306 414	7.886 875	7.498 674	7.315 424	11
12	8.863 252	8.383 844	7.942 686	7.735 278	12
13	9.393 573	8.852 683	8.357 651	8.125 840	13
14	9.898 641	9.294 984	8.745 468	8.489 154	14
15	10.379 658	9.712 249	9.107 914	8.827 120	15
16	10.837 770	10.105 895	9.446 649	9.141 507	16
17	11.274 066	10.477 260	9.763 223	9.433 960	17
18	11.689 587	10.827 603	10.059 087	9.706 009	18
19	12.085 321	11.158 116	10.335 595	9.959 078	19
20	12.462 210	11.469 921	10.594 014	10.194 491	20
21	12.821 153	11.764 077	10.835 527	10.413 480	21
22	13.163 003	12.041 582	11.061 240	10.617 191	22
23	13.488 574	12.303 379	11.272 187	10.806 689	23
24	13.798 642	12.550 358	11.469 334	10.982 967	24
25	14.093 945	12.783 356	11.653 583	11.146 946	25
26	14.375 185	13.003 166	11.825 779	11.299 485	26
27	14.643 034	13.210 534	11.986 709	11.441 381	27
28	14.898 127	13.406 164	12.137 111	11.573 378	28
29	15.141 074	13.590 721	12.277 674	11.696 165	29
30	15.372 451	13.764 831	12.409 041	11.810 386	30
31	15.592 811	13.929 086	12.531 814	11.916 638	31
32	15.802 677	14.084 043	12.646 555	12.015 478	32
33	16.002 549	14.230 230	12.753 790	12.107 421	33
34	16.192 904	14.368 141	12.854 009	12.192 950	34
35	16.374 194	14.498 246	12.947 672	12.272 511	35
36	16.546 852	14.620 987	13.035 208	12.346 522	36
37	16.711 287	14.736 780	13.117 017	12.415 370	37
38	16.867 893	14.846 019	13.193 473	12.479 414	38
39	17.017 041	14.949 075	13.264 928	12.538 989	39
40	17.159 086	15.046 297	13.331 709	12.594 409	40
41	17.294 368	15.138 016	13.394 120	12.645 962	41
42	17.423 208	15.224 543	13.452 449	12.693 918	42
43	17.545 912	15.306 173	13.506 962	12.738 528	43
44	17.662 773	15.383 182	13.557 908	12.780 026	44
45	17.774 070	15.455 832	13.605 522	12.818 629	45
46	17.880 066	15.524 370	13.650 020	12.854 539	46
47	17.981 016	15.589 028	13.691 608	12.887 943	47
48	18.077 158	15.650 027	13.730 474	12.919 017	48
49	18.168 722	15.707 572	13.766 799	12.947 922	49
50	18.255 925	15.761 861	13.800 746	12.974 812	50

YRS	8.0% ANNUAL RATE	8.5% ANNUAL RATE	9.0% ANNUAL RATE	9.5% ANNUAL RATE	YRS
1	0.925 926	0.921 659	0.917 431	0.913 242	1
2	1.783 265	1.771 114	1.759 111	1.747 253	2
3	2.577 097	2.554 022	2.531 295	2.508 907	3
4	3.312 127	3.275 597	3.239 720	3.204 481	4
5	3.992 710	3.940 642	3.889 651	3.839 709	5
6	4.622 880	4.553 587	4.485 919	4.419 825	6
7	5.206 370	5.118 514	5.032 953	4.949 612	7
8	5.746 639	5.639 183	5.534 819	5.433 436	8
9	6.246 888	6.119 063	5.995 247	5.875 284	9
10	6.710 081	6.561 348	6.417 658	6.278 798	10
11	7.138 964	6.968 984	6.805 191	6.647 304	11
12	7.536 078	7.344 686	7.160 725	6.983 839	12
13	7.903 776	7.690 955	7.486 904	7.291 178	13
14	8.244 237	8.010 097	7.786 150	7.571 852	14
15	8.559 479	8.304 237	8.060 688	7.828 175	15
16	8.851 369	8.575 333	8.312 558	8.062 260	16
17	9.121 638	8.825 192	8.543 631	8.276 037	17
18	9.371 887	9.055 476	8.755 625	8.471 266	18
19	9.603 599	9.267 720	8.950 115	8.649 558	19
20	9.818 147	9.463 337	9.128 546	8.812 382	20
21	10.016 803	9.643 628	9.292 244	8.961 080	21
22	10.200 744	9.809 796	9.442 425	9.096 876	22
23	10.371 059	9.962 945	9.580 207	9.220 892	23
24	10.528 758	10.104 097	9.706 612	9.334 148	24
25	10.674 776	10.234 191	9.822 580	9.437 578	25
26	10.809 978	10.354 093	9.928 972	9.532 034	26
27	10.935 165	10.464 602	10.026 580	9.618 296	27
28	11.051 078	10.566 453	10.116 128	9.697 074	28
29	11.158 406	10.660 326	10.198 283	9.769 018	29
30	11.257 783	10.746 844	10.273 654	9.834 719	30
31	11.349 799	10.826 584	10.342 802	9.894 721	31
32	11.434 999	10.900 078	10.406 240	9.949 517	32
33	11.513 888	10.967 813	10.464 441	9.999 559	33
34	11.586 934	11.030 243	10.517 835	10.045 259	34
35	11.654 568	11.087 781	10.566 821	10.086 995	35
36	11.717 193	11.140 812	10.611 763	10.125 109	36
37	11.775 179	11.189 689	10.652 993	10.159 917	37
38	11.828 869	11.234 736	10.690 820	10.191 705	38
39	11.878 582	11.276 255	10.725 523	10.220 735	39
40	11.924 613	11.314 520	10.757 360	10.247 247	40
41	11.967 235	11.349 788	10.786 569	10.271 458	41
42	12.006 699	11.382 293	10.813 366	10.293 569	42
43	12.043 240	11.412 252	10.837 950	10.313 762	43
44	12.077 074	11.439 864	10.860 505	10.332 203	44
45	12.108 402	11.465 312	10.881 197	10.349 043	45
46	12.137 409	11.488 767	10.900 181	10.364 423	46
47	12.164 267	11.510 384	10.917 597	10.378 469	47
48	12.189 136	11.530 308	10.933 575	10.391 296	48
49	12.212 163	11.548 671	10.948 234	10.403 010	49
50	12.233 485	11.565 595	10.961 683	10.413 707	50

PRESENT VALUE OF $1 PER PERIOD

ANNUAL COMPOUNDING

YRS	10.0% ANNUAL RATE	10.5% ANNUAL RATE	11.0% ANNUAL RATE	11.5% ANNUAL RATE	YRS
1	0.909 091	0.904 977	0.900 901	0.896 861	1
2	1.735 537	1.723 961	1.712 523	1.701 221	2
3	2.486 852	2.465 123	2.443 715	2.422 619	3
4	3.169 865	3.135 858	3.102 446	3.069 614	4
5	3.790 787	3.742 858	3.695 897	3.649 878	5
6	4.355 261	4.292 179	4.230 538	4.170 294	6
7	4.868 419	4.789 303	4.712 196	4.637 035	7
8	5.334 926	5.239 188	5.146 123	5.055 637	8
9	5.759 024	5.646 324	5.537 048	5.431 064	9
10	6.144 567	6.014 773	5.889 232	5.767 771	10
11	6.495 061	6.348 211	6.206 515	6.069 750	11
12	6.813 692	6.649 964	6.492 356	6.340 583	12
13	7.103 356	6.923 045	6.749 870	6.583 482	13
14	7.366 687	7.170 176	6.981 865	6.801 329	14
15	7.606 080	7.393 825	7.190 870	6.996 708	15
16	7.823 709	7.596 221	7.379 162	7.171 935	16
17	8.021 553	7.779 386	7.5*8 794	7.329 090	17
18	8.201 412	7.945 146	7.701 617	7.470 036	18
19	8.364 920	8.095 154	7.839 294	7.596 445	19
20	8.513 564	8.230 909	7.963 328	7.709 816	20
21	8.648 694	8.353 764	8.075 070	7.811 494	21
22	8.771 540	8.464 945	8.175 739	7.902 685	22
23	8.883 218	8.565 561	8.266 432	7.984 471	23
24	8.984 744	8.656 616	8.348 137	8.057 822	24
25	9.077 040	8.739 019	8.421 745	8.123 607	25
26	9.160 945	8.813 592	8.488 058	8.182 607	26
27	9.237 223	8.881 079	8.547 800	8.235 522	27
28	9.306 567	8.942 153	8.601 622	8.282 979	28
29	9.369 606	8.997 423	8.650 110	8.325 542	29
30	9.426 914	9.047 442	8.693 793	8.363 715	30
31	9.479 013	9.092 707	8.733 146	8.397 951	31
32	9.526 376	9.133 672	8.768 600	8.428 655	32
33	9.569 432	9.170 744	8.800 541	8.456 193	33
34	9.608 575	9.204 293	8.829 316	8.480 891	34
35	9.644 159	9.234 654	8.855 240	8.503 041	35
36	9.676 508	9.262 131	8.878 594	8.522 907	36
37	9.705 917	9.286 996	8.899 635	8.540 723	37
38	9.732 651	9.309 499	8.918 590	8.556 703	38
39	9.756 956	9.329 863	8.935 666	8.571 034	39
40	9.779 051	9.348 292	8.951 051	8.583 887	40
41	9.799 137	9.364 970	8.964 911	8.595 414	41
42	9.817 397	9.380 064	8.977 397	8.605 753	42
43	9.833 998	9.393 723	8.988 646	8.615 025	43
44	9.849 089	9.406 084	8.998 780	8.623 341	44
45	9.862 808	9.417 271	9.007 910	8.630 799	45
46	9.875 280	9.427 394	9.016 135	8.637 488	46
47	9.886 618	9.436 556	9.023 545	8.643 487	47
48	9.896 926	9.444 847	9.030 221	8.648 867	48
49	9.906 296	9.452 350	9.036 235	8.653 692	49
50	9.914 814	9.459 140	9.041 653	8.658 020	50

PRESENT VALUE OF $1 PER PERIOD — ANNUAL COMPOUNDING

YRS	12.0% ANNUAL RATE	12.5% ANNUAL RATE	13.0% ANNUAL RATE	13.5% ANNUAL RATE	YRS
1	0.892 857	0.888 889	0.884 956	0.881 057	1
2	1.690 051	1.679 012	1.668 102	1.657 319	2
3	2.401 831	2.381 344	2.361 153	2.341 250	3
4	3.037 349	3.005 639	2.974 471	2.943 833	4
5	3.604 776	3.560 568	3.517 231	3.474 743	5
6	4.111 407	4.053 839	3.997 550	3.942 505	6
7	4.563 757	4.492 301	4.422 610	4.354 630	7
8	4.967 640	4.882 045	4.798 770	4.717 735	8
9	5.328 250	5.228 485	5.131 655	5.037 652	9
10	5.650 223	5.536 431	5.426 243	5.319 517	10
11	5.937 699	5.810 161	5.686 941	5.567 857	11
12	6.194 374	6.053 476	5.917 647	5.786 658	12
13	6.423 548	6.269 757	6.121 812	5.979 434	13
14	6.628 168	6.462 006	6.302 488	6.149 281	14
15	6.810 864	6.632 894	6.462 379	6.298 926	15
16	6.973 986	6.784 795	6.603 875	6.430 772	16
17	7.119 630	6.919 818	6.729 093	6.546 936	17
18	7.249 670	7.039 838	6.839 905	6.649 283	18
19	7.365 777	7.146 523	6.937 969	6.739 456	19
20	7.469 444	7.241 353	7.024 752	6.818 904	20
21	7.562 003	7.325 647	7.101 550	6.888 902	21
22	7.644 646	7.400 575	7.169 513	6.950 575	22
23	7.718 434	7.467 178	7.229 658	7.004 912	23
24	7.784 316	7.526 381	7.282 883	7.052 786	24
25	7.843 139	7.579 005	7.329 985	7.094 965	25
26	7.895 660	7.625 782	7.371 668	7.132 128	26
27	7.942 554	7.667 362	7.408 556	7.164 870	27
28	7.984 423	7.704 322	7.441 200	7.193 718	28
29	8.021 806	7.737 175	7.470 088	7.219 135	29
30	8.055 184	7.766 378	7.495 653	7.241 529	30
31	8.084 986	7.792 336	7.518 277	7.261 259	31
32	8.111 594	7.815 410	7.538 299	7.278 642	32
33	8.135 352	7.835 920	7.556 016	7.293 958	33
34	8.156 564	7.854 151	7.571 696	7.307 452	34
35	8.175 504	7.870 356	7.585 572	7.319 341	35
36	8.192 414	7.884 761	7.597 851	7.329 816	36
37	8.207 513	7.897 565	7.608 718	7.339 045	37
38	8.220 993	7.908 947	7.618 334	7.347 176	38
39	8.233 030	7.919 064	7.626 844	7.354 340	39
40	8.243 777	7.928 057	7.634 376	7.360 652	40
41	8.253 372	7.936 051	7.641 040	7.366 213	41
42	8.261 939	7.943 156	7.646 938	7.371 113	42
43	8.269 589	7.949 472	7.652 158	7.375 430	43
44	8.276 418	7.955 086	7.656 777	7.379 233	44
45	8.282 516	7.960 077	7.660 864	7.382 585	45
46	8.287 961	7.964 513	7.664 482	7.385 537	46
47	8.292 822	7.968 456	7.667 683	7.388 138	47
48	8.297 163	7.971 961	7.670 516	7.390 430	48
49	8.301 038	7.975 076	7.673 023	7.392 450	49
50	8.304 498	7.977 845	7.675 242	7.394 229	50

PRESENT VALUE OF
$1 PER PERIOD
ANNUAL COMPOUNDING

	14.0%	14.5%	15.0%	16.0%	
	ANNUAL RATE	ANNUAL RATE	ANNUAL RATE	ANNUAL RATE	
YRS					YRS
1	0.877 193	0.873 362	0.869 565	0.862 069	1
2	1.646 661	1.636 124	1.625 709	1.605 232	2
3	2.321 632	2.302 292	2.283 225	2.245 890	3
4	2.913 712	2.884 098	2.854 978	2.798 181	4
5	3.433 081	3.392 225	3.352 155	3.274 294	5
6	3.888 668	3.836 005	3.784 483	3.684 736	6
7	4.288 305	4.223 585	4.160 420	4.038 565	7
8	4.638 864	4.562 083	4.487 322	4.343 591	8
9	4.946 372	4.857 714	4.771 584	4.606 544	9
10	5.216 116	5.115 908	5.018 769	4.833 227	10
11	5.452 733	5.341 404	5.233 712	5.028 644	11
12	5.660 292	5.538 344	5.420 619	5.197 107	12
13	5.842 362	5.710 344	5.583 147	5.342 334	13
14	6.002 072	5.860 563	5.724 476	5.467 529	14
15	6.142 168	5.991 758	5.847 370	5.575 456	15
16	6.265 060	6.106 339	5.954 235	5.668 497	16
17	6.372 859	6.206 409	6.047 161	5.748 704	17
18	6.467 420	6.293 807	6.127 966	5.817 848	18
19	6.550 369	6.370 137	6.198 231	5.877 455	19
20	6.623 131	6.436 801	6.259 331	5.928 841	20
21	6.686 957	6.495 023	6.312 462	5.973 139	21
22	6.742 944	6.545 871	6.358 663	6.011 326	22
23	6.792 056	6.590 281	6.398 837	6.044 247	23
24	6.835 137	6.629 066	6.433 771	6.072 627	24
25	6.872 927	6.662 940	6.464 149	6.097 092	25
26	6.906 077	6.692 524	6.490 564	6.118 183	26
27	6.935 155	6.718 362	6.513 534	6.136 364	27
28	6.960 662	6.740 927	6.533 508	6.152 038	28
29	6.983 037	6.760 635	6.550 877	6.165 550	29
30	7.002 664	6.777 847	6.565 980	6.177 198	30
31	7.019 881	6.792 880	6.579 113	6.187 240	31
32	7.034 983	6.806 008	6.590 533	6.195 897	32
33	7.048 231	6.817 475	6.600 463	6.203 359	33
34	7.059 852	6.827 489	6.609 099	6.209 792	34
35	7.070 045	6.836 235	6.616 607	6.215 338	35
36	7.078 987	6.843 873	6.623 137	6.220 119	36
37	7.086 831	6.850 544	6.628 815	6.224 241	37
38	7.093 711	6.856 370	6.633 752	6.227 794	38
39	7.099 747	6.861 459	6.638 045	6.230 857	39
40	7.105 041	6.865 903	6.641 778	6.233 497	40
41	7.109 685	6.869 784	6.645 025	6.235 773	41
42	7.113 759	6.873 174	6.647 848	6.237 736	42
43	7.117 332	6.876 135	6.650 302	6.239 427	43
44	7.120 467	6.878 720	6.652 437	6.240 886	44
45	7.123 217	6.880 978	6.654 293	6.242 143	45
46	7.125 629	6.882 950	6.655 907	6.243 227	46
47	7.127 744	6.884 673	6.657 310	6.244 161	47
48	7.129 600	6.886 177	6.658 531	6.244 966	48
49	7.131 228	6.887 491	6.659 592	6.245 661	49
50	7.132 656	6.888 638	6.660 515	6.246 259	50

PRESENT VALUE OF $1 PER PERIOD

ANNUAL COMPOUNDING

YRS	17.0% ANNUAL RATE	18.0% ANNUAL RATE	19.0% ANNUAL RATE	20.0% ANNUAL RATE	YRS
1	0.854 701	0.847 458	0.840 336	0.833 333	1
2	1.585 214	1.565 642	1.546 501	1.527 778	2
3	2.209 585	2.174 273	2.139 917	2.106 481	3
4	2.743 235	2.690 062	2.638 586	2.588 735	4
5	3.199 346	3.127 171	3.057 635	2.990 612	5
6	3.589 185	3.497 603	3.409 777	3.325 510	6
7	3.922 380	3.811 528	3.705 695	3.604 592	7
8	4.207 163	4.077 566	3.954 366	3.837 160	8
9	4.450 566	4.303 022	4.163 332	4.030 967	9
10	4.658 604	4.494 086	4.338 935	4.192 472	10
11	4.836 413	4.656 005	4.486 500	4.327 060	11
12	4.988 387	4.793 225	4.610 504	4.439 217	12
13	5.118 280	4.909 513	4.714 709	4.532 681	13
14	5.229 299	5.008 062	4.802 277	4.610 567	14
15	5.324 187	5.091 578	4.875 863	4.675 473	15
16	5.405 288	5.162 354	4.937 700	4.729 561	16
17	5.474 605	5.222 334	4.989 664	4.774 634	17
18	5.533 851	5.273 164	5.033 331	4.812 195	18
19	5.584 488	5.316 241	5.070 026	4.843 496	19
20	5.627 767	5.352 746	5.100 862	4.869 580	20
21	5.664 758	5.383 683	5.126 775	4.891 316	21
22	5.696 375	5.409 901	5.148 550	4.909 430	22
23	5.723 397	5.432 120	5.166 849	4.924 525	23
24	5.746 493	5.450 949	5.182 226	4.937 104	24
25	5.766 234	5.466 906	5.195 148	4.947 587	25
26	5.783 106	5.480 429	5.206 007	4.956 323	26
27	5.797 526	5.491 889	5.215 132	4.963 602	27
28	5.809 851	5.501 601	5.222 800	4.969 668	28
29	5.820 386	5.509 831	5.229 243	4.974 724	29
30	5.829 390	5.516 806	5.234 658	4.978 936	30
31	5.837 085	5.522 717	5.239 209	4.982 447	31
32	5.843 663	5.527 726	5.243 033	4.985 372	32
33	5.849 284	5.531 971	5.246 246	4.987 810	33
34	5.854 089	5.535 569	5.248 946	4.989 842	34
35	5.858 196	5.538 618	5.251 215	4.991 535	35
36	5.861 706	5.541 201	5.253 122	4.992 946	36
37	5.864 706	5.543 391	5.254 724	4.994 122	37
38	5.867 270	5.545 247	5.256 071	4.995 101	38
39	5.869 461	5.546 819	5.257 202	4.995 918	39
40	5.871 335	5.548 152	5.258 153	4.996 598	40
41	5.872 936	5.549 281	5.258 952	4.997 165	41
42	5.874 304	5.550 238	5.259 624	4.997 638	42
43	5.875 473	5.551 049	5.260 188	4.998 031	43
44	5.876 473	5.551 737	5.260 662	4.998 359	44
45	5.877 327	5.552 319	5.261 061	4.998 633	45
46	5.878 058	5.552 813	5.261 396	4.998 861	46
47	5.878 682	5.553 231	5.261 677	4.999 051	47
48	5.879 215	5.553 586	5.261 913	4.999 209	48
49	5.879 671	5.553 886	5.262 112	4.999 341	49
50	5.880 061	5.554 141	5.262 279	4.999 451	50

Section 6. Partial Payment to Amortize $1.00:

These factors represent the regular and equal payment necessary to be made at the end of each period that will repay both the interest on a loan and the original loan amount. There can be no additional withdrawals or changes in the regular (equal) payments.

In this section the following four (4) periods are presented in detail: monthly, quarterly, semiannual, and annual.

Monthly:

The factors presented on pages 109 through 114 indicate the amount of the monthly payment necessary to repay a loan and the interest. The interest is being charged at the end of each month. This is interest on the entire balance of the loan for one month (or 30 days) plus an amount of money to repay the loan.

Example K

You have a loan for $30,000.00 at 9% interest, to be repaid in 20 years. What is the monthly payment? Turn to page 110 and locate the 9.0% interest rate column. Proceed down that column until you locate the point where the 20 year row intersects the 9.0% interest column. The number is 0.008997. Now multiply 0.00899 by $30,000.00 to get the answer of $269.91. What is th quarterly payment?

Turn to page 116 and locate the 9.0% interest column Proceed down that column until you locate the poir where the 20 years row intersects the 9.0% interes column. The number is 0.027064. Now multiply 0.02706 by $30,000.00 to get the answer $811.92. What is th semiannual payment?

Turn to page 119 and locate the 9.0% interest column. Proceed down that column until you locate the point where the 20 year row intersects the 9.0% interest column. The number is 0.054343. Then, multiply 0.054343 by $30,000.00 to get the answer $1630.29.

What is the annual payment?

Turn to page 121 and locate the 9.0% interest column. Proceed down that column until you locate the point where the 20 year row intersects the 9.0% interest column. The number is 0.109546. Now multiply 0.109546 by $30,000.00 to get the answer $3286.38.

For your interest, here's the formula . . .

$$\frac{1}{a_{\overline{n}|}} = \frac{i}{1 - V^n}$$

$a_{\overline{n}|}$ = Present value of $1 per period
i = interest rate per period
V^n = Present value of $1
n = number of compounding periods
$\dfrac{1}{a_{\overline{n}|}}$ = Partial payment to amortize $1

PARTIAL PAYMENT
TO AMORTIZE $1

MONTHLY
COMPOUNDING

MOS	5.0% ANNUAL RATE	6.0% ANNUAL RATE	7.0% ANNUAL RATE	7.5% ANNUAL RATE	MOS
1	1.004 167	1.005 000	1.005 833	1.006 250	1
2	0.503 127	0.503 753	0.504 379	0.504 692	2
3	0.336 115	0.336 672	0.337 230	0.337 509	3
4	0.252 610	0.253 133	0.253 656	0.253 918	4
5	0.202 507	0.203 010	0.203 514	0.203 766	5
6	0.169 106	0.169 595	0.170 086	0.170 331	6
7	0.145 248	0.145 729	0.146 210	0.146 451	7
8	0.127 355	0.127 829	0.128 304	0.128 541	8
9	0.113 439	0.113 907	0.114 377	0.114 612	9
10	0.102 306	0.102 771	0.103 236	0.103 470	10
11	0.093 198	0.093 659	0.094 122	0.094 354	11
12	0.085 607	0.086 066	0.086 527	0.086 757	12
13	0.079 185	0.079 642	0.080 101	0.080 330	13
14	0.073 681	0.074 136	0.074 593	0.074 822	14
15	0.068 910	0.069 364	0.069 820	0.070 048	15
16	0.064 737	0.065 189	0.065 644	0.065 872	16
17	0.061 054	0.061 506	0.061 960	0.062 187	17
18	0.057 781	0.058 232	0.058 685	0.058 912	18
19	0.054 852	0.055 303	0.055 755	0.055 983	19
20	0.052 216	0.052 666	0.053 119	0.053 346	20
21	0.049 832	0.050 282	0.050 734	0.050 961	21
22	0.047 664	0.048 114	0.048 566	0.048 793	22
23	0.045 685	0.046 135	0.046 587	0.046 814	23
YRS					
2	0.043 871	0.044 321	0.044 773	0.045 000	24
3	0.029 971	0.030 422	0.030 877	0.031 106	36
4	0.023 029	0.023 485	0.023 946	0.024 179	48
5	0.018 871	0.019 333	0.019 801	0.020 038	60
6	0.016 105	0.016 573	0.017 049	0.017 290	72
7	0.014 134	0.014 609	0.015 093	0.015 338	84
8	0.012 660	0.013 141	0.013 634	0.013 884	96
9	0.011 517	0.012 006	0.012 506	0.012 761	108
10	0.010 607	0.011 102	0.011 611	0.011 870	120
11	0.009 864	0.010 367	0.010 884	0.011 148	132
12	0.009 249	0.009 759	0.010 284	0.010 552	144
13	0.008 731	0.009 247	0.009 781	0.010 054	156
14	0.008 289	0.008 812	0.009 354	0.009 631	168
15	0.007 908	0.008 439	0.008 988	0.009 270	180
16	0.007 577	0.008 114	0.008 672	0.008 958	192
17	0.007 287	0.007 831	0.008 397	0.008 687	204
18	0.007 030	0.007 582	0.008 155	0.008 450	216
19	0.006 803	0.007 361	0.007 942	0.008 241	228
20	0.006 600	0.007 164	0.007 753	0.008 056	240
21	0.006 417	0.006 989	0.007 585	0.007 892	252
22	0.006 253	0.006 831	0.007 434	0.007 745	264
23	0.006 104	0.006 688	0.007 299	0.007 614	276
24	0.005 969	0.006 560	0.007 178	0.007 496	288
25	0.005 846	0.006 443	0.007 068	0.007 390	300
26	0.005 733	0.006 337	0.006 968	0.007 294	312
27	0.005 630	0.006 240	0.006 878	0.007 207	324
28	0.005 536	0.006 151	0.006 796	0.007 129	336
29	0.005 449	0.006 070	0.006 721	0.007 057	348
30	0.005 368	0.005 996	0.006 653	0.006 992	360

MOS	8.0% ANNUAL RATE	8.5% ANNUAL RATE	9.0% ANNUAL RATE	9.5% ANNUAL RATE	MOS
1	1..006 667	1.007 083	1.007 500	1.007 917	1
2	0.505 006	0.505 319	0.505 632	0.505 945	2
3	0.337 788	0.338 067	0.338 346	0.338 625	3
4	0.254 181	0.254 443	0.254 705	0.254 967	4
5	0.204 018	0.204 270	0.204 522	0.204 775	5
6	0.170 577	0.170 823	0.171 069	0.171 315	6
7	0.146 692	0.146 933	0.147 175	0.147 417	7
8	0.128 779	0.129 017	0.129 256	0.129 494	8
9	0.114 848	0.115 083	0.115 319	0.115 555	9
10	0.103 703	0.103 937	0.104 171	0.104 406	10
11	0.094 586	0.094 818	0.095 051	0.095 284	11
12	0.086 988	0.087 220	0.087 451	0.087 684	12
13	0.080 561	0.080 791	0.081 022	0.081 253	13
14	0.075 051	0.075 281	0.075 511	0.075 742	14
15	0.070 277	0.070 507	0.070 736	0.070 967	15
16	0.066 100	0.066 329	0.066 559	0.066 789	16
17	0.062 415	0.062 644	0.062 873	0.063 103	17
18	0.059 140	0.059 369	0.059 598	0.059 827	18
19	0.056 210	0.056 439	0.056 667	0.056 897	19
20	0.053 574	0.053 802	0.054 031	0.054 260	20
21	0.051 188	0.051 417	0.051 645	0.051 875	21
22	0.049 020	0.049 249	0.049 477	0.049 707	22
23	0.047 041	0.047 270	0.047 498	0.047 728	23

YRS					
2	0.045 227	0.045 456	0.045 685	0.045 914	24
3	0.031 336	0.031 568	0.031 800	0.032 033	36
4	0.024 413	0.024 648	0.024 885	0.025 123	48
5	0.020 276	0.020 517	0.020 758	0.021 002	60
6	0.017 533	0.017 778	0.018 026	0.018 275	72
7	0.015 586	0.015 836	0.016 089	0.016 344	84
8	0.014 137	0.014 392	0.014 650	0.014 911	96
9	0.013 019	0.013 279	0.013 543	0.013 809	108
10	0.012 133	0.012 399	0.012 668	0.012 940	120
11	0.011 415	0.011 686	0.011 961	0.012 239	132
12	0.010 825	0.011 101	0.011 380	0.011 664	144
13	0.010 331	0.010 612	0.010 897	0.011 186	156
14	0.009 913	0.010 199	0.010 489	0.010 784	168
15	0.009 557	0.009 847	0.010 143	0.010 442	180
16	0.009 249	0.009 545	0.009 845	0.010 150	192
17	0.008 983	0.009 283	0.009 588	0.009 898	204
18	0.008 750	0.009 055	0.009 364	0.009 679	216
19	0.008 545	0.008 854	0.009 169	0.009 488	228
20	0.008 364	0.008 678	0.008 997	0.009 321	240
21	0.008 204	0.008 522	0.008 846	0.009 174	252
22	0.008 062	0.008 384	0.008 712	0.009 045	264
23	0.007 935	0.008 261	0.008 593	0.008 930	276
24	0.007 821	0.008 151	0.008 487	0.008 828	288
25	0.007 718	0.008 052	0.008 392	0.008 737	300
26	0.007 626	0.007 964	0.008 307	0.008 656	312
27	0.007 543	0.007 884	0.008 231	0.008 584	324
28	0.007 468	0.007 812	0.008 163	0.008 519	336
29	0.007 399	0.007 748	0.008 102	0.008 461	348
30	0.007 338	0.007 689	0.008 046	0.008 409	360

PARTIAL PAYMENT
TO AMORTIZE $1

MONTHLY
COMPOUNDING

	10.0% ANNUAL RATE	10.5% ANNUAL RATE	11.0% ANNUAL RATE	11.5% ANNUAL RATE	
MOS					MOS
1	1.008 333	1.008 750	1.009 167	1.009 583	1
2	0.506 259	0.506 572	0.506 885	0.507 199	2
3	0.338 904	0.339 184	0.339 463	0.339 743	3
4	0.255 230	0.255 493	0.255 755	0.256 018	4
5	0.205 028	0.205 280	0.205 533	0.205 787	5
6	0.171 561	0.171 808	0.172 055	0.172 301	6
7	0.147 659	0.147 901	0.148 143	0.148 386	7
8	0.129 733	0.129 972	0.130 211	0.130 451	8
9	0.115 792	0.116 029	0.116 266	0.116 503	9
10	0.104 640	0.104 875	0.105 111	0.105 346	10
11	0.095 517	0.095 751	0.095 985	0.096 219	11
12	0.087 916	0.088 149	0.088 382	0.088 615	12
13	0.081 485	0.081 717	0.081 949	0.082 182	13
14	0.075 973	0.076 205	0.076 436	0.076 669	14
15	0.071 197	0.071 428	0.071 660	0.071 891	15
16	0.067 019	0.067 250	0.067 481	0.067 712	16
17	0.063 333	0.063 563	0.063 795	0.064 026	17
18	0.060 057	0.060 288	0.060 519	0.060 750	18
19	0.057 127	0.057 357	0.057 588	0.057 820	19
20	0.054 490	0.054 720	0.054 951	0.055 183	20
21	0.052 105	0.052 335	0.052 567	0.052 798	21
22	0.049 937	0.050 168	0.050 399	0.050 631	22
23	0.047 958	0.048 189	0.048 421	0.048 653	23
YRS					
2	0.046 145	0.046 376	0.046 608	0.046 840	24
3	0.032 267	0.032 502	0.032 739	0.032 976	36
4	0.025 363	0.025 603	0.025 846	0.026 089	48
5	0.021 247	0.021 494	0.021 742	0.021 993	60
6	0.018 526	0.018 779	0.019 034	0.019 291	72
7	0.016 601	0.016 861	0.017 122	0.017 386	84
8	0.015 174	0.015 440	0.015 708	0.015 979	96
9	0.014 079	0.014 351	0.014 626	0.014 904	108
10	0.013 215	0.013 493	0.013 775	0.014 060	120
11	0.012 520	0.012 804	0.013 092	0.013 384	132
12	0.011 951	0.012 241	0.012 536	0.012 833	144
13	0.011 478	0.011 775	0.012 075	0.012 379	156
14	0.011 082	0.011 384	0.011 691	0.012 001	168
15	0.010 746	0.011 054	0.011 366	0.011 682	180
16	0.010 459	0.010 772	0.011 090	0.011 412	192
17	0.010 212	0.010 531	0.010 854	0.011 181	204
18	0.009 998	0.010 322	0.010 650	0.010 983	216
19	0.009 813	0.010 141	0.010 475	0.010 812	228
20	0.009 650	0.009 984	0.010 322	0.010 664	240
21	0.009 508	0.009 846	0.010 189	0.010 536	252
22	0.009 382	0.009 725	0.010 072	0.010 424	264
23	0.009 272	0.009 619	0.009 970	0.010 326	276
24	0.009 174	0.009 525	0.009 880	0.010 240	288
25	0.009 087	0.009 442	0.009 801	0.010 165	300
26	0.009 010	0.009 368	0.009 731	0.010 098	312
27	0.008 941	0.009 303	0.009 670	0.010 040	324
28	0.008 880	0.009 245	0.009 615	0.009 989	336
29	0.008 825	0.009 193	0.009 566	0.009 943	348
30	0.008 776	0.009 147	0.009 523	0.009 903	360

MOS	12.0% ANNUAL RATE	12.5% ANNUAL RATE	13.0% ANNUAL RATE	13.5% ANNUAL RATE	MOS
1	1.010 000	1.010 417	1.010 833	1.011 250	1
2	0.507 512	0.507 826	0.508 140	0.508 453	2
3	0.340 022	0.340 302	0.340 581	0.340 861	3
4	0.256 281	0.256 544	0.256 807	0.257 071	4
5	0.206 040	0.206 293	0.206 547	0.206 800	5
6	0.172 548	0.172 796	0.173 043	0.173 290	6
7	0.148 628	0.148 871	0.149 114	0.149 358	7
8	0.130 690	0.130 930	0.131 170	0.131 411	8
9	0.116 740	0.116 978	0.117 216	0.117 454	9
10	0.105 582	0.105 818	0.106 055	0.106 291	10
11	0.096 454	0.096 689	0.096 924	0.097 160	11
12	0.088 849	0.089 083	0.089 317	0.089 552	12
13	0.082 415	0.082 648	0.082 882	0.083 116	13
14	0.076 901	0.077 134	0.077 368	0.077 601	14
15	0.072 124	0.072 357	0.072 590	0.072 823	15
16	0.067 945	0.068 177	0.068 410	0.068 644	16
17	0.064 258	0.064 491	0.064 724	0.064 957	17
18	0.060 982	0.061 215	0.061 448	0.061 681	18
19	0.058 052	0.058 284	0.058 518	0.058 751	19
20	0.055 415	0.055 648	0.055 881	0.056 115	20
21	0.053 031	0.053 264	0.053 497	0.053 731	21
22	0.050 864	0.051 097	0.051 331	0.051 565	22
23	0.048 886	0.049 119	0.049 354	0.049 588	23

YRS					
2	0.047 073	0.047 307	0.047 542	0.047 777	24
3	0.033 214	0.033 454	0.033 694	0.033 935	36
4	0.026 334	0.026 580	0.026 827	0.027 076	48
5	0.022 244	0.022 498	0.022 753	0.023 010	60
6	0.019 550	0.019 811	0.020 074	0.020 339	72
7	0.017 653	0.017 921	0.018 192	0.018 465	84
8	0.016 253	0.016 529	0.016 807	0.017 088	96
9	0.015 184	0.015 468	0.015 754	0.016 042	108
10	0.014 347	0.014 638	0.014 931	0.015 227	120
11	0.013 678	0.013 975	0.014 276	0.014 580	132
12	0.013 134	0.013 439	0.013 746	0.014 057	144
13	0.012 687	0.012 998	0.013 312	0.013 630	156
14	0.012 314	0.012 632	0.012 953	0.013 277	168
15	0.012 002	0.012 325	0.012 652	0.012 983	180
16	0.011 737	0.012 067	0.012 400	0.012 737	192
17	0.011 512	0.011 847	0.012 186	0.012 529	204
18	0.011 320	0.011 660	0.012 004	0.012 352	216
19	0.011 154	0.011 500	0.011 849	0.012 202	228
20	0.011 011	0.011 361	0.011 716	0.012 074	240
21	0.010 887	0.011 242	0.011 601	0.011 964	252
22	0.010 779	0.011 139	0.011 502	0.011 869	264
23	0.010 686	0.011 049	0.011 417	0.011 788	276
24	0.010 604	0.010 971	0.011 343	0.011 717	288
25	0.010 532	0.010 904	0.011 278	0.011 656	300
26	0.010 470	0.010 844	0.011 222	0.011 604	312
27	0.010 414	0.010 792	0.011 174	0.011 558	324
28	0.010 366	0.010 747	0.011 131	0.011 518	336
29	0.010 324	0.010 707	0.011 094	0.011 484	348
30	0.010 286	0.010 673	0.011 062	0.011 454	360

PARTIAL PAYMENT
TO AMORTIZE $1

MONTHLY
COMPOUNDING

	14.0%	14.5%	15.0%	16.0%	
	ANNUAL RATE	ANNUAL RATE	ANNUAL RATE	ANNUAL RATE	
MOS					MOS
1	1.011 667	1.012 083	1.012 500	1.013 333	1
2	0.508 767	0.509 081	0.509 394	0.510 022	2
3	0.341 141	0.341 421	0.341 701	0.342 261	3
4	0.257 334	0.257 597	0.257 861	0.258 389	4
5	0.207 054	0.207 308	0.207 562	0.208 071	5
6	0.173 538	0.173 786	0.174 034	0.174 530	6
7	0.149 601	0.149 845	0.150 089	0.150 577	7
8	0.131 651	0.131 892	0.132 133	0.132 616	8
9	0.117 693	0.117 932	0.118 171	0.118 649	9
10	0.106 528	0.106 766	0.107 003	0.107 479	10
11	0.097 396	0.097 632	0.097 868	0.098 342	11
12	0.089 787	0.090 023	0.090 258	0.090 731	12
13	0.083 351	0.083 586	0.083 821	0.084 293	13
14	0.077 836	0.078 070	0.078 305	0.078 776	14
15	0.073 057	0.073 292	0.073 526	0.073 997	15
16	0.068 878	0.069 112	0.069 347	0.069 818	16
17	0.065 191	0.065 425	0.065 660	0.066 131	17
18	0.061 915	0.062 150	0.062 385	0.062 856	18
19	0.058 985	0.059 220	0.059 455	0.059 928	19
20	0.056 350	0.056 585	0.056 820	0.057 293	20
21	0.053 966	0.054 202	0.054 437	0.054 911	21
22	0.051 800	0.052 036	0.052 272	0.052 747	22
23	0.049 824	0.050 060	0.050 297	0.050 772	23
YRS					
2	0.048 013	0.048 249	0.048 487	0.048 963	24
3	0.034 178	0.034 421	0.034 665	0.035 157	36
4	0.027 326	0.027 578	0.027 831	0.028 340	48
5	0.023 268	0.023 528	0.023 790	0.024 318	60
6	0.020 606	0.020 874	0.021 145	0.021 692	72
7	0.018 740	0.019 017	0.019 297	0.019 862	84
8	0.017 372	0.017 657	0.017 945	0.018 529	96
9	0.016 334	0.016 628	0.016 924	0.017 525	108
10	0.015 527	0.015 829	0.016 133	0.016 751	120
11	0.014 887	0.015 196	0.015 509	0.016 143	132
12	0.014 371	0.014 688	0.015 009	0.015 658	144
13	0.013 951	0.014 275	0.014 603	0.015 267	156
14	0.013 605	0.013 936	0.014 270	0.014 948	168
15	0.013 317	0.013 655	0.013 996	0.014 687	180
16.	0.013 077	0.013 421	0.013 768	0.014 471	192
17	0.012 875	0.013 224	0.013 577	0.014 292	204
18	0.012 704	0.013 059	0.013 417	0.014 142	216
19	0.012 559	0.012 919	0.013 282	0.014 017	228
20	0.012 435	0.012 800	0.013 168	0.013 913	240
21	0.012 330	0.012 699	0.013 071	0.013 824	252
22	0.012 239	0.012 613	0.012 989	0.013 750	264
23	0.012 162	0.012 539	0.012 919	0.013 687	276
24	0.012 095	0.012 476	0.012 859	0.013 634	288
25	0.012 038	0.012 422	0.012 808	0.013 589	300
26	0.011 988	0.012 375	0.012 765	0.013 551	312
27	0.011 945	0.012 335	0.012 727	0.013 518	324
28	0.011 908	0.012 301	0.012 695	0.013 491	336
29	0.011 876	0.012 271	0.012 668	0.013 467	348
30	0.011 849	0.012 246	0.012 644	0.013 448	360

PARTIAL PAYMENT TO AMORTIZE $1

MONTHLY COMPOUNDING

MOS	17.0% ANNUAL RATE	18.0% ANNUAL RATE	19.0% ANNUAL RATE	20.0% ANNUAL RATE	MOS
1	1.014 167	1.015 000	1.015 833	1.016 667	1
2	0.510 650	0.511 278	0.511 906	0.512 534	2
3	0.342 822	0.343 383	0.343 944	0.344 506	3
4	0.258 916	0.259 445	0.259 974	0.260 503	4
5	0.208 580	0.209 089	0.209 599	0.210 110	5
6	0.175 027	0.175 525	0.176 024	0.176 523	6
7	0.151 066	0.151 556	0.152 047	0.152 538	7
8	0.133 100	0.133 584	0.134 069	0.134 556	8
9	0.119 129	0.119 610	0.120 092	0.120 574	9
10	0.107 956	0.108 434	0.108 913	0.109 394	10
11	0.098 817	0.099 294	0.099 771	0.100 250	11
12	0.091 205	0.091 680	0.092 157	0.092 635	12
13	0.084 766	0.085 240	0.085 716	0.086 194	13
14	0.079 249	0.079 723	0.080 199	0.080 677	14
15	0.074 470	0.074 944	0.075 420	0.075 898	15
16	0.070 290	0.070 765	0.071 241	0.071 720	16
17	0.066 605	0.067 080	0.067 557	0.068 035	17
18	0.063 330	0.063 806	0.064 283	0.064 763	18
19	0.060 402	0.060 878	0.061 357	0.061 838	19
20	0.057 768	0.058 246	0.058 725	0.059 207	20
21	0.055 387	0.055 865	0.056 346	0.056 829	21
22	0.053 224	0.053 703	0.054 185	0.054 670	22
23	0.051 250	0.051 731	0.052 214	0.052 700	23

YRS					
2	0.049 442	0.049 924	0.050 409	0.050 896	24
3	0.035 653	0.036 152	0.036 656	0.037 164	36
4	0.028 855	0.029 375	0.029 900	0.030 430	48
5	0.024 853	0.025 393	0.025 941	0.026 494	60
6	0.022 246	0.022 808	0.023 377	0.023 953	72
7	0.020 436	0.021 018	0.021 608	0.022 206	84
8	0.019 121	0.019 723	0.020 334	0.020 953	96
9	0.018 136	0.018 757	0.019 387	0.020 027	108
10	0.017 380	0.018 019	0.018 667	0.019 326	120
11	0.016 788	0.017 444	0.018 110	0.018 786	132
12	0.016 319	0.016 991	0.017 674	0.018 366	144
3	0.015 943	0.016 630	0.017 328	0.018 035	156
14	0.015 638	0.016 340	0.017 051	0.017 773	168
15	0.015 390	0.016 104	0.016 829	0.017 563	180
16	0.015 186	0.015 913	0.016 649	0.017 395	192
17	0.015 018	0.015 756	0.016 503	0.017 259	204
18	0.014 879	0.015 627	0.016 384	0.017 149	216
19	0.014 764	0.015 521	0.016 287	0.017 060	228
20	0.014 668	0.015 433	0.016 207	0.016 988	240
21	0.014 588	0.015 361	0.016 141	0.016 929	252
22	0.014 521	0.015 300	0.016 088	0.016 882	264
23	0.014 465	0.015 250	0.016 043	0.016 843	276
24	0.014 418	0.015 209	0.016 007	0.016 811	288
25	0.014 378	0.015 174	0.015 977	0.016 785	300
26	0.014 345	0.015 146	0.015 952	0.016 763	312
27	0.014 317	0.015 122	0.015 931	0.016 746	324
28	0.014 293	0.015 101	0.015 915	0.016 731	336
29	0.014 273	0.015 085	0.015 901	0.016 720	348
30	0.014 257	0.015 071	0.015 889	0.016 710	360

PARTIAL PAYMENT TO AMORTIZE $1 — QUARTERLY COMPOUNDING

QTRS	5.0% ANNUAL RATE	6.0% ANNUAL RATE	7.0% ANNUAL RATE	8.0% ANNUAL RATE	QTRS
1	1.012 500	1.015 000	1.017 500	1.020 000	1
2	0.509 394	0.511 278	0.513 163	0.515 050	2
3	0.341 701	0.343 383	0.345 067	0.346 755	3
4	0.257 861	0.259 445	0.261 032	0.262 624	4
5	0.207 562	0.209 089	0.210 621	0.212 158	5
6	0.174 034	0.175 525	0.177 023	0.178 526	6
7	0.150 089	0.151 556	0.153 031	0.154 512	7
8	0.132 133	0.133 584	0.135 043	0.136 510	8
9	0.118 171	0.119 610	0.121 058	0.122 515	9
10	0.107 003	0.108 434	0.109 875	0.111 324	10
11	0.097 868	0.099 294	0.100 730	0.102 178	11
12	0.090 258	0.091 680	0.093 114	0.094 560	12
13	0.083 821	0.085 240	0.086 673	0.088 118	13
14	0.078 305	0.079 723	0.081 156	0.082 602	14
15	0.073 526	0.074 944	0.076 377	0.077 825	15
16	0.069 347	0.070 765	0.072 200	0.073 650	16
17	0.065 660	0.067 080	0.068 516	0.069 970	17
18	0.062 385	0.063 806	0.065 245	0.066 702	18
19	0.059 455	0.060 878	0.062 321	0.063 782	19

YRS	5.0% ANNUAL RATE	6.0% ANNUAL RATE	7.0% ANNUAL RATE	8.0% ANNUAL RATE	QTRS
5	0.056 820	0.058 246	0.059 691	0.061 157	20
6	0.048 487	0.049 924	0.051 386	0.052 871	24
7	0.042 549	0.044 001	0.045 482	0.046 990	28
8	0.038 108	0.039 577	0.041 078	0.042 611	32
9	0.034 665	0.036 152	0.037 675	0.039 233	36
10	0.031 921	0.033 427	0.034 972	0.036 556	40
11	0.029 686	0.031 210	0.032 778	0.034 388	44
12	0.027 831	0.029 375	0.030 966	0.032 602	48
13	0.026 269	0.027 833	0.029 447	0.031 109	52
14	0.024 937	0.026 521	0.028 158	0.029 847	56
15	0.023 790	0.025 393	0.027 053	0.028 768	60
16	0.022 792	0.024 415	0.026 098	0.027 839	64
17	0.021 917	0.023 560	0.025 266	0.027 032	68
18	0.021 145	0.022 808	0.024 536	0.026 327	72
19	0.020 459	0.022 141	0.023 892	0.025 708	76
20	0.019 847	0.021 548	0.023 321	0.025 161	80
21	0.019 297	0.021 018	0.022 812	0.024 676	84
22	0.018 801	0.020 541	0.022 357	0.024 244	88
23	0.018 353	0.020 112	0.021 949	0.023 859	92
24	0.017 945	0.019 723	0.021 581	0.023 513	96
25	0.017 574	0.019 371	0.021 249	0.023 203	100
26	0.017 235	0.019 050	0.020 948	0.022 923	104
27	0.016 924	0.018 757	0.020 675	0.022 671	108
28	0.016 639	0.018 489	0.020 426	0.022 443	112
29	0.016 376	0.018 244	0.020 200	0.022 236	116
30	0.016 133	0.018 019	0.019 993	0.022 048	120

PARTIAL PAYMENT
TO AMORTIZE $1

QUARTERLY
COMPOUNDING

QTRS	9.0% ANNUAL RATE	10.0% ANNUAL RATE	11.0% ANNUAL RATE	12.0% ANNUAL RATE	QTRS
1	1.022 500	1.025 000	1.027 500	1.030 000	1
2	0.516 938	0.518 827	0.520 718	0.522 611	2
3	0.348 445	0.350 137	0.351 832	0.353 530	3
4	0.264 219	0.265 818	0.267 421	0.269 027	4
5	0.213 700	0.215 247	0.216 798	0.218 355	5
6	0.180 035	0.181 550	0.183 071	0.184 598	6
7	0.156 000	0.157 495	0.158 997	0.160 506	7
8	0.137 985	0.139 467	0.140 958	0.142 456	8
9	0.123 982	0.125 457	0.126 941	0.128 434	9
10	0.112 788	0.114 259	0.115 740	0.117 231	10
11	0.103 636	0.105 106	0.106 586	0.108 077	11
12	0.096 017	0.097 487	0.098 969	0.100 462	12
13	0.089 577	0.091 048	0.092 533	0.094 030	13
14	0.084 062	0.085 537	0.087 025	0.088 526	14
15	0.079 289	0.080 766	0.082 259	0.083 767	15
16	0.075 117	0.076 599	0.078 097	0.079 611	16
17	0.071 440	0.072 928	0.074 432	0.075 953	17
18	0.068 177	0.069 670	0.071 181	0.072 709	18
19	0.065 262	0.066 761	0.068 278	0.069 814	19

YRS					
5	0.062 642	0.064 147	0.065 672	0.067 216	20
6	0.054 380	0.055 913	0.057 469	0.059 047	24
7	0.048 525	0.050 088	0.051 677	0.053 293	28
8	0.044 174	0.045 768	0.047 393	0.049 047	32
9	0.040 825	0.042 452	0.044 111	0.045 804	36
10	0.038 177	0.039 836	0.041 532	0.043 262	40
11	0.036 039	0.037 730	0.039 461	0.041 230	44
12	0.034 282	0.036 006	0.037 772	0.039 578	48
13	0.032 819	0.034 574	0.036 374	0.038 217	52
14	0.031 585	0.033 372	0.035 206	0.037 084	56
15	0.030 535	0.032 353	0.034 220	0.036 133	60
16	0.029 634	0.031 482	0.033 381	0.035 328	64
17	0.028 855	0.030 733	0.032 663	0.034 642	68
18	0.028 177	0.030 084	0.032 044	0.034 054	72
19	0.027 585	0.029 520	0.031 509	0.033 548	76
20	0.027 064	0.029 026	0.031 043	0.033 112	80
21	0.026 604	0.028 593	0.030 637	0.032 733	84
22	0.026 197	0.028 212	0.030 282	0.032 404	88
23	0.025 836	0.027 875	0.029 970	0.032 117	92
24	0.025 514	0.027 577	0.029 696	0.031 866	96
25	0.025 226	0.027 312	0.029 454	0.031 647	100
26	0.024 968	0.027 076	0.029 241	0.031 454	104
27	0.024 737	0.026 867	0.029 051	0.031 285	108
28	0.024 530	0.026 679	0.028 884	0.031 136	112
29	0.024 343	0.026 512	0.028 735	0.031 005	116
30	0.024 174	0.026 362	0.028 603	0.030 890	120

PARTIAL PAYMENT
TO AMORTIZE $1

QUARTERLY
COMPOUNDING

	13.0%	14.0%	15.0%	16.0%	
	ANNUAL RATE	ANNUAL RATE	ANNUAL RATE	ANNUAL RATE	
QTRS					
1	1.032 500	1.035 000	1.037 500	1.040 000	1
2	0.524 505	0.526 400	0.528 298	0.530 196	2
3	0.355 231	0.356 934	0.358 640	0.360 349	3
4	0.270 637	0.272 251	0.273 869	0.275 490	4
5	0.219 916	0.221 481	0.223 052	0.224 627	5
6	0.186 130	0.187 668	0.189 212	0.190 762	6
7	0.162 022	0.163 544	0.165 074	0.166 610	7
8	0.143 963	0.145 477	0.146 998	0.148 528	8
9	0.129 936	0.131 446	0.132 965	0.134 493	9
10	0.118 731	0.120 241	0.121 761	0.123 291	10
11	0.109 579	0.111 092	0.112 615	0.114 149	11
12	0.101 967	0.103 484	0.105 012	0.106 552	12
13	0.095 539	0.097 062	0.098 596	0.100 144	13
14	0.090 042	0.091 571	0.093 113	0.094 669	14
15	0.085 289	0.086 825	0.088 376	0.089 941	15
16	0.081 140	0.082 685	0.084 245	0.085 820	16
17	0.077 490	0.079 043	0.080 613	0.082 199	17
18	0.074 254	0.075 817	0.077 397	0.078 993	18
19	0.071 368	0.072 940	0.074 531	0.076 139	19
YRS					
5	0.068 779	0.070 361	0.071 962	0.073 582	20
6	0.060 649	0.062 273	0.063 919	0.065 587	24
7	0.054 935	0.056 603	0.058 295	0.060 013	28
8	0.050 730	0.052 442	0.054 181	0.055 949	32
9	0.047 528	0.049 284	0.051 071	0.052 887	36
10	0.045 028	0.046 827	0.048 659	0.050 523	40
11	0.043 036	0.044 878	0.046 754	0.048 665	44
12	0.041 423	0.043 306	0.045 226	0.047 181	48
13	0.040 101	0.042 024	0.043 985	0.045 982	52
14	0.039 006	0.040 967	0.042 968	0.045 005	56
15	0.038 090	0.040 089	0.042 127	0.044 202	60
16	0.037 319	0.039 353	0.041 427	0.043 538	64
17	0.036 666	0.038 734	0.040 841	0.042 986	68
18	0.036 110	0.038 210	0.040 349	0.042 525	72
19	0.035 635	0.037 765	0.039 934	0.042 139	76
20	0.035 227	0.037 385	0.039 582	0.041 814	80
21	0.034 876	0.037 060	0.039 283	0.041 541	84
22	0.034 572	0.036 782	0.039 029	0.041 310	88
23	0.034 309	0.036 543	0.038 812	0.041 114	92
24	0.034 082	0.036 337	0.038 627	0.040 949	96
25	0.033 884	0.036 159	0.038 469	0.040 808	100
26	0.033 711	0.036 006	0.038 333	0.040 689	104
27	0.033 561	0.035 873	0.038 217	0.040 587	108
28	0.033 430	0.035 759	0.038 117	0.040 501	112
29	0.033 315	0.035 659	0.038 032	0.040 427	116
30	0.033 215	0.035 573	0.037 958	0.040 365	120

PARTIAL PAYMENT TO AMORTIZE $1

SEMIANNUAL COMPOUNDING

	5.0% ANNUAL RATE	6.0% ANNUAL RATE	7.0% ANNUAL RATE	8.0% ANNUAL RATE	
HALF YRS					**HALF YRS**
1	1.025 000	1.030 000	1.035 000	1.040 000	1
2	0.518 827	0.522 611	0.526 400	0.530 196	2
3	0.350 137	0.353 530	0.356 934	0.360 349	3
4	0.265 818	0.269 027	0.272 251	0.275 490	4
5	0.215 247	0.218 355	0.221 481	0.224 627	5
6	0.181 550	0.184 598	0.187 668	0.190 762	6
7	0.157 495	0.160 506	0.163 544	0.166 610	7
8	0.139 467	0.142 456	0.145 477	0.148 528	8
9	0.125 457	0.128 434	0.131 446	0.134 493	9
10	0.114 259	0.117 231	0.120 241	0.123 291	10
11	0.105 106	0.108 077	0.111 092	0.114 149	11
12	0.097 487	0.100 462	0.103 484	0.106 552	12
13	0.091 048	0.094 030	0.097 062	0.100 144	13
14	0.085 537	0.088 526	0.091 571	0.094 669	14
15	0.080 766	0.083 767	0.086 825	0.089 941	15
16	0.076 599	0.079 611	0.082 685	0.085 820	16
17	0.072 928	0.075 953	0.079 043	0.082 199	17
18	0.069 670	0.072 709	0.075 817	0.078 993	18
19	0.066 761	0.069 814	0.072 940	0.076 139	19
20	0.064 147	0.067 216	0.070 361	0.073 582	20
21	0.061 787	0.064 872	0.068 037	0.071 280	21
22	0.059 647	0.062 747	0.065 932	0.069 199	22
23	0.057 696	0.060 814	0.064 019	0.067 309	23
24	0.055 913	0.059 047	0.062 273	0.065 587	24
25	0.054 276	0.057 428	0.060 674	0.064 012	25
26	0.052 769	0.055 938	0.059 205	0.062 567	26
27	0.051 377	0.054 564	0.057 852	0.061 239	27
28	0.050 088	0.053 293	0.056 603	0.060 013	28
29	0.048 891	0.052 115	0.055 445	0.058 880	29
YRS					
15	0.047 778	0.051 019	0.054 371	0.057 830	30
16	0.045 768	0.049 047	0.052 442	0.055 949	32
17	0.044 007	0.047 322	0 050 760	0.054 315	34
18	0.042 452	0.045 804	0.049 284	0.052 887	36
19	0.041 070	0.044 459	0.047 982	0.051 632	38
20	0.039 836	0.043 262	0.046 827	0.050 523	40
21	0.038 729	0.042 192	0.045 798	0.049 540	42
22	0.037 730	0.041 230	0.044 878	0.048 665	44
23	0.036 827	0.040 363	0.044 051	0.047 882	46
24	0.036 006	0.039 578	0.043 306	0.047 181	48
25	0.035 258	0.038 865	0.042 634	0.046 550	50
26	0.034 574	0.038 217	0.042 024	0.045 982	52
27	0.033 948	0.037 626	0.041 471	0.045 469	54
28	0.033 372	0.037 084	0.040 967	0.045 005	56
29	0.032 842	0.036 588	0.040 508	0.044 584	58
30	0.032 353	0.036 133	0.040 089	0.044 202	60

PARTIAL PAYMENT
TO AMORTIZE $1

SEMIANNUAL
COMPOUNDING

	9.0%	10.0%	11.0%	12.0%	
	ANNUAL RATE	ANNUAL RATE	ANNUAL RATE	ANNUAL RATE	
HALF YRS					HALF YRS
1	1.045 000	1.050 000	1.055 000	1.060 000	1
2	0.533 998	0.537 805	0.541 618	0.545 437	2
3	0.363 773	0.367 209	0.370 654	0.374 110	3
4	0.278 744	0.282 012	0.285 294	0.288 591	4
5	0.227 792	0.230 975	0.234 176	0.237 396	5
6	0.193 878	0.197 017	0.200 179	0.203 363	6
7	0.169 701	0.172 820	0.175 964	0.179 135	7
8	0.151 610	0.154 722	0.157 864	0.161 036	8
9	0.137 574	0.140 690	0.143 839	0.147 022	9
10	0.126 379	0.129 505	0.132 668	0.135 868	10
11	0.117 248	0.120 389	0.123 571	0.126 793	11
12	0.109 666	0.112 825	0.116 029	0.119 277	12
13	0.103 275	0.106 456	0.109 684	0.112 960	13
14	0.097 820	0.101 024	0.104 279	0.107 585	14
15	0.093 114	0.096 342	0.099 626	0.102 963	15
16	0.089 015	0.092 270	0.095 583	0.098 952	16
17	0.085 418	0.088 699	0.092 042	0.095 445	17
18	0.082 237	0.085 546	0.088 920	0.092 357	18
19	0.079 407	0.082 745	0.086 150	0.089 621	19
20	0.076 876	0.080 243	0.083 679	0.087 185	20
21	0.074 601	0.077 996	0.081 465	0.085 005	21
22	0.072 546	0.075 971	0.079 471	0.083 046	22
23	0.070 682	0.074 137	0.077 670	0.081 278	23
24	0.068 987	0.072 471	0.076 036	0.079 679	24
25	0.067 439	0.070 952	0.074 549	0.078 227	25
26	0.066 021	0.069 564	0.073 193	0.076 904	26
27	0.064 719	0.068 292	0.071 952	0.075 697	27
28	0.063 521	0.067 123	0.070 814	0.074 593	28
29	0.062 415	0.066 046	0.069 769	0.073 580	29
YRS					
15	0.061 392	0.065 051	0.068 805	0.072 649	30
16	0.059 563	0.063 280	0.067 095	0.071 002	32
17	0.057 982	0.061 755	0.065 630	0.069 598	34
18	0.056 606	0.060 434	0.064 366	0.068 395	36
19	0.055 402	0.059 284	0.063 272	0.067 358	38
20	0.054 343	0.058 278	0.062 320	0.066 462	40
21	0.053 409	0.057 395	0.061 489	0.065 683	42
22	0.052 581	0.056 616	0.060 761	0.065 006	44
23	0.051 845	0.055 928	0.060 122	0.064 415	46
24	0.051 189	0.055 318	0.059 559	0.063 898	48
25	0.050 602	0.054 777	0.059 061	0.063 444	50
26	0.050 077	0.054 294	0.058 622	0.063 046	52
27	0.049 605	0.053 864	0.058 232	0.062 696	54
28	0.049 181	0.053 480	0.057 887	0.062 388	56
29	0.048 799	0.053 136	0.057 580	0.062 116	58
30	0.048 454	0.052 828	0.057 307	0.061 876	60

PARTIAL PAYMENT
TO AMORTIZE $1

ANNUAL
COMPOUNDING

YRS	5.0% ANNUAL RATE	6.0% ANNUAL RATE	7.0% ANNUAL RATE	7.5% ANNUAL RATE	YRS
1	1.050 000	1.060 000	1.070 000	1.075 000	1
2	0.537 805	0.545 437	0.553 092	0.556 928	2
3	0.367 209	0.374 110	0.381 052	0.384 538	3
4	0.282 012	0.288 591	0.295 228	0.298 568	4
5	0.230 975	0.237 396	0.243 891	0.247 165	5
6	0.197 017	0.203 363	0.209 796	0.213 045	6
7	0.172 820	0.179 135	0.185 553	0.188 800	7
8	0.154 722	0.161 036	0.167 468	0.170 727	8
9	0.140 690	0.147 022	0.153 486	0.156 767	9
10	0.129 505	0.135 868	0.142 378	0.145 686	10
11	0.120 389	0.126 793	0.133 357	0.136 697	11
12	0.112 825	0.119 277	0.125 902	0.129 278	12
13	0.106 456	0.112 960	0.119 651	0.123 064	13
14	0.101 024	0.107 585	0.114 345	0.117 797	14
15	0.096 342	0.102 963	0.109 795	0.113 287	15
16	0.092 270	0.098 952	0.105 858	0.109 391	16
17	0.088 699	0.095 445	0.102 425	0.106 000	17
18	0.085 546	0.092 357	0.099 413	0.103 029	18
19	0.082 745	0.089 621	0.096 753	0.100 411	19
20	0.080 243	0.087 185	0.094 393	0.098 092	20
21	0.077 996	0.085 005	0.092 289	0.096 029	21
22	0.075 971	0.083 046	0.090 406	0.094 187	22
23	0.074 137	0.081 278	0.088 714	0.092 535	23
24	0.072 471	0.079 679	0.087 189	0.091 050	24
25	0.070 952	0.078 227	0.085 811	0.089 711	25
26	0.069 564	0.076 904	0.084 561	0.088 500	26
27	0.068 292	0.075 697	0.083 426	0.087 402	27
28	0.067 123	0.074 593	0.082 392	0.086 405	28
29	0.066 046	0.073 580	0.081 449	0.085 498	29
30	0.065 051	0.072 649	0.080 586	0.084 671	30
31	0.064 132	0.071 792	0.079 797	0.083 916	31
32	0.063 280	0.071 002	0.079 073	0.083 226	32
33	0.062 490	0.070 273	0.078 408	0.082 594	33
34	0.061 755	0.069 598	0.077 797	0.082 015	34
35	0.061 072	0.068 974	0.077 234	0.081 483	35
36	0.060 434	0.068 395	0.076 715	0.080 994	36
37	0.059 840	0.067 857	0.076 237	0.080 545	37
38	0.059 284	0.067 358	0.075 795	0.080 132	38
39	0.058 765	0.066 894	0.075 387	0.079 751	39
40	0.058 278	0.066 462	0.075 009	0.079 400	40
41	0.057 822	0.066 059	0.074 660	0.079 077	41
42	0.057 395	0.065 683	0.074 336	0.078 778	42
43	0.056 993	0.065 333	0.074 036	0.078 502	43
44	0.056 616	0.065 006	0.073 758	0.078 247	44
45	0.056 262	0.064 700	0.073 500	0.078 011	45
46	0.055 928	0.064 415	0.073 260	0.077 794	46
47	0.055 614	0.064 148	0.073 037	0.077 592	47
48	0.055 318	0.063 898	0.072 831	0.077 405	48
49	0.055 040	0.063 664	0.072 639	0.077 232	49
50	0.054 777	0.063 444	0.072 460	0.077 072	50

PARTIAL PAYMENT
TO AMORTIZE $1

ANNUAL
COMPOUNDING

	8.0% ANNUAL RATE	8.5% ANNUAL RATE	9.0% ANNUAL RATE	9.5% ANNUAL RATE	
YRS					YRS
1	1.080 000	1.085 000	1.090 000	1.095 000	1
2	0.560 769	0.564 616	0.568 469	0.572 327	2
3	0.388 034	0.391 539	0.395 055	0.398 580	3
4	0.301 921	0.305 288	0.308 669	0.312 063	4
5	0.250 456	0.253 766	0.257 092	0.260 436	5
6	0.216 315	0.219 607	0.222 920	0.226 253	6
7	0.192 072	0.195 369	0.198 691	0.202 036	7
8	0.174 015	0.177 331	0.180 674	0.184 046	8
9	0.160 080	0.163 424	0.166 799	0.170 205	9
10	0.149 029	0.152 408	0.155 820	0.159 266	10
11	0.140 076	0.143 493	0.146 947	0.150 437	11
12	0.132 695	0.136 153	0.139 651	0.143 188	12
13	0.126 522	0.130 023	0.133 567	0.137 152	13
14	0.121 297	0.124 842	0.128 433	0.132 068	14
15	0.116 830	0.120 420	0.124 059	0.127 744	15
16	0.112 977	0.116 614	0.120 300	0.124 035	16
17	0.109 629	0.113 312	0.117 046	0.120 831	17
18	0.106 702	0.110 430	0.114 212	0.118 046	18
19	0.104 128	0.107 901	0.111 730	0.115 613	19
20	0.101 852	0.105 671	0.109 546	0.113 477	20
21	0.099 832	0.103 695	0.107 617	0.111 594	21
22	0.098 032	0.101 939	0.105 905	0.109 928	22
23	0.096 422	0.100 372	0.104 382	0.108 449	23
24	0.094 978	0.098 970	0.103 023	0.107 134	24
25	0.093 679	0.097 712	0.101 806	0.105 959	25
26	0.092 507	0.096 580	0.100 715	0.104 909	26
27	0.091 448	0.095 560	0.099 735	0.103 969	27
28	0.090 489	0.094 639	0.098 852	0.103 124	28
29	0.089 619	0.093 806	0.098 056	0.102 364	29
30	0.088 827	0.093 051	0.097 336	0.101 681	30
31	0.088 107	0.092 365	0.096 686	0.101 064	31
32	0.087 451	0.091 742	0.096 096	0.100 507	32
33	0.086 852	0.091 176	0.095 562	0.100 004	33
34	0.086 304	0.090 660	0.095 077	0.099 549	34
35	0.085 803	0.090 189	0.094 636	0.099 138	35
36	0.085 345	0.089 760	0.094 235	0.098 764	36
37	0.084 924	0.089 368	0.093 870	0.098 426	37
38	0.084 539	0.089 010	0.093 538	0.098 119	38
39	0.084 185	0.088 682	0.093 236	0.097 840	39
40	0.083 860	0.088 382	0.092 960	0.097 587	40
41	0.083 561	0.088 107	0.092 708	0.097 357	41
42	0.083 287	0.087 856	0.092 478	0.097 148	42
43	0.083 034	0.087 625	0.092 268	0.096 958	43
44	0.082 802	0.087 414	0.092 077	0.096 785	44
45	0.082 587	0.087 220	0.091 902	0.096 627	45
46	0.082 390	0.087 042	0.091 742	0.096 484	46
47	0.082 208	0.086 878	0.091 595	0.096 353	47
48	0.082 040	0.086 728	0.091 461	0.096 234	48
49	0.081 886	0.086 590	0.091 339	0.096 126	49
50	0.081 743	0.086 463	0.091 227	0.096 027	50

	10.0% ANNUAL RATE	10.5% ANNUAL RATE	11.0% ANNUAL RATE	11.5% ANNUAL RATE	
YRS					YRS
1	1.100 000	1.105 000	1.110 000	1.115 000	1
2	0.576 190	0.580 059	0.583 934	0.587 813	2
3	0.402 115	0.405 659	0.409 213	0.412 776	3
4	0.315 471	0.318 892	0.322 326	0.325 774	4
5	0.263 797	0.267 175	0.270 570	0.273 982	5
6	0.229 607	0.232 982	0.236 377	0.239 791	6
7	0.205 405	0.208 799	0.212 215	0.215 655	7
8	0.187 444	0.190 869	0.194 321	0.197 799	8
9	0.173 641	0.177 106	0.180 602	0.184 126	9
10	0.162 745	0.166 257	0.169 801	0.173 377	10
11	0.153 963	0.157 525	0.161 121	0.164 751	11
12	0.146 763	0.150 377	0.154 027	0.157 714	12
13	0.140 779	0.144 445	0.148 151	0.151 895	13
14	0.135 746	0.139 467	0.143 228	0.147 030	14
15	0.131 474	0.135 248	0.139 065	0.142 924	15
16	0.127 817	0.131 644	0.135 517	0.139 432	16
17	0.124 664	0.128 545	0.132 471	0.136 443	17
18	0.121 930	0.125 863	0.129 843	0.133 868	18
19	0.119 547	0.123 531	0.127 563	0.131 641	19
20	0.117 460	0.121 493	0.125 576	0.129 705	20
21	0.115 624	0.119 707	0.123 838	0.128 016	21
22	0.114 005	0.118 134	0.122 313	0.126 539	22
23	0.112 572	0.116 747	0.120 971	0.125 243	23
24	0.111 300	0.115 519	0.119 787	0.124 103	24
25	0.110 168	0.114 429	0.118 740	0.123 098	25
26	0.109 159	0.113 461	0.117 813	0.122 210	26
27	0.108 258	0.112 599	0.116 989	0.121 425	27
28	0.107 451	0.111 830	0.116 257	0.120 730	28
29	0.106 728	0.111 143	0.115 605	0.120 112	29
30	0.106 079	0.110 528	0.115 025	0.119 564	30
31	0.105 496	0.109 978	0.114 506	0.119 077	31
32	0.104 972	0.109 485	0.114 043	0.118 643	32
33	0.104 499	0.109 042	0.113 629	0.118 257	33
34	0.104 074	0.108 645	0.113 259	0.117 912	34
35	0.103 690	0.108 288	0.112 927	0.117 605	35
36	0.103 343	0.107 967	0.112 630	0.117 331	36
37	0.103 030	0.107 677	0.112 364	0.117 086	37
38	0.102 747	0.107 417	0.112 125	0.116 867	38
39	0.102 491	0.107 183	0.111 911	0.116 672	39
40	0.102 259	0.106 971	0.111 719	0.116 497	40
41	0.102 050	0.106 781	0.111 546	0.116 341	41
42	0.101 860	0.106 609	0.111 391	0.116 201	42
43	0.101 688	0.106 454	0.111 251	0.116 076	43
44	0.101 532	0.106 314	0.111 126	0.115 964	44
45	0.101 391	0.106 188	0.111 014	0.115 864	45
46	0.101 263	0.106 074	0.110 912	0.115 774	46
47	0.101 147	0.105 971	0.110 821	0.115 694	47
48	0.101 041	0.105 878	0.110 739	0.115 622	48
49	0.100 946	0.105 794	0.110 666	0.115 558	49
50	0.100 859	0.105 718	0.110 599	0.115 500	50

PARTIAL PAYMENT TO AMORTIZE $1

ANNUAL COMPOUNDING

YRS	12.0% ANNUAL RATE	12.5% ANNUAL RATE	13.0% ANNUAL RATE	13.5% ANNUAL RATE	YRS
1	1.120 000	1.125 000	1.130 000	1.135 000	1
2	0.591 698	0.595 588	0.599 484	0.603 384	2
3	0.416 349	0.419 931	0.423 522	0.427 122	3
4	0.329 234	0.332 708	0.336 194	0.339 693	4
5	0.277 410	0.280 854	0.284 315	0.287 791	5
6	0.243 226	0.246 680	0.250 153	0.253 646	6
7	0.219 118	0.222 603	0.226 111	0.229 641	7
8	0.201 303	0.204 832	0.208 387	0.211 966	8
9	0.187 679	0.191 260	0.194 869	0.198 505	9
10	0.176 984	0.180 622	0.184 290	0.187 987	10
11	0.168 415	0.172 112	0.175 841	0.179 602	11
12	0.161 437	0.165 194	0.168 986	0.172 811	12
13	0.155 677	0.159 496	0.163 350	0.167 240	13
14	0.150 871	0.154 751	0.158 667	0.162 621	14
15	0.146 824	0.150 764	0.154 742	0.158 757	15
16	0.143 390	0.147 388	0.151 426	0.155 502	16
17	0.140 457	0.144 512	0.148 608	0.152 743	17
18	0.137 937	0.142 049	0.146 201	0.150 392	18
19	0.135 763	0.139 928	0.144 134	0.148 380	19
20	0.133 879	0.138 096	0.142 354	0.146 651	20
21	0.132 240	0.136 507	0.140 814	0.145 161	21
22	0.130 811	0.135 125	0.139 479	0.143 873	22
23	0.129 560	0.133 919	0.138 319	0.142 757	23
24	0.128 463	0.132 866	0.137 308	0.141 788	24
25	0.127 500	0.131 943	0.136 426	0.140 945	25
26	0.126 652	0.131 134	0.135 655	0.140 211	26
27	0.125 904	0.130 423	0.134 979	0.139 570	27
28	0.125 244	0.129 797	0.134 387	0.139 010	28
29	0.124 660	0.129 246	0.133 867	0.138 521	29
30	0.124 144	0.128 760	0.133 411	0.138 092	30
31	0.123 686	0.128 331	0.133 009	0.137 717	31
32	0.123 280	0.127 952	0.132 656	0.137 388	32
33	0.122 920	0.127 617	0.132 345	0.137 100	33
34	0.122 601	0.127 321	0.132 071	0.136 847	34
35	0.122 317	0.127 059	0.131 829	0.136 624	35
36	0.122 064	0.126 827	0.131 616	0.136 429	36
37	0.121 840	0.126 621	0.131 428	0.136 258	37
38	0.121 640	0.126 439	0.131 262	0.136 107	38
39	0.121 462	0.126 278	0.131 116	0.135 974	39
40	0.121 304	0.126 134	0.130 986	0.135 858	40
41†	0.121 163	0.126 007	0.130 872	0.135 755	41
42	0.121 037	0.125 895	0.130 771	0.135 665	42
43	0.120 925	0.125 795	0.130 682	0.135 585	43
44	0.120 825	0.125 706	0.130 603	0.135 515	44
45	0.120 736	0.125 627	0.130 534	0.135 454	45
46	0.120 657	0.125 557	0.130 472	0.135 400	46
47	0.120 586	0.125 495	0.130 417	0.135 352	47
48	0.120 523	0.125 440	0.130 369	0.135 310	48
49	0.120 467	0.125 391	0.130 327	0.135 273	49
50	0.120 417	0.125 347	0.130 289	0.135 241	50

PARTIAL PAYMENT
TO AMORTIZE $1

ANNUAL
COMPOUNDING

	14.0%	14.5%	15.0%	16.0%	
	ANNUAL RATE	ANNUAL RATE	ANNUAL RATE	ANNUAL RATE	
YRS					YRS
1	1.140 000	1.145 000	1.150 000	1.160 000	1
2	0.607 290	0.611 200	0.615 116	0.622 963	2
3	0.430 731	0.434 350	0.437 977	0.445 258	3
4	0.343 205	0.346 729	0.350 265	0.357 375	4
5	0.291 284	0.294 792	0.298 316	0.305 409	5
6	0.257 157	0.260 688	0.264 237	0.271 390	6
7	0.233 192	0.236 766	0.240 360	0.247 613	7
8	0.215 570	0.219 198	0.222 850	0.230 224	8
9	0.202 168	0.205 858	0.209 574	0.217 082	9
10	0.191 714	0.195 469	0.199 252	0.206 901	10
11	0.183 394	0.187 217	0.191 069	0.198 861	11
12	0.176 669	0.180 559	0.184 481	0.192 415	12
13	0.171 164	0.175 121	0.179 110	0.187 184	13
14	0.166 609	0.170 632	0.174 688	0.182 898	14
15	0.162 809	0.166 896	0.171 017	0.179 358	15
16	0.159 615	0.163 764	0.167 948	0.176 414	16
17	0.156 915	0.161 124	0.165 367	0.173 952	17
18	0.154 621	0.158 886	0.163 186	0.171 885	18
19	0.152 663	0.156 982	0.161 336	0.170 142	19
20	0.150 986	0.155 357	0.159 761	0.168 667	20
21	0.149 545	0.153 964	0.158 417	0.167 416	21
22	0.148 303	0.152 768	0.157 266	0.166 353	22
23	0.147 231	0.151 739	0.156 278	0.165 447	23
24	0.146 303	0.150 851	0.155 430	0.164 673	24
25	0.145 498	0.150 084	0.154 699	0.164 013	25
26	0.144 800	0.149 420	0.154 070	0.163 447	26
27	0.144 193	0.148 846	0.153 526	0.162 963	27
28	0.143 664	0.148 348	0.153 057	0.162 548	28
29	0.143 204	0.147 915	0.152 651	0.162 192	29
30	0.142 803	0.147 539	0.152 300	0.161 886	30
31	0.142 453	0.147 213	0.151 996	0.161 623	31
32	0.142 147	0.146 929	0.151 733	0.161 397	32
33	0.141 880	0.146 682	0.151 505	0.161 203	33
34	0.141 646	0.146 467	0.151 307	0.161 036	34
35	0.141 442	0.146 279	0.151 135	0.160 892	35
36	0.141 263	0.146 116	0.150 986	0.160 769	36
37	0.141 107	0.145 974	0.150 857	0.160 662	37
38	0.140 970	0.145 850	0.150 744	0.160 571	38
39	0.140 850	0.145 742	0.150 647	0.160 492	39
40	0.140 745	0.145 647	0.150 562	0.160 424	40
41	0.140 653	0.145 565	0.150 489	0.160 365	41
42	0.140 573	0.145 493	0.150 425	0.160 315	42
43	0.140 502	0.145 431	0.150 369	0.160 271	43
44	0.140 440	0.145 376	0.150 321	0.160 234	44
45	0.140 386	0.145 328	0.150 279	0.160 201	45
46	0.140 338	0.145 287	0.150 242	0.160 174	46
47	0.140 297	0.145 250	0.150 211	0.160 150	47
48	0.140 260	0.145 218	0.150 183	0.160 129	48
49	0.140 228	0.145 191	0.150 159	0.160 111	49
50	0.140 200	0.145 167	0.150 139	0.160 096	50

YRS	17.0% ANNUAL RATE	18.0% ANNUAL RATE	19.0% ANNUAL RATE	20.0% ANNUAL RATE	YRS
1	1.170 000	1.180 000	1.190 000	1.200 000	1
2	0.630 829	0.638 716	0.646 621	0.654 545	2
3	0.452 574	0.459 924	0.467 308	0.474 725	3
4	0.364 533	0.371 739	0.378 991	0.386 289	4
5	0.312 564	0.319 778	0.327 050	0.334 380	5
6	0.278 615	0.285 910	0.293 274	0.300 706	6
7	0.254 947	0.262 362	0.269 855	0.277 424	7
8	0.237 690	0.245 244	0.252 885	0.260 609	8
9	0.224 691	0.232 395	0.240 192	0.248 079	9
10	0.214 657	0.222 515	0.230 471	0.238 523	10
11	0.206 765	0.214 776	0.222 891	0.231 104	11
12	0.200 466	0.208 628	0.216 896	0.225 265	12
13	0.195 378	0.203 686	0.212 102	0.220 620	13
14	0.191 230	0.199 678	0.208 235	0.216 893	14
15	0.187 822	0.196 403	0.205 092	0.213 882	15
16	0.185 004	0.193 710	0.202 523	0.211 436	16
17	0.182 662	0.191 485	0.200 414	0.209 440	17
18	0.180 706	0.189 639	0.198 676	0.207 805	18
19	0.179 067	0.188 103	0.197 238	0.206 462	19
20	0.177 690	0.186 820	0.196 045	0.205 357	20
21	0.176 530	0.185 746	0.195 054	0.204 444	21
22	0.175 550	0.184 846	0.194 229	0.203 690	22
23	0.174 721	0.184 090	0.193 542	0.203 065	23
24	0.174 019	0.183 454	0.192 967	0.202 548	24
25	0.173 423	0.182 919	0.192 487	0.202 119	25
26	0.172 917	0.182 467	0.192 086	0.201 762	26
27	0.172 487	0.182 087	0.191 750	0.201 467	27
28	0.172 121	0.181 765	0.191 468	0.201 221	28
29	0.171 810	0.181 494	0.191 232	0.201 016	29
30	0.171 545	0.181 264	0.191 034	0.200 846	30
31	0.171 318	0.181 070	0.190 869	0.200 705	31
32	0.171 126	0.180 906	0.190 729	0.200 587	32
33	0.170 961	0.180 767	0.190 612	0.200 489	33
34	0.170 821	0.180 650	0.190 514	0.200 407	34
35	0.170 701	0.180 550	0.190 432	0.200 339	35
36	0.170 599	0.180 466	0.190 363	0.200 283	36
37	0.170 512	0.180 395	0.190 305	0.200 235	37
38	0.170 437	0.180 335	0.190 256	0.200 196	38
39	0.170 373	0.180 284	0.190 215	0.200 163	39
40	0.170 319	0.180 240	0.190 181	0.200 136	40
41	0.170 273	0.180 204	0.190 152	0.200 113	41
42	0.170 233	0.180 172	0.190 128	0.200 095	42
43	0.170 199	0.180 146	0.190 107	0.200 079	43
44	0.170 170	0.180 124	0.190 090	0.200 066	44
45	0.170 145	0.180 105	0.190 076	0.200 055	45
46	0.170 124	0.180 089	0.190 064	0.200 046	46
47	0.170 106	0.180 075	0.190 053	0.200 038	47
48	0.170 091	0.180 064	0.190 045	0.200 032	48
49	0.170 078	0.180 054	0.190 038	0.200 026	49
50	0.170 066	0.180 046	0.190 032	0.200 022	50

NOTES

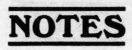

NOTES

NOTES